Lead with Wisdom is a heartfelt, powerful,
compelling and beautifully observed map of leadership.
Sir Robert 'Bob' Harvey KNZM QSO
Chair, Auckland Waterfront Authority

Mark Strom accomplishes a truly extraordinary task: illuminating how wisdom
drives leadership. His approach is intellectually fascinating and practically simple,
and reflects the impressive existential depth of his own life's course.
Pierre Gurdjian
Senior Partner, McKinsey & Company, Brussels

I wish I'd had *Lead with Wisdom* the past three years while our city has been
recovering from a natural disaster. I'm inspired to never give up the hope
of a better future nor the search for a better way of leading.
Ngaire Button
Deputy Mayor, City of Christchurch

A truly original and deeply innovative guide to wise and powerful leadership.
Tom Morris PhD
Author of *If Aristotle Ran General Motors,* and many others.
Former Professor of Philosophy, University of Notre Dame, USA

This is a wonderful and thoughtful treasure chest of the very human talents to be
learned on the journey to wise leadership. It is rich with stories of the ways in which
we can better connect with one another — the foundation of leadership.
Mark has created a special guide for us all, as leaders, and as human beings.
Jo Brosnahan QSO
Founding Chair, Leadership New Zealand, Auckland

Profoundly reframes the connectivity of leadership and wisdom.
Jim Varghese AM
Chairman and Director
Former CEO, Springfield Land Corporation, Brisbane
Former Directors-General of Queensland Main Roads, and Education Queensland

A bright vision of real, true leadership.
Feena May DBA
Head of Global Learning and Development,
International Committee of the Red Cross, Geneva

We have long needed a deeper theory around leadership.
This is it. Mark lifts the whole debate to a new level by aligning
the modern word of 'leader' with the ancient concept of 'wisdom'.
Tony Golsby-Smith PhD
Co-Founder and CEO, Second Road, Sydney

This book is a must. An inspiring, elegant, humanist vision of leadership.
A journey to the heart of being human.
Muriel Hanikenne
Coach and Career Development Manager,
GDF Suez Energy Europe, Brussels

In a world crying out for wise leaders who can speak to the
heart of matters and people, Mark's insights both from the lens
of history and modern day stories will strike a chord.
Martin Tan
Co-Founder and Executive Director, Halogen Foundation, Singapore

Mark partnered me when I saw a real need to infuse
conversation around making a difference in the way my staff
and I catered to the needs of the students in our school.
What came from that partnership was truly remarkable and forever changed
the way we all saw our roles in the students' lives. Mark has had an everlasting
and positive impact both on the school and on me personally.
Toni McKinnon
Former Principal, Liverpool West Primary School

The best book on the practical application of wisdom for life and leadership
I've ever read. This book needs to become the alternative
leadership guide for the 21st century.
Mike Thompson PhD
Visiting Professor of Management Practice
China Europe International Business School, Shanghai
Co-founder and Chief Integrity Officer, Good Leaders Online (GLO), Shanghai

If you've ever felt unsettled by a formulaic approach to change
or hoped that there is a deeper and more noble path,
this is probably the alternate wisdom you've been looking for.
Ann Austin
National Sustainability Manager, Lend Lease — Building, Sydney

A compelling map, guide and inspiration to those willing
to think and grow as leaders.
Selwyn D'Souza
Partner, Head of Strategy, Deloitte Consulting Australia, Sydney

An inspiring and artful weaving together of ancient insight and modern realities.
Bessi Graham
CEO and Co-Founder, The Difference Incubator, Melbourne

This deceptively simple book provides profound advice and insight.
Bernard McKenna PhD
Associate Professor, University of Queensland Business School

It would be foolish to claim any book can turn you or anyone into a wise leader. But
this book is likely to set you, like it did for me,
on a path to dare to become one.
Laurent Ledoux
President of the Executive Committee,
Federal Public Service for Mobility & Transports, Brussels

Offers a fundamental schema for effective leadership with humanity,
integrity and brilliance.
Mark Diamond
Instructional Leader and Leadership Mentor,
Department of Education and Communities NSW, Sydney

A hymn to our history, our nature, and the beauty of inspiring the best in others.
Ana de Montvert
Business Ethics Work Stream Leader, Caux Initiatives for Business, Zurich

Poignant, elegant, substantive, profound, simple.
Theary Seng
President, CIVICUS, Phnom Penh

MARK STROM

LEAD WITH WISDOM

HOW
WISDOM
TRANSFORMS
GOOD
LEADERS
INTO
GREAT
LEADERS

WILEY

First published in 2014 by John Wiley & Sons Australia, Ltd
42 McDougall St, Milton Qld 4064
Office also in Melbourne

Typeset in Avenir LT Std and Amatic SC

National Library of Australia Cataloguing-in-Publication data:

Author:	Strom, Mark, author
Title:	Lead with Wisdom: how wisdom transforms good leaders into great leaders / Mark Strom
ISBN:	9780730344889 (pbk.)
	9781118637579 (ebook)
Subjects:	Wisdom.
	Leadership.
Dewey Number:	153.4

Cover image: Alexandra Modie
Book design and illustration: Alexandra Modie

10 9 8 7 6 5 4 3 2 1

Disclaimer
The material in this publication is of the nature of general comment only, and does not represent professional advice. It is not intended to provide specific guidance for particular circumstances and it should not be relied on as the basis for any decision to take action or not take action on any matter which it covers. Readers should obtain professional advice where appropriate before making any such decision. To the maximum extent permitted by law, the author and publisher disclaim all responsibility and liability to any person, arising directly or indirectly from any person taking or not taking action based on the information in this publication.

To the generations that follow: Miriam, Luke & Jo, Hannah & Leon, and your little ones on the way. You teach me what it is to walk and lead in wisdom and grace.

CONTENTS

INTRODUCTION

Mud. That's what Aussie bricklayers call mortar. Leadership is a lot like laying bricks. Every day you handle 'bricks'. These are the substantial things that have to be done, delivered, checked, and signed off. But in and around them is the 'mortar' of countless small things. Like the words you use. Or the corridor chats. Or what you did with that nagging intuition. Or if you were really present in that conversation yesterday. Or whether you believe your own strategy. The strength of a wall is in the mortar, not the bricks. This is a book about laying bricks. The 'mud' is wisdom.

Leadership needs wisdom. Every day you face oddities that need more than standard answers. Sometimes you just need a great question to unearth what's really going on. But how do you find a great question? How do you craft a compelling argument for moving forward? How do you do this so people come with you as active authors rather than as passive readers? How do you help them find their brilliance? For that matter, how do you find your own brilliance and become more deliberate about leading from it? This is the stuff of wisdom.

None of this is about numbers and formulas, or even processes. It's not even so much about answers. It's deeper and simpler and more human. This is about how words shape our experience. About how people interpret and form meaning. About the power of questions and stories. More than anything, it's about relationships. How you build true authority and influence. What it takes for people to trust you. How you stay true in the face of fear or opportunity. What it means to be present and attentive to people and ideas. And how you bring conversations alive that stimulate serious innovation and deep, lasting change.

None of this comes quickly or easily. I've been a CEO twice as well as advising many leaders over many years. I know that the expectations of leadership can be overwhelming. A lot pushes back at you from outside and inside. The good news is that we don't need to master any of this. What we need is the desire and confidence to grow.

Wisdom is for dining rooms, lunch rooms, board rooms, and parliaments. *Lead with Wisdom* offers a map of wisdom for leaders and clues for navigating from it. You can see that map on page 2 and repeated at the start of each section. There are four parts to the map and the book, and thirteen chapters.

In Part I: Wisdom and Leadership, I view wisdom as reading the patterns of life with discernment and applying your insights with integrity and care. I then look at leadership as a pattern of human experience. My aim is to dignify leadership while demystifying it.

In Part II: Patterns, I examine four patterns of human experience that you deal with every day. I call them Naming, Conversation, Influence, and Character. Simply, they are about how language shapes reality, how meaning is formed in dialogue, how relationship shapes influence, and how the will faces uncertainty and fear.

In Part III: Arts, I examine four arts for working with the patterns. I call them Story, Brilliance, Promise, and Grace. Simply, we learn to work with story to shape identity, intent and community; we learn to draw out people's capacity to shine; we learn to speak so as to deepen character and hope; and we learn how to strengthen heart through dignity and kindness.

In Part IV: Applying the Patterns and Arts, I share three stories central to how I came to see these patterns and arts and work with them. The first is my own story. I tell it to encourage you to know and tell your own. The second is the story of my friendship with my son Luke through rich and difficult years. The third is an ancient story whose legacy is the contradictions that shape our ongoing attempts to lead with wisdom.

A simple idea underpins the design of the book. Apart from the final three stories and chapters, there is a single idea to each page or double page spread. Think of them as conversation starters that build one upon the other. There are also specific layouts throughout to distinguish different types of content that build and crystallise the whole meaning.

There are one and two page 'articles' where I address important tangents. For example, this isn't a book on strategy but when you link wisdom and leadership to strategy you get some interesting ideas. The illustrations help illuminate the ideas, make key concepts accessible, and hopefully take some stuffiness out of leadership. The 'Question and Answer' sections in each chapter are a personal favourite where I've tried to anticipate what a reader might want to ask at those points. And every chapter mixes ideas from history and even a little philosophy with everyday stories and practical how-to suggestions. It's full of tips.

Wisdom is big and old, but it should also stay accessible and fresh. This is a book you can dip in and out of, go deeper on certain topics, pause, skip forward, and easily come back later. You can read from start to back, a chapter at a time, or just browse. May it refresh your heart and mind to lead with wisdom.

PART I

Wisdom and Leadership

Leadership needs wisdom. Although we can gain wisdom and still not lead well, no-one leads well without wisdom.

WISDOM AND LEADERSHIP

Why do we need to lead with wisdom?

PATTERNS

ARTS

How do we lead with wisdom?

APPLYING THE
PATTERNS AND ARTS

Where must we lead with wisdom?

THE STORY BEHIND WISDOM AND LEADERSHIP

Leadership needs wisdom

I never particularly liked the word leadership. I always knew it could be a rich word full of nobility and people doing bold or selfless things to open up a way through great difficulties. But it could also mask something narcissistic or even darker.

Gandhi, Mother Teresa, Mandela, and Mary Robinson are all called leaders who served their people well. We hear stories of unsung people who lead people to safety and action in the face of floods, fires, famine, and war. We've also seen and heard manipulation, intimidation, belittling, and hype called 'being a leader'. Everyone who accepts the call to lead must find a way to think about leadership. For my part, I put it inside the bigger idea of wisdom.

In Chapter 1: Wisdom, I view wisdom in terms of reading the patterns of life. It's an old idea found in traditions from the ancient Near East to the First Peoples of America. The ways most things happen in the human and non-human worlds forms patterns. We grow wise by paying attention to them and drawing conclusions that help us live well. And living well brings integrity and care into the picture.

In Chapter 2: Leadership, I apply this old insight to leadership itself. What is leading if it too is a pattern? I think this helps sort out some old questions, like: born or made, position or person, formal or informal. Since we were kids just about everyone has led at some time. And, no matter who you are, or what your title or role, you still have to follow. It's the pattern. That means our positions don't make us leaders. Our positions are our contexts, where we can lead wisely or foolishly. But we want to lead wisely. So let's start with wisdom.

WISDOM READS LIFE'S
PATTERNS WITH
DISCERNMENT, INTEGRITY
AND CARE. SO MUCH
DEPENDS ON HOW
ATTENTIVE AND PRESENT
WE ARE TO LIFE.

CHAPTER 1

Wisdom

Wisdom is the stuff of life

We know it when we see it

Plato recalled Socrates saying, 'the unexamined life is not worth living'. Whether the old sage was right, we cannot say. But what we surely can say is that the unreflective life seldom leads to wisdom.

No definition will do wisdom justice. It's simply too vast, subtle, and profound. Yet wisdom is not utterly mysterious to us: we recognise it in the words, actions and characters of people. Perhaps, like love, we know wisdom more tacitly than overtly: we know more than we can say or define. We know love, and wisdom, as much by its absence as its presence, and we can discern the genuine article from pretence. And, like love, we long for the ways wisdom enriches and completes us.

Wisdom is as old as humanity: the accumulated insights of cultures and traditions gained over vast generations. At our best, we live, we notice, we learn, we remember, and we bequeath a better legacy.

Wisdom is as varied as we are. It lives in all our glory and profundity, contradiction and absurdity. We glimpse it in fleeting insights as often as in settled understanding. We name an enduring relationship with our dearest ones as a life of love. Yet not every moment of even the most intimate relationship bears all the marks of love. We cannot live with such intensity. Likewise no-one, not even the wisest, thinks and acts with unbroken wisdom. Just as we lapse into forgetfulness and thoughtlessness toward the ones we love most, so even the wisest lapse into folly.

Wisdom is disarmingly human: always within reach, yet somehow elusive. So how do we recognise it?

Wisdom is close at hand

We recognise wisdom

We recognise wisdom in those we admire as honourable, perceptive or grounded. We bring to mind those we believe have made the world a better place. We recall those who have touched our own lives for good.

Imagine if we could invite them all to dinner, the famous along with our own dear friends. What a conversation that would be! One thing's for sure: they would disagree as often as they agreed. Few would have made the same decision in the same way in the same context. At some point, the simplest might stump the smartest. The obscure might confound the famous. The uneducated might instruct the learned. No-one has a mortgage on wisdom. Wisdom crosses culture and geography, education and accomplishment, personality and experience.

The most precious resource we have for coping with life in an unstable, discontinuous and revolutionary world is not information, but each other. Wisdom is not to be found in a database; it grows out of the experience of living the life of the human herd and absorbing the lessons which that experience inevitably teaches us about who we are.[1]

HUGH MCKAY

We have known the wise

In seminars and workshops over the years I have asked people to recall those whom they considered wise. People for whom we are grateful, whose words and lives have influenced ours for good. Many find it odd to speak of others as wise but, as we recall the stories, the word begins to feel apt.

It feels natural to compile a list of attributes. But no list will do justice to experience: stories are the key. The subtlety and depth of the friends we recall lies in their stories. It is here that the textures and hues of wisdom become apparent.

Some speak of friends who gave strong and emphatic direction and counsel. Other friends would not give advice. Instead they made room for us working things out ourselves, and for learning from our own mistakes. Wisdom came in gentle tones—or like a whack on the side of the head! I commend to you the same exercise: to consider those who have been wise in your own life.

We begin to sense that wisdom is contextual. An action in one place may be wise, but in another context it may be foolish. The wisdom sayings are commonly misunderstood as rules or moral guidelines. Sometimes this may be part of the original authors' intent, but generally they are better read as observations of life. Not 'life should be this', but 'this is what I have seen'.

THE PRIORITY OF WISDOM

The sages differed on many things. But they agreed on one big thing. Wisdom matters most to people and communities who seek to live well.

Wisdom is supreme; therefore get wisdom. Though it cost you all you have, get understanding.[2]
SOLOMON

He who knows others is clever, he who knows himself has discernment.
He who masters others has force, he who masters himself is strong.
He who knows contentment is rich, he who perseveres is a man of purpose.[3]
LAO-TSE

At fifteen I set my heart on learning; at thirty I took my stand; at forty I had no doubts; at fifty I was conscious of the decrees of heaven; at sixty I was already obedient to these decrees; at seventy I just followed my heart's desire, without overstepping the boundaries (of what is right).[4]
CONFUCIUS

Imperturbable wisdom, being most honorable, is worth everything.[5]
DEMOCRITUS

A man, though wise, should never be ashamed of learning more, and must unbend his mind.[6]
SOPHOCLES

Everybody ought by all means to try and make himself as wise as he can.[7]
PLATO

Each one has just so much of happiness as he has of virtue and wisdom, and of virtuous and wise action.[8]
ARISTOTLE

There is no purifier in this world like wisdom.[9]
BHAGAVAD-GITA

No man is ever wise enough by himself.[10]
PLAUTUS

If wisdom be attainable, let us not only win but enjoy it.[11]
CICERO

Wisdom is the conqueror of fortune.[12]
JUVENAL

For what is more agreeable than wisdom itself, when you think of the security and the happy course of all things which depend on the faculty of understanding and knowledge.[13]
MARCUS AURELIUS

Wisdom has an advantage: She is eternal.[14]
BALTHASAR GRACIAN

Where is the wisdom we have lost in knowledge? Where is the knowledge we have lost in information?[15]
TS ELIOT

A useful distinction: Wisdom is observation and insight, not law, morality, or formula

Law, morality, and formula view life as binary — as involving choices between in/out, good/bad, best/worst. Wisdom views life as a whole — a vast complex tapestry.

For millennia people have looked to their wisdom traditions for guidance. These profound observations of life have instructed and warned generations. But the traditions cannot tell us what to do. The decisions remain ours and through them we grow wise … or foolish.

The wisdom traditions reflect life as it was experienced, not as a moralist might claim it should be. Wisdom is therefore always contextual.

The sayings of the wisdom traditions are very often imbalanced, incomplete and liable to misunderstanding. They cannot offer prescriptions for life since, again, wisdom needs to be related to a specific context. So wisdom leaves us the task of discernment. We must say how, or even whether, their observations speak to our particular situation.

In the Hebrew Proverbs we find two curious contradictory pieces of advice:

Do not answer a fool according to his folly, or you will be like him yourself. Answer a fool according to his folly, or he will be wise in his own eyes.[16]
SOLOMON

These two sayings, arranged one after the other, advise opposite courses of action when confronted by someone spouting nonsense. 'Do not answer a fool according to his folly'. How many would-be critics end up looking as foolish as the people they judge! Yet sometimes foolishness should be exposed. 'Answer the fool according to his folly'. There is a time to play the court jester, lampooning the king with his own foolishness.

So how do I know which strategy to choose? I have to make a wise response to my particular context. But how do I make this wise response? By becoming wise! Wait: I'm going in a circle! Yes, it *is* a circle and there's only one way ahead: it's back to reading patterns.

Wisdom views life as a whole — a vast complex tapestry. It urges us to watch, to listen, to read, to discern, and to store up insights we can draw from later.

We recognise wisdom. We know it even though we can't define it. We see wisdom, and foolishness, most easily in people. And we know that wisdom depends on context. This makes wisdom far richer and subtler than rules, morals systems, or processes.

Wisdom addresses a management paradox. We commonly say that complexity, connectivity, and the pace of change are increasing. We stress 'big picture' thinking but may defer to analysing the parts rather than reading the whole. This is the domain of wisdom.

Wisdom reads well the patterns of life

Reading life

No definition does justice to wisdom. Wisdom is as broad as the ability to live well grounded in good understanding. We grow in knowledge of ourselves and of the world around us, and we learn to make good choices and to live well with others.

Life seems an impossibly complex tapestry. We have the sense of 'weaving' — of colours and hues that suggest everything is somehow connected — but the scale of it overwhelms. We would be utterly lost in the vastness of life were it not for our ability to see similarities between situations despite their myriad differences.

Reading is the metaphor used by the ancients:

The mark of wisdom is to read aright the present, and to march with the occasion.[17]

HOMER

The wisdom traditions speak of reading life's 'patterns'. We see analogies, links and levels in every facet of life. We see patterns in the natural world. Humility is likened to a river: the river only becomes greater by always descending to a lower place. The industry of ants is a provocation to human diligence. We see patterns in each other — in our behaviours, personalities, and characters. And we see patterns in the events that fill our lives. These patterns are our pathways to understanding.

Reading and living patterns

So here is a working definition of wisdom:

Wisdom is reading and living the patterns of life well.

Let me expand that in two halves:
1. Wisdom is ways of being and knowing by which we indwell and read the patterns of life insightfully — the patterns of our own lives, of each other, and of the wider world.
2. Wisdom is then bringing this indwelling and insight to specific contexts with attentiveness and discernment, integrity and care.

Finding patterns

Patterns simplify complexity. We collect memories and hunches of things that went together. Bringing them to mind we say, 'I've seen that before!' But what's a pattern?

There's no end to patterns because patterns are not 'out there' like rocks on the ground. The patterns are similarities we notice. They are more in our heads than out there in the world, though they fit what's out there. I think of them as 'Ways life goes together that I have noticed'. Kind of like the 'books of life' I've read.

'LIFE IS A GOOD READ'.

Watch life's patterns and learn

The patterns of nature teach us

In many traditions, nature is infused with wisdom and the wise read this:

There is no river that permits itself to be concealed; that is, it breaks the dam by which it was hidden. So also the soul goes to the place which it knows, and deviates not from its way of yesterday.[18]

THE INSTRUCTION OF KING MERI-KA-RE

Earth teach me quiet — as the grasses are still with new light.
Earth teach me suffering—as old stones suffer with memory.
Earth teach me humility—as blossoms are humble with beginning.
Earth teach me caring — as mothers nurture their young.
Earth teach me courage — as the tree that stands alone.
Earth teach me limitation — as the ant that crawls on the ground.
Earth teach me freedom—as the eagle that soars in the sky.
Earth teach me acceptance — as the leaves that die each fall.
Earth teach me renewal — as the seed that rises in the spring.
Earth teach me to forget myself — as melted snow forgets its life.
Earth teach me to remember kindness — as dry fields weep with rain.[19]

NATIVE AMERICAN UTE PRAYER

The patterns of people teach us

The traditions urge us to read people well to live well. Watch how people deal with one another. Imitate the ways of the wise. Shun the way of fools:

Do not set out to stand around
in the assembly.
Do not loiter where there is a
dispute, for in the dispute they will
have you as an observer.
Then you will be made a witness for
them, and they will involve you in a
lawsuit to affirm something that does
not concern you.
In case of a dispute, get away from it,
disregard it.
A dispute is a covered pit, a ... wall
which can cover over its foes;
it brings to mind what one has
forgotten and makes an accusation
against a man.[20]

THE INSTRUCTIONS OF SHURUPPAK

Is a man not superior, who without anticipating attempts at deception or presuming acts of bad faith, is, nonetheless, the first to be aware of such behaviour?[21]

CONFUCIUS

Learning wisdom from the human and non-human world.

Words change things

Our lives are shaped by words. An apt word can bring life. An ill-considered word can bring ruin. The wisdom traditions placed great emphasis on a word in or out of season, on speech, and 'the tongue':

More than all watchfulness watch thy mouth, and over what thou hearest harden thy heart. For a word is a bird: once released, no man can recapture it.[22]

THE WORDS OF AHIQAR

Do not associate thyself to the heated man,
Nor visit him for conversation.
Preserve thy tongue from answering thy superior,
And guard thyself against reviling him.
Do not make too free with thy answer.[23]

THE INSTRUCTION OF AMEN-EM-OPET

My son, chatter not overmuch so that thou speak out every word that comes to thy mind; for men's eyes and ears are everywhere trained upon thy mouth. Beware lest it be thy undoing.[24]

THE WORDS OF AHIQAR

Reckless words pierce like a sword, but the tongue of the wise brings healing. Truthful lips endure forever, but a lying tongue lasts only a moment.[25]

SOLOMON

Many men perform the foulest deeds and practice the fairest words.[26]

Fine words do not hide foul actions nor is a good action spoiled by slanderous words.[27]

DEMOCRITUS

To fail to speak to a man who is capable of benefiting is to let a man go to waste. To speak to a man who is incapable of benefiting is to let one's words go to waste. A wise man lets neither men nor words go to waste.[28]

CONFUCIUS

Words are the primary tool of every leader. So much depends on the words we use, the ways we speak, and the language and conversations we foster among others. Foolish words bring ruin. Words of value build people of value.

Ancient speech tips

- Let another praise you, not you.
- Don't say every word you think of!
- To answer before listening: that is folly.
- Even a fool is thought wise if he keeps silent.
- When words are many, evil is present.
- Whoever spreads slander is a fool.
- A flattering mouth works ruin.
- A fool shows his annoyance at once.
- Arrogant lips are unsuited to a fool.
- Fine words do not hide foul actions.
- A fortune made by a lying tongue is a fleeting vapour and a deadly snare.[29]
- Don't loiter where there is a dispute.
- Watch your mouth and heart.

THE BIG IDEA OF THE
ONE AND MANY

Corporations, governments and not-for-profits have adopted a common vocabulary. Merger. Acquisition. Divestment. Centralisation. Decentralisation. Restructuring. Unification. Diversification. Sounds very modern. But they are actually our institutional versions of an ancient question.

Where philosophy began
Ever wondered how philosophy began? To oversimplify greatly a very long story, Western philosophy began with one big question: How come there is unity — coherence, order, meaning — within the bewildering diversity of life? (In different ways, this question shaped both Western and Eastern traditions of philosophy.) What we call unity and diversity, the ancients called 'the One and the Many'. The 'One' as in the whole; the 'Many' as in the parts.

Ideas arise in social contexts; so did the question of One and Many. Life in each city-state *(polis)* of what we now call Greece was largely self-contained. The seventh century BC began unprecedented access to other peoples and ideas.

This brought unsettling questions. In what ways were other peoples and conventions the same (One) and in what ways different (Many)? It seemed, for example, that every city had an idea of justice; but not always the same idea. Was justice merely a convention, or was there something universal to the idea? So how should a city frame its laws?

How Plato split the world
Surely, the ancients reasoned, even though there's so much change (Many), some things must stay the same (One). Or does life swing between being ordered and coherent (One) and fragmented and chaotic (Many)? We aren't the first ones to feel like life goes back and forth between the two:

At one time they grew to be one alone from being many, and at another they grew apart again to be many from being one.[30]
EMPEDOCLES

The philosophers pondered whether something, somehow, might unify all the diversity they experienced. But what? This was the appeal of the four elements — earth, fire, air, and water. Perhaps individually, or as a whole, the elements were what held everything together.

Then again, some argued, maybe life only looks ordered (One). Perhaps it's actually really fragmented and chaotic and only change is constant (Many). Heraclitus thought so. Or maybe it's the exact opposite: that change is an illusion. That was Parmenides' choice. The pre-Socratic philosophers explored every possibility.

The solution put forward by Plato hugely influenced Western thought. Returning to our topic of justice, Plato argued that there is one true, eternal Form (Pure Idea) of Justice, and that every instance of justice we see is a poor copy of that Form. Likewise there is a Form of Goodness, and of Beauty, and of everything else that unifies our diverse experiences and ideas. Every single thing we see is a corrupted copy (Many) of a perfect original idea (One):

We distinguish between the many particular things which we call beautiful or good, and absolute beauty and goodness.[31]

PLATO

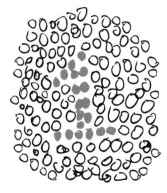

Sometimes we see the whole, the One.
Sometimes we see the parts, the Many.
Our eyes and mind move between both.

Plato's answer split the world in two. On the one hand, the Forms — pure ideas, eternal and unchanging. On the other hand, Matter — the changeable world of everyday experiences and things. Okay, time for a ditty: In Plato's scheme, Matter doesn't matter; only what isn't Matter, matters. (Did you get that?!)

This strange answer mirrored society. Plato lived a privileged life in a city stratified from those who mattered (high rank) to those who didn't (low rank). I think we can link his theory with his life: Plato philosophised a picture of ultimate reality that mirrored his own privileged life as an educated man of rank.

This influential theory of a split world — philosophers call it dualism — yielded an 'upstairs downstairs' world view. Plato saw people as a microcosm of this split universe: each of us, he said, has a divine element (mind, soul) that grasps the Forms; but we are trapped within corrupt physical Matter (body). This idea reinforced the prejudice of those of high rank against those who 'worked with their own hands', a put-down that recurs in over a thousand years of classical literature.

Plato's vision of reality shaped and was shaped by his belief that we should place greater trust in reason than in our senses (mere 'opinion and irrational sensation'). Our senses are too caught up in Matter. Only reason, Plato believed, could let us distance ourselves enough from Matter to gain some knowledge of the Forms. More on reason later. For now, we note that wisdom holds in tension the parts and the whole, and that we need a fuller account of knowing than reason alone.

HOW TO PICK A
SPLIT WORLD

Plato sold us a dud when he split the world into what matters and what doesn't. We keep buying it.

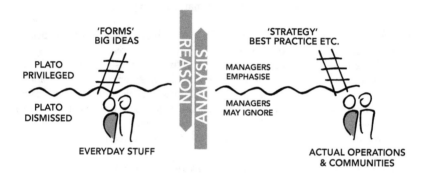

Plato's legacy lives on

Look for false distinctions about what's supposedly most 'real' and ways of knowing that are more 'true'.

You may hear forced distinctions like...
- Reason vs emotion.
- Theory vs practice.
- Intellectual vs practical.
- Analysis vs imagination.
- Centralised vs decentralised.
- Best practice vs our best stories.
- Knowledge work vs craft work.

For Plato, reason was like a ladder: we must lift our thinking from what we see to the 'real truth' of pure ideas.

For managers, statistics, analysis, and models of best practice can seem 'higher' or more rational than the day-to-day realities of how people actually work and relate.

Plato's legacy shapes management

Look for ways analysis, models and plans are given more weight than what people actually say and do in context.

You may hear ideas like ...
- Importing 'world's best practice' without asking if it fits the context.
- Treating all 'problems' as solvable by right model + data + analysis.
- Using restructures to (supposedly) change how people think, work and 'engage' (i.e. 'cultural change').
- Ignoring the pride in craft of workers, calling them unengaged because our vision/mission/values hold no interest for them.

All possible brain work should be removed from the shop and centered in the planning or laying-out department.[32]
FREDERICK TAYLOR

Abstraction, or the curse of the school project

The gift and curse of abstraction

The Greek philosophers gave greater weight to ideas than to their expression. As philosophy and science became detached from people, '(the philosophers became) locked into an abstract cycle of debate in general terms, driven more by the sheer rationality of the tradition than by reference to any actual social situation'.[33]

The intellectual method of abstraction evolved. The idea is to extract the essence of something from the details — like a kernel from the husk. Linked to this is 'boxed' thinking: breaking things into categories (boxes) to put everything in its box. If something doesn't fit the box, it must be irrelevant.

In medicine, science, engineering, and more this thinking enabled amazing discovery and invention. But it can also reduce what is living and changing to fixed and clumsy categories:

If theory attempts to displace skill and understanding in concrete situations, it becomes first a nuisance and later a hindrance to both thought and action.[34]
DAVID TRACY

Fighting an educational legacy

Do you remember doing 'projects' in early school? A collage of pictures and words arranged and decorated on a sheet of cardboard? Mum and Dad 'helping' at the kitchen table the night before it was due?

The topic was always broad, like 'Frogs' or 'Parliament' or 'Tasmania'. Occasionally we (or our parents!) got interested and learned something. But that was optional.

The real task was to fill up the sheet with anything we thought was relevant.

Moving to high school, we progressed to essays. Now we had to deal with plagiarism. We decided which quotes to footnote, discard, or 'put in our own words'. The game was the same: fill the essay with whatever we could find. Now there was a word count. Even at university the game was often still the same. I think we still do it.

Think of boring meetings, presentations, and reports. The slides are full of words and numbers but you can't find the point. The presenter says everything he thinks he should say, but there's no argument or key question. It's like a grown-up school project.

Great ideas need life. Cut the jargon. Find grounded questions. And turn those meetings into places of making.[35]

WISDOM TRANSLATES WELL
THE PATTERNS OF LIFE

Wisdom helps us read complexity and ambiguity. Often balance is the need, but not always. What matters most is to translate wisdom well in each context.

Wisdom is not always balanced

The ancient Greeks believed that balance was the key to resolving the One and Many. Perfection for them was balance, moderation, lack of excess, harmony, the middle way. But balance, what they called the 'mean', is an abstract ideal that never occurs.

Half a world away from Athens, Mencius saw the problem well:

To lay hold of the mean without
taking into account the occasion,
is like grasping one thing only.[36]
MENCIUS

Balance is rarely the answer. What we need is the intellectual and emotional strength to hold both One and Many in tension. A wise path way well lie between two extremes, though sometimes an 'extreme' might be just what's needed. But the better path almost certainly does not lie in the middle.

Here's a simple example. At an offsite to set business plans for the next year, the agenda turned to sales forecasts. There was no shortage of spreadsheets. Then the auction started: 'Sales will be up by 20 per cent next year'. 'I think more like 10 per cent'. You guessed it, they settled for 15 per cent. (Funny isn't it how

no-one settles for an 'irrational' number like 16.486 per cent, yet it's all supposed to be based on analysis.) Meanwhile, several seasoned executives have the sinking feeling that the whole discussion is missing the realities of what's actually happening in the marketplace and internal operations.

Wisdom doesn't rush to such 'balanced' solutions. Wisdom can sit with ambiguity.

We don't need and can't have a complete view of anything. Rather, we move between the one and the many — the pattern or principle and the specifics of a given context — searching for insight.

What we need is the ability to consider things from multiple perspectives. This is the heart of thinking contextually and systemically. But only seeing patterns would make us armchair philosophers. Translating these patterns to the contexts around (and within) us takes us into engagement and action.

Wisdom requires the hard work of discerning context. From the storehouse of patterns we have observed, and the instinct to read the present, we choose and translate a particular line of speech or action to meet the challenges of the particular context.

Translating takes perspective

It's an iterative process

First we read the patterns: we attend to them and interpret them. Next we take the meaning we have seen and creatively bring these insights to our own contexts: we translate.

None of this happens like one, two, three. It is iterative. Reading, attending, interpreting, translating — all happen together.

We know by analogies and systems

Life is mind-bogglingly inter-connected. So is our knowledge of it. All our knowing uses analogy — we know something by reference to something else.

One of our most successful tricks is to bundle bits of this complexity together and call it a system. Thinking in analogies and systems is a great tool but limited.

We learn to multiply perspectives

Even the systems we create in our minds are too complex. One part of the system, or a big theme in how we think about the system, can serve as a perspective on the whole. Like looking at a scene through a window or pair of glasses.

Once we realise how perspectives enable us to see, we can become skilled at finding and shaping them. And we learn to multiply perspectives. We start to gain richer insights. Then whole new possibilities for interpretation and translation become possible.

Searching for perspective

1. Immerse yourself in what you're reading. You won't get it all.
2. Find the passion.
3. Move between looking at the whole (One) and parts (Many) — you can start with either.
4. Listen for key stories.
5. Listen for how your language, or others', opens up or shuts down your reading.
6. Try a metaphor. Make links. Sit with it. Don't get too attached. Expect it to change.
7. Ask if you have succumbed to the 'school project' — just saying everything. Put people back in the centre.
8. Try telling a new story. Watch if people come with you.

Themes can help us find perspective. Finding more themes multiplies perspectives.

THREE TESTS FOR
STRATEGY

Maybe talking about patterns, One and Many, dualism, and abstraction seems too philosophical and impractical — especially to business. Here are three quick tests to see if these ideas really do have an impact on us today. For any strategy look for one or more of these fallacies:

1. The fallacy of balance

Sound familiar?

'Sales will be up by 20 per cent next year'.

'I think we can only expect 10 per cent'.

'Okay, we'll plan for 15 per cent'.

I have heard this kind of bargaining at the centre of many strategy and planning sessions. It seeks balance, or consensus.

There are always lots of numbers to back it up.

But we can be pretty sure the future is not going to lie in the middle of any set of numbers.

It looks rational. But it's not.

2. The fallacies of order and certainty

Sound familiar?

'Did we include all the data from all the sites?'

'No, some just didn't match the model'.

'So how do we know the model is right?'

'Well it fits the data we used'.

I have seen this kind of selective data used to make the most ambiguous context look ordered, bounded, and able to be analysed.

The spreadsheets seem irrefutable. Besides things look messy without them.

It looks analytical. But it's not.

3. The fallacy of presentation

Sound familiar?

'We've started a project.'
'How far are you?'
'Just beginning. What should we do?'
'A slide presentation'.
'What should I include?'
'Everything. Best Practice. Articles. Lots of stats. Just cut-n-paste your last presentation'.

I have seen this kind of presentation convince a group they are ready for a solution when they haven't even started to explore the issue.

It looks professional. But it's not.

There are ways to shape intelligent, even wise, strategy. This is where we are headed.

Q. # Wisdom is so big. Where do you start?

A. Personally I find it helpful to think in terms of attentiveness and presence. Wisdom asks me to pay attention to life; to notice and wonder and consider. Life is so big. Sometimes I can't start 'out there'; I have to start 'in here'. It isn't natural for me to pay attention or to be present to what is happening around and within me. I'm too busy. Too distracted. But sometimes, without warning, a door opens to wonder. I start to pay attention. Stillness becomes possible. I may find myself uncommonly present to others and to the world, its beauty and its travail. This is where my learning starts.

Wisdom stays open to the patterns of life

We know and we notice

We read and we translate that which comes to our attention. Or so it seems. Yet most knowing is tacit: we don't know what we know (more in *Chapter 3: Naming*). Indeed, we read far more than we realise: in a sense, we are always reading. Wisdom builds upon this knowledge that we absorb.

You can become blind by seeing each day as a similar one. Each day is a different one, each day brings a miracle of its own. It's just a matter of paying attention to this miracle.[37]
PAULO COELHO

To learn we must pay attention to life within us and beyond us. We must learn to discern the presence and significance of patterns, picking up nuance and subtlety, congruence and anomaly.

Attentiveness brings wisdom and it is urged in many traditions. We are asked to open our ears and eyes to the significance of the everyday:

Turn your ear to wisdom and apply your heart to understanding.[38] My son, pay attention to my wisdom; turn your ear to my words of insight.[39]
SOLOMON

To be attentive is more than thinking. It is to draw near to engage, not to stand apart. It requires us to be present to what is emerging around us and within us. We enter into that which we seek to know; whether ideas, events, other people, or even our own hearts.

If we liken reading life's patterns to making maps of reality, then our goal is not to be great map-makers, but to travel. There is an attentiveness to every facet of this: reading the terrain, drawing a map, locating ourselves, plotting a path, and journeying itself.

On staying open

Let yourself be open and life will be easier. A spoon of salt in a glass of water makes the water undrinkable. A spoon of salt in a lake is almost unnoticed.[40]
BUDDHA

If someone is able to show me that what I think or do is not right, I will happily change, for I seek the truth, by which no-one was ever truly harmed. It is the person who continues in his self-deception and ignorance who is harmed.[41]
MARCUS AURELIUS

It is never too late to give up our prejudices.[42]
HENRY DAVID THOREAU

Open-mindedness should not be fostered because, as Scripture teaches, Truth is great and will prevail, nor because, as Milton suggests, Truth will always win in a free and open encounter. It should be fostered for its own sake.[43]
RICHARD RORTY

Attention is as varied as we are

'Pay attention!' Mrs Monaghan was my third grade teacher. For a sweet, kind teacher she had a wicked habit. She would sneak up behind anyone daydreaming and whack the desk with a three-foot ruler! She got me several times even though, due to illness, I wasn't at school all that often. Seems attentiveness wasn't a strong point for me.

Now I may just be making excuses but I'd like to think my inattentiveness in class masked an attentiveness of another kind. School certainly did not hold my attention; but life did.

I've known many children who were fascinated by life but not by school; my own included. I can't help feeling that the attentiveness valued at school is too often contrived. The goal seems to be compliance, not curiosity; an attentiveness without presence.

At its worst, a child may learn to pay enough attention to repeat what is given to her, without actually engaging with what is being offered.

Running a massive educational system will always work against this. But I do daydream about education that values and encourages the different ways that children attend to life and its patterns. I can't help but think it would help nurture integrity and care. That 'distracted' schoolgirl or boy may be enthralled with another 'curriculum'. Thankfully there are many, many teachers who know and nurture this deeper fascination.

So what can we say about attentiveness? Why some things more than others come to hold our attention is perhaps unfathomable. One thing's for sure, it's as varied as we are.

Tell me to what you pay attention and I will tell you who you are.[44]
JOSE ORTEGA Y GASSET

What we pay attention to may not be what is 'prescribed', but what is most valued.

THOUGHTS ON ATTENTIVENESS

People are attentive to life in different ways. For some it seems more about thinking. For others, more about feeling. I think it's always both. How do you attend to life?

I posted a question on Facebook: 'What comes to mind when you think of being attentive to life?' Here, with their permission, are my paraphrases of some of my connections' responses:

When curiosity meets empathy, we learn to attend to life and to each other.
RICHARD

Attentiveness is like a vulnerable embrace.
IMMANUEL

When we are thankful, stillness settles in us … (and) we may read life's patterns.
TARA

Attentiveness, encounter, vulnerability, gratitude, and curiosity are most present in the moment of giving and gift.
JOHN

Wisdom does not dissect life into parts. Perhaps wisdom is the way of the undivided life.
MEREDITH

Attention looks for wholes, for significance, for meaning. The contradictory and incoherent aspects of experience help hone this skill.
BRYCE

Attentiveness and presence takes the courage to look seriously into the paradox of our own glory and brokenness.
JAYME

Think of the fracturing forces that have shaped our lives. Perhaps we are only able to face different things at different stages of life.
DAVID

Attentiveness and presence is not dissociation: it is the courage and vulnerability of being still and listening deeply.
EMMA

Speech is a kind of risk: to be attentive and present is to trust another and to guard the trust given in return.
SCOTT

Paradoxically, attentiveness helps us see life's 'non-patterns' — the discontinuities. Here too lie the things of wisdom and of what it is to be truly human.
KENNETH

Could a greater miracle take place than for us to look through each other's eyes for an instant?[45]
HENRY DAVID THOREAU

There is a lovely extra layer of meaning in what my friends have provided. Simply, we need others' insights.

Wisdom lives the patterns with integrity

Small stuff matters

Someone may read life well and have a fine sense of judgement. But if her personal integrity is questionable, we might call her clever or astute, but never wise. Wise leadership needs integrity.

If character is who we are when no-one can see us, then integrity is being the same person no matter who we are with or where we are. It is a living commitment to be true to oneself and to others equally.

If a man is correct in his own person, then there will be obedience without orders being given; but if he is not correct in his own person, there will not be obedience even though orders are given.[46]
CONFUCIUS

My dad taught me that two things test who I am:

First, who do I become when things go wrong? This is the test of truth: what is the truth of my life?

Second, who do I become when I am asked to do 'lesser' things? This is the test of humility: how do I really see myself in relation to others?

Anyone can appear to have integrity when things go well. But when things go wrong, then I'm put to the test.

Will I blame, or shift responsibility, or will I humbly acknowledge my own shortcomings? Will I tear down individuals before their peers, or do I build up the whole? Will I feed gossip, or growth? Will I follow the crowd, or embrace the one who is shunned? These are tough choices.

Integrity reveals wisdom. But I think it runs much deeper. I think we learn what it is to be wise through every small choice to live with integrity.

Small stuff matters. The insights and choices that change us are likely to be small, unheralded, counter-intuitive, even paradoxical. These glimpses of everyday glory and brokenness — wonder, frailty, joy, grief, vulnerability, delight, shame — ground us in life, in integrity, in wisdom.

Practice yourself, for heaven's sake in little things, and then proceed to greater.[47]
EPICTETUS

There are three topics in philosophy, in which he who would be wise and good must be exercised: that of the desires and aversions, that he may not be disappointed of the one, nor incur the other; that of the pursuits and avoidances, and, in general, the duties of life, that he may act with order and consideration, and not carelessly; the third includes integrity of mind and prudence, and, in general, whatever belongs to the judgment.[48]
EPICTETUS

Wisdom lives the patterns with care

Always ask 'on behalf of' whom
Some words and phrases take us straight to the heart of things.

It was my privilege to work closely with the leaders of a large public education system. I heard leaders there use a little phrase — 'on behalf of' — to provoke serious reflection on policies, strategies, and initiatives.

How was such-and-such a policy, they asked, genuinely on behalf of teachers? How was a strategy genuinely on behalf of schools and their communities? How was a pedagogical or curriculum reform on behalf of children, their learning, and their futures? I learned that there is always an 'on behalf of' to consider.

The wise act with care. It is care that gives heart to their integrity and makes it more than duty. Like attentiveness, care can be starkly evident where we least expect it.

There is always tremendous power in genuine acts of care by people of high position who act without regard for their own status.

'THINK, SPEAK, ACT... ON BEHALF OF'.

What we care about defines who we are and how we act in the world. Wisdom is often evident in selfless acts of care.

Some years ago I was in an airport and noticed a woman shining shoes. I had never had my shoes shined and I had some time so I sat down. We started to talk. She was from Africa. All her family had been massacred except for three children. She had found her way to America with the remaining children about fifteen years before.

Trained as an engineer, the only work she had been able to get was shining shoes, and she had done it cheerfully to put all her children through university. She was a woman of extraordinary pain, dignity, courage, and faith. Her presence was powerful. She lived and worked 'on behalf of' her children. As she shined my shoes and we chatted that day, I had the sense that for those few minutes she was also there 'on behalf of' me.

It is care that makes the best students of the patterns of the world. It is care that moulds discernment and thoughtful application. It is care, love even, that sustains one's commitment to grow in wisdom and to live for a better world.

As the great Russian dissident and novelist observed:

It is a mistake to think that there are times when you can safely address a person without love. In the same way as you cannot work with bees without being cautious, you cannot work with people without being mindful of their humanity.[49]
LEO TOLSTOY

Q. # How does wisdom help you lead?

A. Wisdom is not a formula or process. Leaders know instinctively that it's the people stuff that matters most. But reading people is hard work. Where do we start? Wisdom nurtures attentiveness in us. We listen for the words that free people to give their best and those that rob them of the power to act. We look beyond assured explanations. We learn to give equal weight to unity and diversity, and to give up the illusion of balance. We learn not to panic at complexity and ambiguity. Nor to dumb things down. We begin to think and communicate by stories more than by abstract definitions. These are some of the ways wisdom helps me lead. But we've only just begun to address that question.

Positions are contexts for leading; they don't make anyone a leader. Since we were children we have led and we have followed others. The wise still do.

CHAPTER 2

Leadership

Leading well is bringing wisdom to life

We lead on behalf of others

It's rare that everyone in a group sees the same possibility at the same time. Someone sees a way forward before others do. An industry of leadership advice has grown around this simple pattern of life.

At the start of retreats I sometimes ask, 'What do you hope we won't talk about?' The answer is clear: they do not want to hear clichés and formulas. No-one wants to hear the 'Seven Assured Steps of Leadership'. So what do they want?

They come seeking thoughtful, human ways to meet the challenges for which there are no easy answers. They might not use these words but in effect they seek leadership grounded in substance and character. That's the conversation they want.

Few use the word, but they seek wisdom. They seek ways to lead thoughtfully and humanly in situations where no textbook can give the answers: After decades of silos and stand-offs, how do you get managers and engineers to design a sustainable system together? How do you turn the mood of a group that has lost heart? How do you draw the best from people even when you doubt that such a 'best' is there—in them or you?

Wisdom is not about the individual for himself or herself. Wisdom is about living well with and for others. And leadership is always on behalf of others.

So to lead well is to bring wisdom to life in two senses: First, we help bring needed wisdom to a context. Second, we help bring to life the wisdom that is already there. Living wisely and leading well go hand in hand.

People have reflected on leadership for millennia. So how have we understood it and what if anything has changed?

It's a cliché, but leading is a journey

Leadership was superiority

Being a leader was always about being superior. We may not like it but that's the historical reality. Our word 'leader' is a relatively new invention. The 'leader' was (is) the chief, hero, head of clan, general, gentleman, captain, owner, conqueror, sage, king, imam, emperor, shaman, priest, and lots more. The terms are almost all masculine: that is the prejudice of history.

It's somewhat anachronistic to use our term 'leadership' to describe people and roles in cultures and traditions that lacked the term (and some still do). Yet the idea is clear enough: one or more person was owed loyalty and obedience by virtue of their rank. Whether inherited or won, this rank signalled not only authority, but superiority.

Ancient thoughts on leading

As early as the second millennium BC we begin to encounter literary reflections on the character and success of persons of rank and authority. In the royal autobiographies and wisdom literature of ancient Near Eastern cultures we read how men (always men) elicit loyalty and obedience, dissent and rebellion.

In the first millennium BC we hear sympathetic echoes of these sources in the ancient Jewish wisdom literature, and the beginnings of a critique. Around the sixth and fifth centuries BC, major traditions about the character and conduct of the leader emerged independently in China and Greece.

Among the Greeks we read of the demagogue. For us the term is negative. Originally it was the one who 'leads' (Gk. *ago* 'to go') the 'assembly' (Gk. *demos*).

In time the Greek and Roman consensus of the superior man (always a man) was confronted and reframed by the Christian message of a humble and humiliated messiah. Within a few centuries the fusion of these traditions produced various forms of the Christian superior man (still a man). Today we hold a fascinating, contradictory expectation of a leader: one who is superior, but humble. Or to go right back to the heart of the word, as we'll see, we expect a guide who is also a fellow traveller.

Leadership is a walk with others

The English word 'lead' in our sense has emerged since medieval times from words for 'to go'. At its most basic, we picture people 'going' somewhere and expecting someone to walk in front. Clichéd or not, the metaphor is a journey. Consider the words we use:

- We are 'here' but we want to be 'there'.
- We pursue a vision (ahead of us), our destination, and goal.
- Moving forward, we scan the horizon, look over the hill, around the corner, wondering what may be coming at us.
- We build a bridge, clear the way, and navigate unchartered territory.
- We know it will be a long haul on a rocky path with roadblocks.

- We look for guides with a sense of direction and a sure compass to open space, find a path, set a course, walk the talk, walk in our shoes, and help us progress.

The ideal of walking together

Whatever our favourite definition, here is the core pattern we know and assume:

We find ourselves part of a group who, metaphorically or literally, are going somewhere, want to go somewhere, or need to go somewhere. What makes someone a leader is the group's acceptance or invitation, then expectation that he or she will guide; whether from the front, the back, or in the middle.

Watch children play. One suggests a game and others follow. Then someone else steps forward. Lead and follow: we've been doing both since we were kids in all kinds of contexts.

Today, a new ideal has emerged. We want to move forward together. Sometimes I see a way ahead. I put it to you. Maybe I persuade you, maybe not. Then you have the better view and it's your turn to persuade me to follow.

We no longer assume that rank makes a guide worth following. We want the guide to prove his or her credibility in character, word, and action.

Going slowly doesn't stop one arriving.[1]
GUINEAN PROVERB

You can only go halfway into the darkest forest; then you are coming out the other side.[2]
CHINESE PROVERB

The traditional notion of 'leader' as superior may be true in the hierarchy of an organisation, but does not reflect the true character of a successful leader.

You're superior!

'Bringing wisdom to life'

We're in this together

Authority and character are always in the mix

Authority is unavoidable

Our peep at history suggests that authority — both position and power — can't be wiped from the leadership map. Nor need it be. I understand why we are reticent to talk about power, but it needs to be faced.

Authority and position are always part of the mix when anyone leads. They may be grasped, hijacked, or held humbly in trust. Likewise power need not be power *over*. It can be a welcome energy grounded in an intent and heart to serve.

Once a group asks someone to lead them, or accepts being led by him or her, the relationship between that person and the group is altered. The social 'contract' around invitation, acceptance, and expectation changes the person's relationship to the group (position) and brings an authority to think and act. And position and authority create the dynamic of power: sooner or later a leader and a group will face the possibility of a struggle for control. Then character becomes clear.

As a former CEO engaged to turn around a public institution, I know that position does matter, that authority is vital, and that power is always present. To put the institution back in the black and ready it for a new future, I had to strengthen governance, close most operating centres, wind back many programs, and make almost half the staff roles redundant.

Leadership is shaped by character

But if position, authority, and power are unavoidable in leading, they are neither sufficient nor even most important. Position is only a context for leading. Authority must have boundaries. And power is always susceptible to misuse in service of ego and personal gain.

Authority, power, and influence are critical tools, but they do not define leadership.[3]
RONALD HEIFETZ

My position enabled me to make the calls to restructure the college. It was my responsibility to do so and the board backed me with their authority. Power was unavoidable: I alone could make calls to hold up a process or to press ahead; to manipulate or to honour; to patronise or to listen; to shut down or to give voice. I can't say I got all these right, but we did find ways to move ahead well.

Anyone who has led such changes knows it takes considerable management skill to do it well, but skill is not enough. More than anything, the outcome is shaped by the character, authenticity, persuasion, presence, and relationships of the leader(s).

If a man is correct in his own person, then there will be obedience without orders being given; but if he is not correct in his own person, there will not be obedience even though orders are given.[4]
CONFUCIUS

A useful distinction: Formal authority extends to lists. Informal authority extends to hearts and minds.

Formal or informal?

Was a project delivered on time and budget? Did staff complete performance reviews? These things require the formal authority to hold people accountable. But it takes the informal 'authority' of character, presence, and relationship to touch hearts and minds.

A skilled leader can use her or his position to ensure a change program is delivered; but it may not influence a single belief or behaviour.

With formal authority we can influence *what*. With informal authority we can influence *who*. The formal always sits within the informal. This distinction helps us keep the emphasis on the ways we influence others and can help us address some perennial questions.

Born or made?

Run, listen, love — most of us can do what everyone else can do. But some do it better, earlier, and with an unlearned flair. I suggest it's the same with leading.

Whether by skill or some intangible, some children end up leading, and being expected to lead, more often. This may continue their whole lives. But like there are late-bloomers at sports or the academy, some people start to lead later, often in response to a crisis.

By a 'born' or 'natural' leader we usually mean charisma. True, for some leaders charisma is part of their effectiveness. But many effective and admired leaders lack charisma, and many with charisma have turned out to be appalling leaders. Charisma is important, but it's no guide to leading wisely.

True or false?

Leadership can express the noblest and darkest aspects of being human. We judge leaders not only by whether we reached the destination. We judge their influence upon us and upon the world along the way.

Were Hitler and other despots leaders? Of course. But I want nothing to do with their kinds of leading or influence.

To define or not to define?

Leadership is not about getting the same group of people to do the same things in the same ways in a stable context. Leadership is the domain of adaptation, translation, and improvisation. The ways to do this are as varied as the people and the context.

No formula will capture the humanity and effectiveness of those in whom authority and character kiss.

What we need is not so much a definition but the ability to see the impact of one life upon another across the spectrum of human experience.

The advantage of formal positions of authority is breadth. The disadvantage is distance from raw and relevant detail.[5]
RONALD HEIFETZ

A TALE OF
MANA

We learn how to hold authority well and how to match character to authority from experience.

I count myself greatly blessed for the friendship of a man in whom authority is character, and character is authority. I sketch our story with his permission.

In 2004 the chairman of a college sought my interest in the role of CEO. Founded in 1922, the odds were not in my favour to turn around this iconic, loved New Zealand institution. First, I'd never been a CEO. Second, I was an Aussie. If you don't know what that means, watch the 2012 Rugby World Cup semi-final between Australia and New Zealand. But I was to face a much deeper challenge.

I SENSED MY LEADERSHIP
WOULD MEAN NOTHING IF
I IGNORED THIS.

In 1840 a treaty was made between the first peoples of Aotearoa New Zealand and the colonising British. Every year on February 6 the signing of the treaty, Te Tiriti O Waitangi, is remembered at Waitangi in the beautiful Bay of Islands. My first weekend in the role coincided with Waitangi Day and the college Runanga, Maori elders, hosted Sue and me. We thought we were going for a tourist experience. Little did we know.

A kaumatua is a highly esteemed man or woman who holds deep knowledge of Maori tradition. The kaumatua of the college, Hoani 'John' Komene, was also kaumatua of Te Tii marae, the meeting place at the centre of Waitangi, the treaty, and the protests.

We were watching the powhiri (welcoming) from the crowd when John slipped out of the ceremony and found me. Next thing I was seated in the whare (meeting house) alongside prominent political leaders. As I 'listened' to the speeches — all in Te Reo — I was told my turn was coming. You can imagine my relief when a breach of protocol ended the meeting prematurely and we began an hour of hongi (touching forehead and nose).

There was no escape the next morning. I spoke at dawn in the whare near where the Treaty was signed. Later that day I spoke on live national television. I wondered what on earth I had fallen into.

Not long after, I heard suggestions of an unresolved injustice toward our kaumatua. Most cautioned me to leave it alone. Knowing little about Maoritanga (Maori tradition) I knew I could make things worse. But I sensed my leadership would mean nothing if I ignored this.

I invited John to spend an afternoon together so I could hear his story. After a long and awkward conversation we arrived at what we both felt was an appropriate way to address the injustice and hurt.

Sitting opposite me at a small table, John began to pray. In Maoritanga, karakia (prayers) and waiata (songs) accompany significant meetings. An orator and warrior, John's karakia carries the formidable weight of his integrity and heart.

As he prayed, John took my hand in an arm-wrestling grip and, without a hint of competition, focused his formidable strength into me. As he prayed on, tears streaming down his face, the strength of his grip and exertion grew greater. My arm and shoulder ached but I knew I had to meet strength with strength. Standing, John drew me into a lingering hongi. There I began to glimpse its meaning: an exchange of 'the breath of life'.

My inauguration was soon after. Waiting with the Runanga to enter the auditorium, John cloaked me with his own first cloak as a kaumatua. No principal had been cloaked and few pakeha (Europeans) are ever cloaked. Physically heavy, the responsibility was unbearably heavier. A true statesman was calling me, an iconoclastic Aussie, to grow into statesmanship.

JOHN HAD CLOAKED ME TO PLACE AN UNQUESTIONABLE AUTHORITY, MANA, UPON ME.

John repeated the honour six years later at my farewell. Reminiscing recently, I asked him why he cloaked me the first time. I knew it was partly about addressing the old wrong. But now, long after leaving the college, he told me what he couldn't tell me before.

John had cloaked me to place an unquestionable authority, mana, upon me. He believed I was the right leader for the college. He knew the authority I needed and how hard it would be to win. So, without precedent, for my sake and the college's, he bestowed on me the one emblem of formal and informal authority esteemed unequivocally by all peoples of the land.

In cloaking me, John set my life's work: to grow into a mana of character that could bear the mana of the cloak.

'Naku te rourou nau te rourou ka ora ai te iwi ...'

'... With your basket and my basket the people will live'.

QUALITIES THAT
SHAPE A GROUP

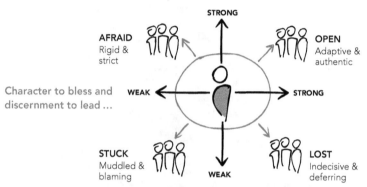

Authority to initiate and
presence with others …

STRONG

AFRAID
Rigid &
strict

OPEN
Adaptive &
authentic

Character to bless and
discernment to lead …

WEAK

STRONG

STUCK
Muddled &
blaming

LOST
Indecisive &
deferring

WEAK

We lead from who we are
The ethos of the group depends on the strength or weakness of our Authority and Presence, Character and Discernment. According to our leadership, and the context, a group may feel stuck, afraid, lost, or open. What does this mean for us and for our group?

Authority — Formal or informal, we need authority to discharge responsibility.

Presence — There's always a human link. Whether we stand with, for, or against those we lead, we're there.

Character — Intent is never purely pragmatic. Our hearts — our disposition and will — are inclined to bless, or not.

Discernment — Everything happens in a context. So much depends on how well we discern the people and context.

Leadership impacts possibility
The strength (S) or weakness (W) of a leader's qualities impacts the group:

Muddled + blaming — Authority is lost. Presence is remote or stifling. Reading lacks a big picture. Character is victim-like or accusatory. Group feels stuck.

Indecisive + deferring — Authority is embarrassing. Presence only affirms. Reading sees risks but lacks judgement. Character seems limp. Group feels lost.

Rigid + strict — Authority is law-like. Presence is harsh or rude. Reading is reductionsitic and unsubtle. Character is demeaning. Group is afraid.

Adaptive + authentic — Authority fits context. Presence enlivens. Reading wrestles with complexity. Character honours others. Group feels open.

DEEP CHARACTER

Deep character enables deep change. Below are two short stories about Australian leaders whose strength of character brought innovation and hope.

Sir Edward 'Weary' Dunlop

The indefatigable Captain Edward 'Weary' Dunlop was the senior medical officer and sometimes commanding officer among Australian and Allied prisoners of war in Burma during World War II.

Weary made brilliant surgical innovations using bamboo and other improvised aids. He fearlessly confronted and wooed the Japanese guards and officers to win relief and supplies for his men. He spoke out against the vengeful treatment of many former guards after the Japanese surrender.

Weary worked tirelessly for the returned prisoners and their families until he died. When he resumed his surgical career in Australia, some peers were jealous of the goodwill shown to him. They sought to taint his efforts on behalf of others with the smear of mixed motives.

His biographer recounts Weary's explanation of why he led as he did: 'Hintok 1943 is the key, when (Weary) read the Sermon on the Mount in the midst of "all the misery, the squalor, the grey rain and slush and sick and dying people" ... It was then that he was possessed by a "marvellous ... happiness. I understood what it would mean to love your neighbour more than yourself"'.[6]

David Bussau

In 2008 David Bussau AM was Senior Australian of the Year. In 2003 he was the Ernst & Young Australian Entrepreneur of the Year. In 2001 he received the Order of Australia. In 2000 he featured in the ABC television series *Australian Story* and was hailed 'one of Australia's 10 most creative minds'. But in 1940 he was left in an orphanage. The common link lies in David's unique and deep response to poverty.

David is a pioneer of microfinance in the developing world. On Christmas Eve 1974, Cyclone Tracy devastated Darwin. Having built several successful businesses, David took his teams to Darwin to rebuild homes at his own expense. Shortly after this incident, David responded to an earthquake in Indonesia. There he saw handouts have little impact on poverty, but a $50 loan to an Indonesian farmer changed that man's life. Decades later, Opportunity International has helped end poverty for thousands.

I've been blessed, and ... I have a responsibility to give that blessing back to others ... I happen to believe that everybody is gifted, and that everybody really has the potential to make a difference in the lives of others.[7]

DAVID BUSSAU

Q. # Why put authority and character at the heart of leadership?

A. For many people 'authority' will ring alarm bells. It may sound a hair's breadth from advocating (inappropriate) control and power. I'm not arguing for that. Definitely not. Rather I'm starting from the root metaphor of a journey and the formal or informal 'contract' between a group and a leader. A group wants direction and is prepared to give position and back it with authority. This is the *what* of leadership. It can go well or badly. *How* depends on the intangibles of wisdom, character, presence, and relationship.

Blessing expresses deep intent

An old idea worth reclaiming

Since its misty origins in medieval Anglo-Saxon and Old English the word 'bless' has conveyed religious ideas. The same can be seen in older European and other traditions. In medieval Europe, the innocuous 'Bless you!' to a sneeze was an invocation against the 'evil' of the Black Plague.

Less religiously, parents, kings, and sages spoke blessings over their children, people, and followers. A blessing was a statement of one's strongest wishes of well-being for another. In some cases the blessing was held to possess the power to actualise what was spoken and the sense of invoking magic was not far away.

But there's something rich here for our leadership contexts no matter how secular.

In ancient Near Eastern literature, a delightfully human meaning arises from the divine in accounts of creation. God or the gods create with a word, animate what is made with another word, and sometimes affirm what is made with a further word. It's as though one word summons potentiality and, another, actuality.

The wisdom traditions put great emphasis on language and speech. The power of language links the acts of knowing, making, relating, and bringing change.

Translating blessing to today

I warm to the idea that to lead is to speak and act in ways that bless others. When we live and speak in ways that are life-affirming, we may help people move from potentiality to actuality. What might that mean in practice?

Personally, when I work with people I try to pause and ask myself how I can bless them. Now I know that could sound and even be patronising or demeaning, as well as just plain old-fashioned. But it does several tangible things for me.

The idea of blessing helps me focus. I'm not there for myself, but on behalf of others. Blessing helps me see these people with respect. And blessing helps put words like serve, enable, and empower in a bigger, richer human context.

Blessing in this sense captures the deep disposition of one who leads well. Present. Attentive. Caring. Imaginative. Positioning ourselves in terms of blessing helps us look beneath the surface to what might add life.

Before that big meeting
- Take some time on your own.
- Put your notes away.
- Think about the people.
- See them as people, not colleagues.
- Imagine them flourishing.
- Commit to being present to bless.

BUILD ON BRILLIANCE

'Engagement' usually means the wider staff should engage with the messages and ideals of executives. Wise leaders engage with the craft and community of their people.

Turn engagement upside down

I love this word 'brilliance'.

I don't mean IQ but the ability of everyone to shine. Today we talk about 'empowerment'. But sometimes this may be little more than a slogan. Brilliance is deeper and more challenging.

A leader may have to break from management tradition to genuinely honour and work from brilliance. Start from what gives meaning rather than from the system.

Once we grasp the brilliance in the craft and community of our people, an extraordinary possibility opens up — we can turn engagement upside down.

We need to recognise two aspects of meaning that underpin brilliance:
1. Making — our sense of craft.
2. Relating — the communities in which we apply our craft.

This is about more than mood and camaraderie. Being able to articulate and honour the brilliance of people offers a rich perspective on strategy and innovation.

In my experience, campaigns to 'engage' workers in managers' slides and slogans are useless. I suggest managers put aside their campaigns, slides, and slogans. I suggest they engage with the craft and community of workers' brilliance and pride.

This means shifting to lead with an 'upside down' authority.

Tips for finding brilliance
1. Look for brilliance in stories of pride.
2. Understand people may not know their brilliance.
3. Expect brilliance in the unlikely.
4. Look for brilliance in craft and community.
5. Take an interest in people beyond the work environment.
6. Engage in conversation.
7. Learn what people care about.
8. Relate what you learn to what people care about.

Presentations do not engage people to be part of a community — people do.

Create the space to find voice

A usefully mixed metaphor

It is one thing for a person to name and own their brilliance. It is another to find one's voice to articulate this brilliance in the context of what challenges the community. It is yet another to know that there is space — trust, respect, dialogue, openness — to speak and to be heard.

I don't think it's a leader's place to name another's brilliance. If invited, we may coax the questioning and story-telling. Likewise, it's not possible for us to give another their voice. But if invited, we might echo their own sense of resonance and dissonance.

What a leader can do is help create the space — trust, respect, dialogue, openness — where someone can find their brilliance and voice.

The drawing below is adapted from the Reader to Author Model™, by Tony Golsby-Smith of Second Road. This model represents the transformation of people who find voice through agency.

From reader to authors

My good friend Tony Golsby-Smith has a marvellous image of this process that takes it deeper.[8]

Drawing on his considerable experience and research, Tony critiqued the modern organisation as rendering workers as passive readers bombarded with messages and no basis for discerning what is or isn't significant. At its worst, this can be dehumanising.

In a lovely play on words, Tony speaks of the 'author-ising' organisation (and leader) that equips people to be the authors of a new organisational narrative and design. As readers people are resources. As authors they are agents of design and purpose.

I think this is a rich perspective on the work of blessing: opening a path to brilliance and finding voice by author-ising people.

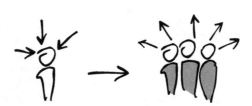

From lone and passive
readers of messages

To communities of
authors writing the script

TRUTH, BEAUTY, GOODNESS &
LIVING WELL

If leading is guiding as we walk with others, then we need some sense of where we are going. If the end is to live well together, then many of the great minds of antiquity urge us to set our compass to truth, beauty, and goodness.

Learning from ancient Athens

Athens is famous as the birthplace of the idea of democracy. It turns out the story is a bit more complicated. First, there were other ancient experiments in democracy. Second, democracy didn't mean to them what it means to us.

To qualify for the demos a man (only a man) had to be free and of high rank, and own sufficient property. We would call it oligarchy (even though the Greeks thought their form of democracy would stop oligarchy). Today we insist on equality with our democracy.

DEMOCRACY WAS A HOW, NOT A WHAT: A WAY OF ORGANISING SOCIETY, NOT A THEORY OF SOCIETY. FOR THAT WE CAN LOOK TO TWO OF GREECE'S MOST FAMOUS SONS: TO PLATO'S REPUBLIC AND ARISTOTLE'S POLITICS, AND THE STORY BEHIND THEM.

Pericles, the great statesman of Athens in the fifth century BC, had committed the city to a bold strategy to rid themselves of Sparta, their age-old rivals. But Sparta formed an alliance with their common enemy, the Persians. Pericles' plan turned into a nightmare of siege, plague, starvation, and near anarchy.

Socrates was one of the few who stood against this madness. He urged the citizens to think for themselves. This is the background to his conviction and execution for 'corrupting the minds of Athens' youth'.

Naming 'partnerships in living well'

Plato was with Socrates when the old man drank the poison. In time, he wrote the Republic to answer two questions: How could a city kill its brightest and fairest? And how do we stop this happening again? His answer was a regime of three classes ruled by a philosopher-king.

Aristotle, Plato's student, argued in a different direction. His lecture notes were gathered together by his students into the work we now know as Politics, a work not about politics in the narrow sense, but about how the affairs of the polis (city or state) should be ordered and led. Aristotle gives numerous images of the polis. One of his most succinct and suggestive definitions is this: 'The polis is a partnership of families and clans in living well, and its object is a full and independent life'. [9]. We lead on behalf of partnerships in living well.

Partnership. It's a great description not only of Aristotle's polis but of the groups we lead. A significant naming: communities, companies, organisations, or schools are partnerships. To lead with wisdom is to enable partnership.

The polis is a partnership in living well.[10]
ARISTOTLE

What did Aristotle mean by 'living well'?

Aristotle presumed the great ideals of the classical age: Truth, Beauty, and Goodness. (Funnily enough, 'everyone' appealed to those three ideals for over 1000 years but I still can't find a sentence that includes all three!)

In his wonderful book, *If Aristotle Ran General Motors*, Tom Morris, a former professor of philosophy, linked unity to these ideals in a fourfold model of excellence: truth, beauty, goodness and unity.[11] Unity was a favourite word for Plato, but he meant conformity.

That's possibly why Aristotle didn't like the word unity. But Tom is right. The idea is there. For Aristotle, unity was about connectedness, not uniformity.

Building 'partnerships in living well'
Truth? No-one can live well feeling patronised and treated as a fool. We need to know how things really are.

Truth, beauty, goodness

TRUTH YIELDS CLARITY. BEAUTY YIELDS ELEGANCE. GOODNESS YIELDS STRENGTH OF CHARACTER. UNITY-IN-DIVERSITY YIELDS HEART.

Beauty? Think of the effects on people of some public housing and bland featureless offices.

Goodness? How can we live well without the confidence that basic human rights will be honoured?

Unity-in-diversity? We can't live well without a strong sense of belonging (unity) and individuality (diversity).

Truth yields clarity. Beauty yields elegance. Goodness yields strength of character and unity-in-diversity yields heart.

This is the story behind the Arts in Chapters 7 to 10. The Art of Story builds and nurtures clarity with a heart and mind fixed on truth. The Art of Brilliance builds and nurtures elegance with a heart and mind fixed on beauty. The Art of Promise builds and nurtures strength of character with a heart and mind fixed on goodness. The Art of Grace builds and nurtures heart with a heart and mind fixed on unity-in-diversity.

41

LEADERS
(RE)SHAPE THE SYSTEM

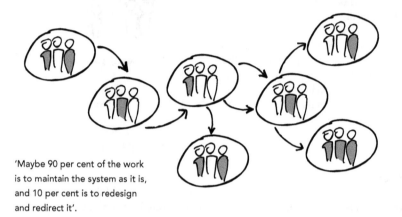

'Maybe 90 per cent of the work
is to maintain the system as it is,
and 10 per cent is to redesign
and redirect it'.

Sustain the system and subvert it

I have been privileged to work alongside some remarkable leaders. One day I was talking to one of the ones I admire most, a former senior public servant in education. I was disparaging bureaucracy when he pulled me up short:

'Mark, maybe 90 per cent of my work is to keep the system exactly as it is. The other 10 per cent is about subverting it, redesigning it, and doing everything I can to bring it back to its core mission of making children life-long learners. What you don't understand is that I only get to do the 10 per cent because I am so competent and well respected at the 90 per cent'. That gives me the freedom and authority to change the system'.

At the time I had not been a CEO and thought he was overstating the case. Now I know he was dead right.

What do re-shapers need?

- To learn how to learn.
- To think systemically.
- To see patterns and make models.
- To see the brilliance in people.
- To engage through conversation.
- To master language as an art of creation.
- To make convincing imaginative arguments.

How do we reshape systems?

- Name current reality candidly.
- Never dumb down complexity.
- Subvert elitism.
- Subvert unhelpful abstraction.
- Mobilise people as agents and authors.
- Enrich identity, intent and context through (new) story.
- Look for a new metaphor of organisation.
- Look for stories of innovation at the grass roots.

LEADERS WHO
LEAD LEARNERS

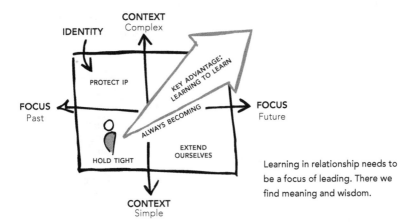

Learning in relationship needs to be a focus of leading. There we find meaning and wisdom.

Identity is complex

How well a group embraces learning depends on the complexity of the context, and where they are focused. At least four 'learning' scenarios are possible.

'Hold tight' — The future is a threat. It threatens every way we could name ourselves. Hold to the past and resist.

'Protect IP' — Our smarts have carried us through major changes. They put us ahead of the game. The future will only be incrementally different.

'Extend ourselves' — We have always adapted and extended our IP and service to every incremental change in our context.

'Always becoming' — In complex and changeable contexts a leader can't know exactly what to do. Every challenge urges us to learn and to change.

Leaders of learning to learn

Learning alone may not equip someone to lead, but those who lead well, learn well. In a sense this is the point of *Lead with Wisdom*. The leader as learner.

Change is no longer about time frames and faster, smarter technology. Deep underlying assumptions are undergoing massive upheaval: What is knowledge? What is it to know? What does it mean to be human and in a community? Boundaries are collapsing and reforming around disciplines, communities, and unfathomable possibilities.

The unfamiliarity created by ambiguity, complexity, and change requires leaders to become leaders of learners. Yet few of us know how we learn. This is the challenge: to develop an attentiveness to our own learning and to nurturing the learning of others.

43

Failure is an anvil for wisdom

Leading well makes us vulnerable

I once said it was best to lead as 'a belligerent, hard-nosed bastard'.

A group was debating whether wisdom makes leaders more successful. At a particularly raucous moment I said, 'If success is an expanded balance sheet, inflated share price, fat bonuses, and a golden handshake every 2.5 years, then forget wisdom and just be a belligerent, hard-nosed bastard!'

It was an exaggeration of course. I'm not anti balance sheets and bonuses, I just want to tell my kids a story of how I helped people to flourish as much as I helped an institution to succeed. But better stories cost.

A writer is somebody for whom writing is more difficult than it is for other people.[12]

THOMAS MANN

Good writing is hard: it takes vulnerability as much as skill. In the same spirit I wonder if 'a (wise) leader is somebody for whom leading is more difficult than it is for other people'.

I had the privilege to hear and meet cartoonist Michael Leunig. Michael called vulnerability 'an opening of our senses that is its own kind of intelligence and that welcomes intelligence of all kinds'. I think this is also true of leading. In finding an appropriate vulnerability we open ourselves to learn and to lead as learners.

Failure can be an anvil for gaining wisdom. Our deepest learning is sometimes hammered out on our worst leading.

Sometimes it takes suffering for bravado to be tempered to real courage. Sometimes it takes failure to learn to move past blame to humility. Sometimes we may only create genuine vision on the other side of our fears and chaos.

I think it takes a little bit of the fool to seek that kind of wisdom.

Leading from vulnerability
- Find a wise confidant.
- Deal with your issues first.
- Ask what you need to learn.
- Keep a learning journal.
- Think Truth, Beauty, Goodness.
- Live three words: On behalf of.
- Think about how to bless.
- Focus on hearts and minds.
- Let informal strengthen formal.
- Ask if it's time to lead or follow.
- Lead from back or middle.
- Step back to enable agency.
- Choose present before clever.
- Admit when you don't know.
- Choose to listen.
- Go for walks with people.
- Ask others about their stories.
- Wonder at their brilliance.
- Let status go.
- Show uncontrived kindness.
- Choose small things.
- Praise meaningfully often.
- Thank everyone.

Q. # This stuff sounds so old. Is there a danger of losing relevance?

A. If the mark of relevance is a quick fix, then what I'm saying won't sound relevant. But relevance is a poor cousin to wisdom. I think the greater danger is in being distracted by slogans of relevance. Ronald Heifetz famously talked about 'Leadership when there are no easy answers'. It takes more than formulas and street cunning to wend one's way through structures and systems, expectations and traditions, politics and emotions. We need the patience to not overreact, the integrity to not become complicit, and the will to hold in tension the expedient with the true, the good, and the beautiful.

PART II

Patterns

Naming, Conversation, Influence, and Character shape life.
Learning to read these well cannot guarantee that we will lead
wisely, but we're sunk if we don't.

WHY?

WISDOM AND LEADERSHIP
1 Wisdom
2 Leadership

Why do we need to lead with wisdom?

PATTERNS
3 Naming
4 Conversation
5 Influence
6 Character

WHAT?

HOW?

ARTS
7 Story
8 Brilliance
9 Promise
10 Grace

How do we lead with wisdom?

WHERE?

APPLYING THE
PATTERNS AND ARTS
11 Leader's Journey
12 Leading One
13 Leading Many

Where must we lead with wisdom?

THE STORY BEHIND PATTERNS

Wise leaders read life well

For millennia people have understood wisdom in terms of reading life's patterns. This has much to offer leadership today. But which patterns should we be reading? There are millions! I've chosen four: Naming, Conversation, Influence, and Character. I could have chosen others and I have changed their names a few times. There's no single reason why I settled on these. In the end, they are what I notice more than anything as I work alongside leaders in organisations large and small, and read old and new works in the history of ideas. Here they are.

In Chapter 3: Naming, I look at how language shapes reality. New words don't necessarily change anything, but nothing changes without new words. Naming throws light on how certain ways of thinking and speaking work against finding new possibilities and ideas. Wise leaders help people name themselves, their work, and the world truly and strongly.

In Chapter 4: Conversation, I look at how meaning is created by talking together. Communication is about sharing already created meaning. Conversation is about creating new shared meaning. Conversation is particularly important for leading. Wise leaders help people bring alive the conversations that create new possibilities.

In Chapter 5: Influence, I look at how relationships make or break change. No-one can have more influence than their relationships will bear. Formal authority can influence people to comply. Informal authority expressed in relationship can reach hearts and minds. Wise leaders help people build the relationships that support new understanding and change.

In Chapter 6: Character, I look at how our wills hold steady in the face of adversity and fear. If everyone shares an intrinsic and equal dignity, then character is how we 'carry' this dignity through our inner life and relationships. Wise leaders help people deepen integrity, trust, and perseverance.

New words may not change anything. But nothing changes without new words.

CHAPTER 3

Naming

We live and lead in language

Whether we know it or not

There's a big idea in this chapter. At its simplest, we need to use language well as leaders. At its most profound, everything we do — relating, thinking, knowing, holding hope, and bringing change—is created and mediated in language. That's a big idea.

My friend David Jones and I call this big idea naming.[1] Here, in a few short sentences, is what we mean. Take your time with them:

We shape reality with language whether we know it or not. We can bring truth and strength to our own lives and to others' through our words. New words may not change anything. But nothing changes without new words.

Working on this book, I asked alumni of my retreats two questions: First, of all the ideas, what was the hardest to grasp? Second, what's been the most powerful? Naming, both times! The power and the difficulty of naming lies in the big ideas it tries to hold together.

Knowledge and knowing, language and meaning, relationships and change. Too often education and management theory pulls these ideas apart and dumbs them down. What do I mean?

Think of a bucket. Knowledge is the things we have in the bucket. Knowing is tipping things into the bucket. Language is labelling what's in the bucket. Change is swapping things in and out of the bucket. And relationships, well, maybe that's putting things into the bucket nicely. I hope you know I'm joking!

Life and language, knowing and relating, are obviously infinitely subtler than my silly bucket analogy. Yet in many ways we were taught to see these big ideas that way. I use 'naming' to hold these big ideas together in a way that I hope is far more human. We begin with a story of naming.

HOW NAMING CAN
TRANSFORM

I'll never forget how one young teacher's renaming of herself began the transformation of a public school in a tough part of the city.

Looking for a puzzling story

The principal of the school had invited me to play the role of 'critical friend' to her staff. The teachers loved the kids but behavioural management filled their days. On a two-day retreat they had begun an important conversation. I was following up with anyone who wanted to look at their own teaching and learning.

MICHELLE AND HER COLLEAGUES HAD NO RICHER NAMING OF BEING A TEACHER THAN 'I'M A THIRD-GRADE TEACHER', AND 'I MUST FOLLOW LESSON PLANS'.

Six teachers crammed into the tiny office. I had asked them to bring stories of teaching experiences that didn't fit the norm. Reluctantly, Michelle told us about a 20-minute art lesson with her Year 3 class. The lesson, as she put it, got out of hand. 'It probably looked chaotic to anyone walking past the window', she said. Art flowed into reading into conversation into work on their theme of national parks and other topics.

I sensed something good had happened but I needed more to go on. I asked about the children.

Several children noted for behavioural difficulties did not bite, kick, or swear that afternoon! At the start of the afternoon a board at the back was near empty; at the end it was full of things the children wanted to learn. As teachers say, the kids were engaged.

Stuck with a poor naming

It was a great story, yet Michelle was apologetic. She had 'not followed the lesson plan' and gone 'off task'. If following a lesson plan is the measure of good teaching then, yes, she had failed. But it isn't. All the workshops and books on creativity, gave her no way to name what had happened that afternoon.

Michelle and her colleagues had no richer naming of being a teacher than 'I'm a third-grade teacher', and 'I must follow lesson plans'. The definitions and prescriptions were clear: set a lesson plan, teach the plan, achieve the learning outcomes, deal with behavioural problems, and so on. Certainly each has its place in being a teacher.

But those definitions and prescriptions name every teacher, any teacher, and no teacher in particular. They offer no room for individuality. Michelle could not see herself in this purely functional naming. Nor did it do justice to her as a professional, or to what happened that afternoon.

Looking for a better naming

My instincts were that something good had happened and that Michelle needed to pay attention to it. As the conversation continued she began to get inside her story and to rename what had happened. 'Perhaps I wasn't off task at all. If it's all about student engagement', she began to enthuse, 'perhaps I was more on task than I've ever been'. Her colleagues pitched in with other stories. Again, I asked Michelle to pay attention to the story.

'I AM A TEACHER WHO PAINTS WITH CHILDREN'. COMPARE THAT NAMING TO 'JUST A THIRD-GRADE TEACHER'.

A month later Michelle came up to me in the school grounds. 'Mark, I know my name. I am a teacher who paints with children', she said. 'I don't know if I'm the colours or the canvas, or if they're the brushes! What I do know is that afternoon I taught like I paint. And it's not the only time it's happened'.

Perhaps her naming sounds too cute. But Michelle is, in fact, an artist, so the name has a deep resonance for her. She found a strong sense of analogy between when she paints and when she teaches from her best. 'I am a teacher who paints with children'. Compare that naming to 'just a third-grade teacher' and its loaded double-meaning.

A new naming takes hold

Along with the retreat, Michelle's story was a catalyst for the transformation of the school. Her colleagues too shared their stories and named their brilliance. By the end of the year the story-telling had worked its way across the staff. Their new openness enabled a superb teaching practitioner seconded as an assistant principal, to draw alongside them as a mentor and coach.

As the months passed, it became clear that something had shifted in many of them. Children and parents noticed. Conversations in the staff room were now about teaching and learning. Behavioural and learning indicators began to improve. Parent and community involvement increased. That was ten years ago and the school has never looked back.

When Michelle told her story, a better intuition about herself as a teacher had already started to find words. That's why she came to that tiny office. She knew intuitively that 'following a script' is a poor naming of teaching. In her story Michelle began to speak a new possibility. When she named herself 'a teacher who paints with children' a door opened to a richer practice for her and for others.

'Naming' is critical to finding voice and agency.

A useful distinction: Naming is letting meaning unfold in language, not forcing precision through definition

Definition views language as a problem to solve. Naming views language as vital to how we know and relate to each other.

Words express identity

I love how my friend David Jones puts it: 'Naming is a different concept to definition — as different as explore is to analyse'.[2] Naming encourages us to make room for new possibilities to unfold even when we haven't quite found the words. We saw this in Michelle's story.

When Michelle named herself as 'a teacher who paints with children' she was naming her particular brilliance as a teacher. The point wasn't to find words that made her feel good. What she needed were words that named her brilliance as a teacher. Likewise her colleagues, none of whom named themselves the same way because their brilliance was different.

I think Michelle had begun to rename her teaching long before the session with me. She sensed that her best teaching broke the norms. But she still couldn't name what she was doing when she taught at her best. Once she named it, she became more deliberate about teaching that way more often.

Words close or open conversation

Neither naming nor definition is 'better'. The difference is our disposition to the broader context of words and life. Definition closes. Naming opens.

Definition is about deciding on a core of meaning that excludes all other meanings. Naming is about staying open to outlying meanings.

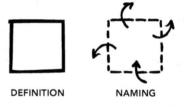

DEFINITION   **NAMING**

Definition — Finds clarity by excluding outlying meanings and finalising conversation.

Naming — Finds clarity by staying open to outlying meanings and conversation.

Consider Michelle again. Certain elements of the definitions of teaching remained important to her. But they ruled out meanings and experiences such as the art class. Her naming — 'I am a teacher who paints with children' — brought her outlying experiences and meaning into the heart of her identity.

As data is to definition, so stories are to naming. If definition offers precision, naming expresses identity.

Here's a tip. The louder a speaker gets, the less he knows his point. Likewise, the more we insist on a certain word, the less we know our own point. This is how some vision statements read like a pastiche.

Language shapes reality

Language is integral to life

Leaders certainly need to use language well. But, far bigger than that, everything we do is somehow created and mediated by language.

Later I will introduce thinkers I draw on regarding naming. For now, here are four big hypotheses about life behind what I mean by naming.

We speak to know who we are and where we are.

We live in relationships — We only know ourselves in relationships. We live 'in', with, and for others.

We live in stories — We are our stories, not bundles of traits or facts. We live by our openness to meaning unfolding within and around us.

We live by interpreting — We create meaning more than discover it. We live by attributing significance to ideas and events.

We live in language — We speak to know who we are. We name who we are first to ourselves, then to the world.

Language shapes our relationships and stories, and how we interpret both. As life unfolds, we feel the need to describe, to name, ourselves differently. What begins as a hunch may end up changing our lives. It is fascinating how something is triggered in us by speaking about ourselves in a new way.

A name allows and limits possibility

New words may not change anything, but nothing changes without new words.

It's tempting to think we can change our lives by just changing our words. We can't. No matter how religiously we repeat the motivational one-liners we put on the fridge, we might not change one whit. Yet equally our lives won't change until we find new words we can speak truly and strongly.

Sue and I were married in 1979. 'Married' remains a precious naming for us. But with the years, our marriage has come to mean new things to us, and we have found new ways to name the bond, the understanding, and the possibilities we share.

Each name links to those before; each with its own possibilities. Some names limit us; some enrich us.

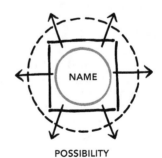

POSSIBILITY

Change can only occur through a rich and meaningful naming of our past and present that enables possibilities.

Naming is more than positivity

Selling naming short
Motivational hype is not the way of transformation.

A renowned motivational speaker dialogues with a young man in a vast audience. The crowd wills its banter deeper. Artfully the speaker reframes each self-defeating phrase the young man utters. The optimism is intoxicating. The young man rises from his seat to the promise of power and wealth.

The speaker draws out another and another. His rhetoric pervades and persuades. Some certainly leave better. The influence lingers in the tapes and books and coffee mugs. Others will crash to earth with a thump in the days and weeks that follow.

What do we make of this phenomenon? I don't wish for a moment to deny the genuine change that some experience at these kinds of seminars. But the way the speaker uses language disturbs me.

The speaker in part honours and in part misrepresents a truth. Our language does shape our lives. If I have to keep quoting one-liners to remain emotionally buoyant, then my underlying defeatist self-naming still rules. Worse, I might try to be what I'm not. Motivational phrases are not the way of deep transformation.

Naming truly and strongly
The wise leader enables others to name themselves more truly and strongly.

Hype seems strong but is false and thus weak. I'm talking about a deeper dynamic. I want to understand how the subtle inner conversation — between the sense we make of our lives and how we describe ourselves — impacts our choices and experiences.

For many years clients asked, 'Mark, when will you take up a CEO role?' I always answered, 'I'm not CEO material', and they always challenged me. One day I wondered, 'Why do I always say that? What if it's not true?' Not long after I was CEO of a public institution.

Saying those words didn't change anything — except in me. But that's what had to change first.

When we wonder at what might be, an inchoate musing begins to find shape in language. If this fledgling naming is weak and untrue, nothing good will come of it. But if it's strong and true, and we dare to speak it, then we stand on the edge of new possibility.

'JUST SAY THE WORDS!'

Naming and maturity

The power of past naming

Have you ever said something and wished you could shove the words back in your mouth?

Those of us with children know the experience only too well. At one level we might think, 'What's the big deal?' Words are only sounds, right? Wrong.

It turns out that our words can have a huge effect on ourselves, others, and even the world.

One child grows up hearing words of affirmation and encouragement. Another hears only disparagement or abuse. No one's destiny is fixed in these words, yet very often they continue to echo in the now adult's sense of identity and worth.

Other words shape us too. Though we may be blind to them, stories from the past carry their own profound impact. Our history in close relationships, family, and community sets limits on how we can see ourselves and speak about life.

The broader past too shapes us. Cultural norms that seem natural to us — like justice, democracy, equality — arose in the complex tapestry of our culture's past and are now woven with the drives, the desires, and the actions of the present.

Maturity is a journey to name well

Think again of the child demeaned and abused with weak and false naming.

Perhaps she had a kind grandmother or teacher who encouraged her with stronger, truer namings. Over time this young woman must:

1. Hold on to each older naming that still rings true and strong.
2. Reject each naming that no longer or never was true or strong.
3. Embrace new namings that better say who she is and desires to become.

This is a lifetime's work, and a hard road. Every false and weak naming needs to be rejected. And every strong and true naming, whether given by ourselves or others, retained and deepened. But if we are to help others name themselves truly and strongly, it is a road we must take ourselves.

Reflect on your own names

- How were you named as a child? Which helped you live well? Which didn't?
- How have these names lingered with you?
- How do you name yourself now? Which ones feel true and strong? Which don't?
- Which ones help you engage fully with others?
- What do you need in order to give them due attention?

CAVEAT: Some people have been hurt deeply by the names others gave them. Please don't continue any exercise that triggers distress.

THE SIGNIFICANCE OF
NAMING OUR PAST WELL

It would be nice to think that naming and renaming could be easy and automatic. Often it is not. Usually it involves a measure of standing alone, while those around us see things in the old ways. To name ourselves strongly and truly will call upon our deepest resources of character.

A tortured man

Fernando Flores was Minister of Finance in Chile at the time of Pinochet's military coup.[3] He was gaoled for three years and was subjected to torture and solitary confinement. Early in his incarceration, Flores named his challenge powerfully: not to live or die, but to grow or die.

'When I left prison, I had to figure out how to embrace my past', Flores says. 'Those three years represented a tragedy that I used to recreate myself, not something that was done to me. I never blamed Pinochet, or my torturers, or external circumstances. I feel "co-responsible" for the events that took place'.

As Flores explains, it matters deeply what story we tell: 'I never told a victim story about my imprisonment. Instead, I told a transformation story — about how prison changed my outlook, about how I saw that communication, truth and trust are at the heart of power. I made my own assessment of my life, and I began to live it. That was freedom'.

Renaming tragedy

Consider what Flores did. He 'embraced' his past. He named his story truly and strongly — it was a 'tragedy'. But it wasn't only tragedy. He sensed he must also name his story another way. He refused to name himself as a 'victim'. He refused to hand power to his gaolers and torturers by blaming them. Flores named his own place in the life of Chile before the coup. But he sensed a further possibility. He could tell a 'transformation story'. He could change his 'outlook'. He could find 'power' to live. Flores found 'freedom' in living a new naming of his life.

POWERLESS INTERPRETATIONS SHRINK OUR LIVES. POWERFUL INTERPRETATIONS ENLARGE US.

Flores named a possibility he sensed in his story and in himself. Then he began to speak and live this possibility, this naming, into being.

Later, Flores reflected on the connection between language and action: 'We don't realise how much we create reality through language', he says. 'People talk about changing their thinking, but they have no idea what that is, let alone how to do it. The key is to stop producing interpretations that have no power'.

How well do we name?

We interpret — and then we name — ourselves and our worlds. What we think about ourselves and life, how we interpret and name ourselves, has a way of coming to the surface. Powerless interpretations shrink our lives. Powerful interpretations enlarge us.

Naming is integral to how we live. The question is, how well do we name?

Like Flores, sometimes we have an intuitive sense that there is more to who we are and what we have experienced. We move towards naming ourselves more strongly. We begin to name our community more truly. We name ourselves in community with new insight. Our intuition links us in new ways to those around us. We sense the presence of something greater that links us to the best of being human. We also sense something unique, some possibility that only we as individuals can know and realise. We wonder what might be if we dared to name ourselves more truly and strongly.

'PAST'

Poor naming of our circumstance and blaming gives power to those who do not deserve it.

A caveat for 'victims'

I admire Flores and his choice not to name himself a 'victim'. However, for others, especially for those abused as children, they may first need to name themselves as victims.

Too often silence has shrouded this horrendous injustice. To refuse the shame that is not hers, a woman abused as a child must first name herself a victim. In time, to live well, she may grow to name herself a survivor.

There is a big difference between Flores' circumstances and those abused as children. Flores was an adult. He acknowledged some complicity in the circumstances that led to his imprisonment. This is not the case with children abused by adults.

This is a book on leadership. We must acknowledge that in many cases children were abused by leaders whom sections of society subsequently protected more than the children.

I offer this caveat out of respect for friends whose lives were traumatised as children by the violence of trusted adults. Likewise for friends, sometimes the same, who work alongside those who were abused as carers, activists, social workers, and therapists. I salute you all.

Q. **What is the importance of naming in leading?**

A.   I have likened leading to the mortar in a brick wall. The strength lies in the smaller, less substantial fill. Small things can have disproportionate impact. There is not much that is 'smaller' than a word — but few things are more powerful. We have all known the impact of a careless word or a well-chosen word. We have endured presentations where bland, predictable language cut off all hope of dialogue and discovery. To change a culture one must change the way some words are used and introduce others. Of course, new words may not change anything. But nothing will change without new words.

Strong naming subverts clichés

When 'creative thinking' isn't

At the close of the first day of their planning retreat, I was to give an address on leadership to the partners and directors of a practice within a global professional services firm. Although previously renowned for their entrepreneurial flair and positive culture, the practice and the firm had slumped in best employer surveys and they were losing market share. They had chosen 'Difference' as the guiding theme for the retreat.

I joined them for the afternoon's 'creative thinking' workshop before my address. Brightly coloured pipe cleaner sculptures now covered the tables. The walls were papered with brainstorming ideas from small groups. It had been a lively session and the group had enjoyed spending time together. With only a handful of exceptions, however, the walls were covered in clichés.

I discarded my address and asked a simple question: 'If your competitors had done this exercise, would the words on the walls still be the same?' The answer was embarrassing: 'yes'. But more had happened that afternoon than the sculptures and clichés suggested.

Naming is always messy at first

On five occasions they had engaged in real conversation. The insights had been rich but messy and inconclusive. Each conversation had departed from the facilitator's process; so although the insights were the best of the day,

none had been captured. Rather than embracing these conversations, the facilitator had cut each one short and steered the group back to their pipe cleaners and butcher's paper. And no-one challenged this.

The words on the walls were 'best practice' and vacuous. The naming was bullish but empty; positive but false. We began a new conversation that afternoon. What might 'different' mean without the clichés? As well as being renowned for its competence, how could the practice earn a reputation for being brilliant?

Twelve months later the practice was living this richer naming. Every staff member had named their own professional brilliance. Unsurprisingly, little of it mapped onto the firm's competency matrices. Significant innovations emerged as they learned to leverage their brilliance. At the next survey, the practice was rated equal best in the firm and positioned in the best employer bracket nationally.

'... BUT WE'RE NAMING SOMETHING IMPORTANT'.

'STICK TO THE PROCESS!'

BEHIND THE IDEA OF NAMING STAND SOME
SIGNIFICANT THINKERS

Good theory, after all, is both an abstraction from, and an enrichment of, our concrete experience.[4]

DAVID TRACY

Knowing is not only intellectual but personal and relational. We know through our feelings, imagination, and even our bodies. Language plays a vital role in this full-bodied knowing. Isn't it fascinating how we don't quite know what we think or feel until we speak or write it! When we do name it, no matter how inarticulate, something begins within and beyond us.

No philosopher talked about naming quite like this, but some big names prepared the way.

Martin Heidegger (1889–1976) showed the limits of self-awareness. A carpenter hammers nails. He can bend a nail and hit his thumb occasionally without really being aware of his hammering. But if he bends several nails, or hits himself repeatedly, he becomes aware! He wonders if the nails are weak, or maybe he's tired. Sometimes his hammering changes.

Heidegger's student, **Hans-Georg Gadamer (1900–2002),** extended this insight to language: 'The more language is a living operation, the less we are aware of it'.[5] The new word was 'interpretation'. Interpreting life is a bit like interpreting a text. We learn to negotiate and 'fuse' different 'horizons'; like an author's intention, culture and history, the details of the text, and our contexts and 'prejudices'. But as far as we know we're just reading.[6]

Michael Polanyi (1891–1976) explored knowing in scientific discovery and everyday experiences. He saw knowing as 'tacit' and personal. Looking at a painting, we're only 'subsidiarily' aware of colours and brush marks. A face anchors us while our minds rearrange the details into a meaningful whole. In the end, we may encounter the painting and be changed by it. Knowing, then, is a kind of indwelling; like the way we learned to ride a bike.

The 'early' **Ludwig Wittgenstein (1889– 1951)** believed philosophical problems were linguistic puzzles that could be solved by tighter language and logic. Language was almost mathematical. Later he radically challenged this view. Definitions he realised 'only lead us to other undefined terms'.[7] Instead of definitions, he spoke now of 'language-games'; of the fluid yet meaningful role of language within communities of speakers.[8]

Dispelling the idea of science as neutral, **Thomas Kuhn (1922–1996)** showed that 'normal science' actually suppresses discoveries if these subvert a scientific community's basic commitments.[9] Young scientists, or those new to a field, ask different questions because they see from a different 'paradigm'. If this alternative paradigm prevails, it is the new 'normal science', as shown in the shifts in physics from Newton to quantum mechanics.

The 'postmodern turn' exposed how power works through language. **Michel Foucault (1926–1984)** wrote searing critiques of the impact of definitions of 'normal' and 'abnormal' in the history of mental institutions and prisons. **Jacques Derrida (1930–2004)** believed all speech and texts must be 'deconstructed' to reveal their complicity in oppression. But **Paulo Freire (1921–1997)** invoked a very different power behind the role of language and conversation in the struggle for liberation:

Dialogue cannot exist … in the absence of a profound love for the world and for men. The naming of the world, which is an act of creation and co-creation, is not possible if it is not infused with love.[10]

PAULO FREIRE

Certainty — exhaustive knowledge — has been the Holy Grail of Western philosophers. Most assumed that reason is capable of reaching this certainty. Plato anchored his confidence in the Forms. That was too woolly for Aristotle. He looked to the *telos* or purpose inherent in things. Descartes looked inside himself: he doubted, therefore he thought, therefore he is, or was! In the twentieth century we kept moving inward. To structures of the mind. To experiences of meaning and power. To phenomena of personal existence. To language. To interpretation. To the social, even relational, structures of knowing.

Insights for leading in language

From these thinkers and more, I have drawn this composite of naming:

- Our words shape our lives and others' whether we know it or not.
- Our language conveys commitment, not simply information.
- Language is not capable of exhaustive precision.
- Every naming is provisional — we never name with finality.
- We do not master language but indwell it.
- Language means what it comes to mean in a community.
- Every naming helps us see something, yet blinds us to other possibilities.
- The more abstract we make our language, the more it reduces us.
- 'The naming of the world (wisely)… is not possible if it is not infused with love'.[11]
- All naming begins in inchoate and inarticulate musings.
- 'Naming is our way of making knowledge personal'.[12]
- To name truly and strongly is to make hope tangible.
- A wise leader enables others to name themselves more truly and strongly.
- Use plain words if possible.

Naming complexity by systems

Systems are in our minds

One of the ways we manage complexity and ambiguity is to think in terms of systems. We see the body as having a skeletal system, nervous system, circulatory system, and so on. We group oceans, mountains, rivers, and weather and name this the water cycle.

Faced with phenomena that we want to understand, we bundle it up, draw a boundary, ascribe a purpose, and name it the 'such-and-such' system. It's amazing how well this thinking works considering we can never name precisely where the boundaries lie. The boundaries may appear to be 'just there' — like cell walls and shorelines and national borders — but they're as much the products of our naming of them as of any physical demarcation from what they surround.

It's virtually impossible to conceive of modern life without this idea of systems. We speak of information systems, safety systems, education systems, transport systems, economic systems, political systems, and more. Something as big as a global mining corporation or a public health service would hopelessly confuse us if we couldn't mentally put a boundary around it and name it as a system.

Naming patterns as systems

Systems don't exist in the same way as a tree, or the Eiffel Tower, or Aunt Suzanna. What I mean is this: What we name as a system is never exactly what's 'out there'. It's an idea that helps us hold the whole and parts together (One and Many) so we can talk meaningfully and act purposefully. Sometimes breakthroughs come 'simply' by redrawing the boundaries and renaming the context.

Sir Geoffrey Vickers, the eminent systems theorist, served as a British officer during World War I. In a seminal article, he argued that naming complex contexts as 'problems' promoted ineffectual 'solutions'. Vickers recalled a speech from the ceasefire on November 11, 1918. Hours earlier they had been shelling Germans to free the French. Now the British general brilliantly renamed their context:

'Gentlemen, have you considered how you are going to manage without the Germans? ... For more than four years France has been divided into an occupied zone — occupied by the Germans — and a free zone, defended by us. Now all the Germans will be gone in a few weeks but we shall be here for months ... Meantime we shall be the occupiers'.[13] With those words the world shifted.

'GENTLEMEN, FORGET THE GERMANS —THINK OF THE FRENCH!'

POETS, WIZARDS, AND MISFITS

My deepest inspirations are some wily poets, wizards and misfits from literature. Let yourself soak in these gorgeously human images of naming.

The poetry of naming
When the mind is at sea, a new word provides a raft.[14]
JOHANN WOLFGANG VON GOETHE

The Word became flesh ... and dwelt among us ... full of grace and truth.[15]
GOSPEL OF JOHN

An entire mythology is stored within our language.[16]
LUDWIG WITTGENSTEIN

The wizardry of naming
My favourite fantasy novel is *Earthsea* by Ursula Le Guin. I love the deeply flawed humanity of the characters and how naming is the deep magic of life.

Need alone is not enough to set power free: there must be knowledge.[17]

'Let him be named as soon as may be', said the mage, 'for he has need of his name'.[18]

'When will my apprenticeship begin, Sir?' 'It has begun', said Ogion. There was a silence, as if Ged was keeping back something he had to say. Then he said it: 'But I haven't learned anything yet!' 'Because you haven't found out what I'm teaching', replied the mage.[19]

To change this rock into a jewel, you must change its true name. And to do that, my son, even to so small a scrap of the world, is to change the world.[20]

For magic consists in this, the true naming of a thing.[21]

'For a word to be spoken', Ged answered slowly, 'there must be silence. Before, and after'.[22]
URSULA LE GUIN

The places we find names
Our greatest stupidities may be very wise.[23]

Don't for heaven's sake, be afraid of talking nonsense! But you must pay attention to your nonsense.[24]

Never stay up on the barren heights of cleverness, but come down into the green valleys of silliness.[25]
LUDWIG WITTGENSTEIN

The deep humanity of naming
Human existence cannot be silent, nor can it be nourished by false words, but only by true words, with which men and women transform the world. To exist, humanly, is to name the world, to change it. Once named, the world in its turn reappears to the namers as a problem and requires of them a new naming. Human beings are not built in silence, but in word, in work, in action reflection. [26]
PAULO FREIRE

THE UNUSUAL STORY OF
NAMING AS LEARNING

We say we 'live and learn'. Well, we live, but we may not always learn. One such failure led to a new picture of learning.

An 'Oh, S@#*!!' experience

Early in the 1990s one of the world's biggest mining operators was in the final stages of planning a new mine. But the executives harboured a growing unease. After a long day holed up in a hotel room, one wrote three figures on a transparency — time to build, cost to build, annual tonnage output — and placed the damning numbers on the overhead projector. Another simply wrote across those figures, 'Oh, S@#*!!'.

Two things followed. A better, cheaper mine was built in less time. And the event passed into folklore as a great story of 'organisational learning' and 'thinking outside the box'.

I'M VIEWING LEARNING AS THE CAPACITY TO CRAFT DEEP INSIGHTS INTO OURSELVES, OTHERS AND THE WORLD.

The CEO was delighted by the better mine that the team eventually built. But he saw no evidence they were better able to achieve future breakthroughs. If they couldn't explain how they had reached the first (bad) design, or how they had come to rethink the second, then could they say they had learned?

Learning as insight by naming

My colleague David Jones [27] and I were invited to study the experience and develop a commensurate theory of organisational learning. The result was this working model and description of learning:

Learning is moving from one naming to the next open to the significance of both.

Learning — We are clearly a million miles from training. I'm viewing learning as the capacity to craft deep insights into ourselves, others, and the world — and to be changed by the ways we hold those insights.

The mining executives could reconstruct their story using the clichés of 'breakthrough thinking' and innovation. But superimposing explanations is not learning. Like the teacher Michelle, deep learning requires us to be present to our stories. The executives' growing unease before the breakthrough — why they hadn't addressed it — was ample raw material. They only needed to pay attention to their instincts.

From one naming to the next — No name ever says everything. Every name is provisional. A way of naming feels right at one point in time. Later it doesn't say enough or may be misleading. We have changed. A new naming begins to emerge.

A name is not a label. Sue and I are married but we name what that label means to us in ways we never could 34 years ago. The Australian Taxation Office still bears that label. In a stable taxation system, it was enough to say it was 'the collector of revenue'. But when global commerce changed the game, it had to become the primary 'shaper of the taxation system'. The mining executives had a dramatic story but it failed to fire new understanding. They had new numbers, but no new naming.

Open to the significance — Initially David and I wrote 'fully open to the significance of both'. But Heidegger was right: we are never fully open. So when do we know we have learned? Perhaps when we know why one naming gave way to another. Perhaps also when we know this well enough to be more open to the next.

Deep learning requires humility. The first mine design was embarrassing. But dismissing it stifled learning. Questions, without blame, needed to be asked: About how the original design unfolded and was approved. About why the misgivings were suppressed. About how key conversations lost their way. About how the legend of 'Oh, S@#*!!' stopped reflection. Stories are the raw materials of learning. Ignore them to stay ignorant. Embrace them to grow.

Of both — We must respect our stories even as we surrender the past. It is unhelpful to romanticise or denigrate the past. Nor to speak naïvely or cynically of the future. If we cut off our past, we cut off our identity. If we won't face the past, we lose our conviction to rename. If we won't face the future, we die. And if we fantasise a bright tomorrow, we lack the conviction to act truly and strongly.

No-one intended to design an under-performing, over-priced mine that would take too long to build. Rubbishing the past marks an unwillingness to learn. Deep learning is markedly different. First, respect toward the first designers and their outputs. Second, insights into the time of growing unease. Third, clarity about what happened between 'Oh, S@#*!!' and 'Why don't we try this!' And fourth, a new openness of conversation across the mine.

Indeed learning is moving from one naming to the next open to the significance of both.

Reflect on a positive change

1. Before the shift, what ways of naming were part of the problem?
2. What role did changing language play in creating change?
3. How do people describe the change and what it means to them?
4. What story do they tell?
5. What evidence is there of learning at the time?
6. What is the learning that you see is still to be gained?
7. Try naming the shift that took place: From 'this' to 'that'.
8. Are they still open to learn?

Hunting for a name

My messy process

A client is an expert in project management (PM) with an impressive portfolio of turning around stalled projects. She tells a compelling story of the failure of PM as a discipline. Like many innovators and entrepreneurs, she has struggled to name what she does. So she asked me to help her name all this. What did I do?

What I most want to hear first is dissonance. I look for confusion, ambiguity, anomaly, and contradiction; for insights carried in stories and hunches that don't (yet) cohere. This proves to be fertile ground.

Side anecdotes interest me as much as the stories that seem most relevant. I try to catch both the cascades of ideas and the quieter, less confident, moments that often reveal rich confusion.

I search my storehouse of patterns for One and Many, abstraction and story, knowing and meaning, and more. An earlier story comes back. I ponder an analogy. I bridge history and philosophy, my stories, clients' stories, and hers. I sense a pattern that I can't yet name.

Feeling I have nothing often precedes insight. Half a question forms. If I ask it too soon I see the eyes glaze. I never reach a good question without fumbling over others too abstract.

I draw and map the whole time. I have a bag full of little hieroglyphs for paradox,

change, system, relationship, dualism, abstraction, perspective, dialogue, argument, story, and naming. I play with words: singly, in pairs, and triplets.

Cautiously I suggest a naming of what she does. I keep it very simple. A metaphor or analogy. I don't use management terms.

I glimpse parallels in the sense she makes of her own life and of her clients' projects. I have no desire to intrude but suggest my intuition. With permission I look; without it, I don't.

On a walk or in a café I see what I hadn't seen. I write and draw quickly. I juxtapose ideas that haven't been connected.

I see vision as a future story and strategy as an argument for that story. I try to imagine the story she imagines. I share my storyboard of the argument. She begins to tell the story her way and it's far better than mine.

As best I can look inside my own 'hammering', I think that's what I do when I help someone name more truly and strongly.

Q. # How is language and naming vital to organisations?

A. People are creating meaning all the time. Our only access to this changing meaning is in the words people use. But the official labels or definitions rarely carry the key meanings. We find those in the informal languaging: in the anecdotes, analogies, and metaphors that people use to assure themselves they know what's going on. These might be true and strong, or false and weak. If a leader is to stimulate change, she must get inside this language and — subtly — strengthen or subvert it as appropriate.

Conversation may not yield new meaning. But new meaning will not take hold without conversation.

CHAPTER 4

Conversation

We construct meaning in conversation

Meaning-making is an art of leadership

Twenty-five years ago my former colleagues and I began to frame ways to construct and lead conversations that were genuinely strategic.[1]

We were struck by how many meetings seemed to meander for want of clear intent. Agendas, reports, and minutes didn't seem to help and people struggled to name with real insight the purpose for meeting. Colleagues met and talked but rarely seemed to engage with each other.

We watched the ways language and conversation would open or close the space to imagine and frame a strategic argument. We began to build into our practice the patterns we saw in these conversations. Increasingly, clients embraced the kinds of dialogue that fostered creativity and innovation.

What we saw was a shift in meaning-making: from struggling to find or clarify meaning, to becoming adept at constructing new meaning.

Genuine breakthroughs may arise from inspired moments for individuals, but they don't take effect without conversation. Meetings, however, rarely become the kind of conversation that leads to breakthroughs and new meaning. In fact, formal meetings, presentations and reports are more likely to stifle inspiration. So what does it take for people to grapple well with ambiguity and complexity? It takes the informality and egalitarianism of coffee and whiteboards.

Meaning-making is an art of leadership. I'm not suggesting that the leader necessarily makes the meaning. I'm suggesting that a leader is uniquely placed to influence the conditions necessary for conversations to reach breakthroughs and new meaning.

Leaders facilitate meaning-making. By the ways they are present, and the ways they name the context and challenge, leaders set the ethos for imagination, insight, deliberation, and choice.

So what do I mean by conversation?

A useful distinction: Conversation is not the same as communication

Conversation opens space

Communication is sharing created meaning.

Conversation is creating shared meaning.

I don't want to be precious about this. At a certain level communication and conversation are synonyms. Yet the distinction is not just playing with words. The bigger picture is our assumptions about knowing and meaning.

Communication — Sharing created meaning—suggests there already exists some knowledge that others need to know. We need to communicate: clearly, concisely, and relevantly. This is crucial in every kind of enterprise. Sometimes things are straightforward, and the last thing we need is a never-ending process of consultation that's supposed to deliver consensus.

Communication tends to assume that knowledge and meaning are things to be discovered and passed on.

Conversation— Creating new meaning — suggests that the meaning or the message is not yet fixed. This kind of unscripted interaction can be a doorway to new meaning and new knowledge.

Conversation tends to assume that knowledge and meaning take shape through interaction. Conversations highlight how meaning is tied to relationship.

Conversation is a leader's work

Conversation is to leading as communication is to managing.

Communication is crucial to operations and execution. I know that well as a former CEO leading a turnaround. Everyone needs to hear the same message at the same time or as soon as possible.

Conversation is particularly crucial to strategy and design. But strategy has come to be dominated by analysis and planning. The data may be relevant and the analysis expert, but no-one analyses their way to the future. Communication can't create strategy.

I think of strategy as an act of human imagination. Our vision is a future story. Our strategy is our argument for that story. And that argument becomes the basis of new design work. All this involves creating new meaning. That's the domain of conversation.

Conversations like this only happen where a leader makes room for them. The art here is to stay open to the unexpected, while bringing clear intent. Here new meaning can unfold.

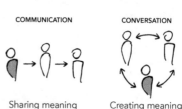

COMMUNICATION · Sharing meaning

CONVERSATION · Creating meaning

Meaning unfolds in relationship

Meaning emerges as we engage

Knowledge and meaning are not things 'out there' waiting to be discovered. Knowing and meaning are tied into relationship. That's as true of how we know ideas and things as it is with personal relationships. It's when we bring people, ideas, and things together that we see something new.

So meaning emerges as we engage in each other's lives. That means we can't stand at a distance and hope to learn or make anything new. We have to enter into each other's ways of thinking and talking, and especially share our stories.

Few instances of knowing and meaning are as profound as the bond of a mother and child.

Find a lovely photo of a mother and child. (Seriously, go find one.) Think about how they know each other. That child knows the mother and she knows the child. But there's more. The child will come to know herself or himself by the mother knowing her or him. And it's the same for her.

We come to know ourselves through others knowing us.

Attachment shapes our knowing

In *A General Theory of Love*, Lewis, Amini, and Lannon bring neuroscience to this experience with a theory of how love impacts the brain.[2] First, they show how experience lays down neural pathways. Second, they show how limbic connections are established between people. Last, they illustrate the impact of love on the brain. The child's and the mother's brains will mirror each other depending on the presence or absence of love. I find that extraordinary!

So love, or lack of love, shapes how a child grows and knows for the rest of his or her life. And it's not just about children and mothers.

Attachment is a form of knowing. What happens between all people shapes how they see themselves, each other, and the world. This is why I say that somehow all our knowing occurs in and for relationship. Even inanimate things make sense to us because of the relationships we indwell between people, experiences, ideas, history, and much, much more.

This is why conversation in workplaces is so important. We only develop new possibilities to the degree that we engage with our colleagues.

'THE MORE I KNOW YOU, THE MORE I KNOW MYSELF'.

Knowing and meaning begins with the bond between mother and child.

TWO ROADS FOR
ENGAGEMENT

Conversation is vital to engagement, the holy grail of organisational leadership.

Two roads to understanding

I remember a CEO presenting over fifty slides covering vision, mission, values, and so on. His aim was to engage his top 100 managers in changing the culture of the business. Each manager received his own slide pack to repeat the presentation and engage the next few hundred. And so on. He achieved culture change, but for the worse. I suggest we rethink engagement.

In 1986 I was part of the start-up of the strategy and design firm now called Second Road. Later I served as its CEO. The name comes from something Aristotle said.[3]

Famous for framing the rules of logic, Aristotle also saw the limitations of logic as a 'path to truth'. Logic or the syllogism, he said, worked for 'things that cannot be other than they are' — that is, things that don't change.[4] He suggested a different set of thinking tools for things that *can* be other than they are — things that can change — for anything involving people.

Aristotle used different words for this alternative toolkit. One of his favourites was rhetoric, a word with as much bad press in his day as it has in ours. Our picture of rhetoric is pretty much limited to how a speaker uses language to persuade. While Aristotle included persuasion under rhetoric, he began with invention: what we would call imagination, creativity, invention, and design. My friend Tony Golsby-Smith named this the 'Second Road'.

	1st road	2nd road
For Aristotle:	Logic	Rhetoric
For us:	Analysis	Story + design

The 'first road' has produced the astonishing accomplishments of engineering, medicine, and so much more. It used to take a year to get a message across the world; now it takes milliseconds. People used to die from what we can treat with a pill. (Sadly, many people do still die: equity hasn't always followed technology.)

(Dis)engaging on the two roads

One road is not better or worse than the other. They are both important. Nor does knowing and leading map neatly across the distinction I'm making between the roads. But the idea of 'two roads' is a powerful heuristic on leading change.

The 'second road' without the first can lead to flights of imagination and even decisions that lack an anchor in verifiable evidence or experience. The 'first road' without the second can produce bureaucracies and systems that stifle creativity and innovation, and ultimately alienate workers.

We seem to have forgotten Aristotle's caveat: that logic and analysis are not suited to things concerning people. Ironically, like my example above, many so-called 'Engagement Programs' are structured as though a process or theory of change is more relevant than any actual people and context. Predictably such programs only alienate people more.

Engagement requires a different posture of the heart and mind:

1st road	2nd road
Certainty	Confidence
▼	▲
Command	Community
▼	▲
Control	Co-design
▼	▲
Communication	Conversation

Okay, I know eight C's is a bit naff. The four words on the left help explain why many engagement programs don't work. The four words on the right suggest what enables real engagement. Note the contrasts from left to right, and up and down.

Organisational management and analysis is largely built on the 'first road'. Its key assumption and goal is certainty. Nestled behind certainty is another assumption: the ideal of the autonomous individual knower. Management theorists did not invent these assumptions, ideals, and goals. They have driven the history of Western philosophy for millenia.

If I assume I can and I must have certainty, then I'll put my trust in data and plans, expecting the world to follow suit. But it never does. So I might revise my expectations. Or I might fake the analysis. Either way, I lock myself into leading by command and control. My interactions are one-way: I communicate the messages I decide everyone needs to hear.

So here's the difficult truth. We can't have certainty and we were never autonomous. What we need is an intelligent level of confidence with which to face the unknown.

Embracing conversation

Engagement on the 'second road' runs the other direction. It starts with the people and by shifting from communication to conversation. Leadership based on conversation enables people to find their unique voices. This opens the way to new meaning and to co-designing new futures. And that's how community forms.

The more we lead this way the more our expectations of engagement will change. Compliance with slides and slogans says little. People feeling confident to write their own stories within a bigger story — that says volumes.

Leaders can turn engagement upside down. Rather than ask people to engage with our words, we lead engagement by engaging with those we lead.

We know by indwelling

Knowing by experiencing

Think about how you learned to ride a bicycle, play an instrument, juggle, or swing a bat or club. Think about anything you do without concentrating. Musicians might like to try this experiment (if you don't play an instrument, pick some other skill):

- Play a piece with which you are familiar.
- Now do it again paying attention to your muscle movements.

What happened? Most likely your playing lost fluency. You may have had to stop. Why?

First, your fluency depends on not knowing what you are doing — at least not explicitly. Sounds odd, doesn't it? But the better you know something, the less you need to think about it. Details like musical notes and finger movements live somewhere in the background for a musician.

Second, your fluency depends on knowing the parts and the whole — the One and the Many — at the same time. When we try to concentrate on one without the other, we become lost.

Think about how a professional learns a craft. A young doctor may master every textbook, but only the experience of diagnosing and misdiagnosing will lead her into true expertise. It's the same for an athlete, architect, artist, builder, chef, designer, engineer, or mechanic.[5]

As Michael Polanyi put it, our knowing is a kind of immersion or indwelling. We can't know someone or something by holding them at a distance. We must move toward and even 'into' what we hope to know.

This is a difficult concept but our experience bears it out. We don't assemble facts and ideas to learn how to ride a bike, or recognise a face, or admire a painting. We throw ourselves into the experience in order to know it. And this is what happens in conversation.

As we will see, how we know is mirrored in how we talk to each other.

'HOW DID YOU DO THAT?' 'I HAVE NO IDEA'.

Fluency depends on not knowing what you are doing — at least not explicitly.

HOW WE KNOW SHAPES
HOW WE TALK

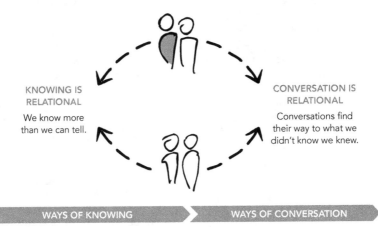

KNOWING IS RELATIONAL

We know more than we can tell.

CONVERSATION IS RELATIONAL

Conversations find their way to what we didn't know we knew.

WAYS OF KNOWING ▸ WAYS OF CONVERSATION ▸

Ways of knowing

- Knowing is as much about encounter and indwelling as it is about thinking.
- Most of our knowledge is like clues that we don't even know we know.
- When something comes into focus, clues form into patterns of meaning.
- Integration comes as 'Ah I see it!' moments when we make a new whole.
- Knowing anyone or anything transforms us and what we know.
- Our deepest need in knowing is a sense of meaningfulness, not certainty.

Ways of conversation

- The more we engage, the more we know ourselves and each other, and the more likely we are to find new meaning.
- We talk in order to think. Discussion brings clues to light. 'Bouncing ideas around' is a search for patterns.
- It may only be one person who sees or says it first. But dialogue gives shape, texture and colour to the new whole.
- We have meaningful dialogue as we are attentive and present to each other. In respect we find insight.

Conversation brings strength

We can't predict meaning

Similar in spirit to Michael Polanyi, the hermeneutical philosophers draw our attention to the open-ended experience of conversation and to the role of commitment:

No-one knows what will 'come out' in a conversation... All this shows that a conversation has a spirit of its own, and that the language used in it bears its own truth within it, i.e. that it reveals something which henceforth exists.[6]

HANS-GEORG GADAMER

Conversation itself is another kind of game... It is not an exam. It is questioning itself. It is a willingness to follow the question wherever it may go... We learn to play the game of conversation when we allow questioning to take over. We learn when we allow the question to impose its logic, its demands, and ultimately its own rhythm upon us.[7]

DAVID TRACY

Conversation may take many different directions leading to insight.

Conversation is a core process

Can you recall a professional or personal conversation that changed things for the better for you or others? How would you describe the path of the talking and listening?

Most likely it wasn't straightforward. You start with something familiar. Then find yourself talking about it differently. Or you go in a whole new direction. Someone introduces an idea or phrase. It sounds odd. Then 'it just makes perfect sense'. Someone tells a story that triggers an insight. You glimpse a new perspective. Along the way, together, you are creating meaning that is new for you.

This simple unpredictable human interaction is the unseen life of any organisation. Strategy, innovation, engagement, and empowerment need ways for people to bring their brilliance, experience, and imagination. This is the domain of conversation.

To build organisational resilience and competitive advantage, we need to ask how healthy are the conversations in the business. Are we creating room for them? Do we understand and foster the conversations that make innovation and excellence flourish?

Leaders must communicate well. Again, I do not mean to minimise the difficulty or importance of communicating well. But conversation is another order, and so much harder.

Q. # How do you work with the uncertainty of conversation?

A. It's hard to shake the desire for certainty. We think if we master the parts, we know the whole. But we can't and don't. So how do I proceed? I need to be open. Time and again I've seen brilliant ideas come from the people I didn't expect. If I try to contrive the 'right' conversations, I'm likely to end up outside where new things are really happening. Or I can embrace my unease and lean into others' conversations. I find that the more present I can be in those conversations, the more likely I might influence and welcome what emerges.

Breakdown enables new meaning

Shared ground will give way
Conversation is possible to the degree we share understanding and reciprocate commitment.

Quite a lot needs to be held sufficiently in common. We need a shared language. We need tacit agreement about how conversations work. Simple things, like taking turns to speak and not walking off mid-sentence (yes, some people don't seem to know the rules).

We also need to share some general assumptions about life and people. Like what's funny or sad. Or what you can or can't say when you don't know each other. And about how reciprocity works in sharing stories.

With enough skill we can keep a conversation comfortable. It might be bland but it's safe. But comfortable rarely moves anyone anywhere. Moving a conversation beyond comfortable and maintaining respect — now that takes great maturity and skill. People might refuse. They don't want to talk because the other party 'isn't on the same page' or 'wouldn't understand'.

It is an act of leadership to reach across differences in background to create new possibilities.

A conversation then is an exchange of far more than words and ideas. At the heart of it is commitment. We commit to staying in it and to following where it goes. This commitment is rarely explicit, but we are highly attuned to it. We read each other. We sense when someone is 'present' and when they're not.

This doesn't mean we agree on everything; quite the contrary. Imagine how unconstructive, not to mention boring, conversation would be if we simply agreed about everything.

Agreement is not the basis for continuing conversation. The will to stay open to new meanings that go beyond what we share — that's the basis. And that means old meanings must break down.

So how do we face it?

SHARED MEANING AND BACKGROUND

PRESENT   NOT PRESENT

Staying present in conversation enables old meanings to break down and new shared meaning to emerge.

Breakdown enables new meaning

Here's the rub ...

Breakdown in conversation does not guarantee new meaning. But new meaning will not emerge without breakdown.

Nobody likes breakdowns. Awkward and unpleasant at best, any breakdown in understanding or communication is likely to be painful, even destructive. Our natural instinct may be to retreat.

We need to grasp a profound but counter-intuitive point about how meaning is formed. New meaning only emerges when conversation passes beyond what is shared. New meaning arises on the other side of a breakdown in shared understanding, if commitment holds.[8]

It seems so counter-intuitive. Surely, we think, new ideas come from everyone getting along well. But if everyone always agrees, nothing new emerges.

When the conversation gets stuck or hits a barrier, most people walk away. But that's when new meaning becomes possible. And the more important the issue and relationship, the more likely it is that the conversation will break down at some point.

So how do we lead at these times? It's tempting to want to smooth and fix everything. But sometimes the mark of leadership and wisdom is not to avoid breakdown, but to help others walk well through it.

We've all experienced it

The conversation breaks down. We can't make sense of what we're hearing. We don't like it. Our attempt to bridge our differences collapses. We might retreat and close the door. Then something stirs us to re-engage. A real meeting of heart and mind is risky. It might change us. We might not like changing. We might grow. We might have to rethink. We might have to learn — even from those we didn't like or respect. New meaning will change the relationships and responsibilities. Again, the conversation may not yield new meaning. But if there is to be new meaning, it will only come by getting to the other side of breakdown.

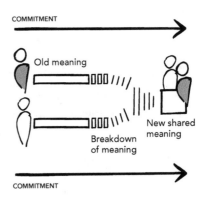

Barriers in conversation are actually turning points where new meaning becomes possible.

Maintain commitment

Conversation is vital to resilience

It's easy to see how this pattern of background, commitment, breakdown, and meaning plays out in personal relationships. But it's just as true of life in an organisation. The conversations can be healthy, unhealthy, underground, near dead, or simply gossip.

We can see resilience I think in how well we keep talking and engaging in the face of uncertainty and change. This is why I am placing so much emphasis on a leader understanding what a conversation is and does, and on the arts necessary to making them flourish.

Conversation isn't a soft option. It is indispensable to great thinking, design, operations, and service delivery. A leader must certainly communicate well. But we bear a particular responsibility to create contexts for dialogue that foster respect, imagination, and engagement.

Some argue that the right method plus the right statistics solves everything. Not much room there for dialogue. I don't buy it. Certainly conversation isn't like that. It's not a method.

At some point, a leader has to leap into the uncertainty and possibility of conversation.

Commitment tips

Moving through breakdown to new meaning

1. Stay committed to the conversation partners. Even above the outcome.
2. Stay committed to the conversation.
3. Make your commitment tangible.
4. Model the openness you seek.
5. Admit your limits of understanding.
6. Frame a question.
7. Name the breakdown if it happens.
8. Search for someone's story that helps refocus on common desire.

'I'LL JUMP IF YOU DO'.

Leaders must brave the ambiguity of conversation as part of their commitment.

Moving to questions

Method isn't enough

If conversation is such a natural part of life, why is it so often stifled in organisations? Why is communication championed as the key to engagement and cultural change?

A key figure is the French philosopher René Descartes (of 'I think, therefore I am' fame). The title of his 1637 work, *A Discourse on Method* is suggestive. His legacy pervades management: a right use of the right method is assumed to solve any problem. This trust in method has teamed with a naïve view of statistics. If the numbers say 'x', then 'x' is the reality. This is the 'first road' at its worst.

Don't get me wrong: measuring and controlling is vital. As a CEO I have experienced first hand the problems of inadequate data and analysis. The problem comes when this faith in method and measurement is applied to people and we are told to trust the system!

From answers to questions

This is hard for many managers to grasp. We seem hard-wired to see the world as measurable and controllable. We expect charts and presentations. It's hard to challenge these constructs.

Since we were children we were examined at virtually every step of our education. We learned that answers trump questions. When teachers set a question, they did not want to hear a

better question in response. The path of professionalism is likewise a path of answers. A reputation for asking tough questions can be career limiting.

Shifting from this mode is hard. That's the vital step I have inserted below between the last two rows of the eight Cs for engagement.

Engagement needs great questions.

If I frame a searching question, I can't know what it might challenge. If I create room for a real conversation, there's no way of knowing where it will go.

From certainty to confidence

When I speak of challenging analysis and questioning certainty, I'm not advocating sloppiness. There is an appropriate logical and statistical rigour. Grappling with strategic options for major corporations is fraught without deeply insightful analysis and modelling.

Data and analysis need a question grounded in a context. Then analysis can serve imagination. We seek confidence to act, not the illusion of certainty.

THE ARTS OF ASKING
GROUNDED QUESTIONS

Socrates was famous for modelling the power of the question, and the difficulty of framing a good one. He's still right.

An irritating philosopher

In Plato's dialogues, Socrates wears down someone with his relentless questioning.[9] Eventually, these companions complain that the enquiry is unfair since Socrates is asking all the questions. So he offers to change places. But soon the other swaps back saying it's harder to ask a good question than to answer one.

This exchange has come to be known as the Socratic dialogue: a conversation or argument in which truth is uncovered by the asking of questions that build upon one another.

The school project again

Do you remember 'Tasmania'? Not the place (it's beautiful by the way), but how the school project illustrates the problem of inappropriately abstract thinking.

At about twelve years of age, Hannah came home from school and announced, 'Daddy, we have to do a project on Parliament'. Notice the 'we'! With three children under three, I'd watched her older siblings do the same project and emerge none the wiser. Then I discovered Hannah's teacher knew little better.

So I asked Han, 'Why do we drive on the left hand side of the road'? (We live in Australia.) She guessed there were laws. So I asked how we get laws. She guessed it might be the police. Informing her that the police only enforce the laws, Hannah asked the key question, 'So who makes laws'? Try as I might she wouldn't drop the project and follow the question. This child was focused.

GROUNDED QUESTIONS TAKE US TO STORIES. THIS IS KEY. STORIES CARRY OUR SENSE OF IDENTITY AND MEANING.

But if Hannah had pursued the question, she might have arrived at the rationale and function of Parliament. Instead of a collage of buildings, different coloured seats, and Prime Ministers, she might have found her way to understand a central convention of democracy.

All it would take was a question within reach of her own experience. A grounded question.

Why grounded questions?

Consulting over many years with complex socio-technical systems I have seen firsthand an entrenched faith in ideas lifted out of any human context.

Once we put people back into the frame, however, we realise we can only address things that matter by crossing organisational or disciplinary boundaries, or going right outside them. I would love to see this thinking taught and encouraged in all education.

In tackling complexity, the deep insights are where experts rarely look. They're in simple human stories. The only way to unearth them is to ask a question that can't be answered with bullet points.

What makes a question grounded is the soil of people's lives. It's the kind of question that makes us reach behind abstract explanations into lived experience.

Grounded questions take us to stories. This is key. Stories carry our sense of identity and meaning. That's never just cognitive but something arising from and shaping the whole person. In these stories we find the deep insights that enable us to work for change in natural uncontrived ways.

Framing a grounded question

Marks of a grounded question
1. Brings people to the fore.
2. Starts in curiosity and respect.
3. Draws us to engage.
4. Will subvert an unhelpful meeting agenda.
5. Triggers conversations that renew heart and pride.
6. Draws stories. Abstract questions draw bullet points.
7. Is very often a 'sideways' question.
8. Tends to be an open question.

Try a 'sideways' question
This is a question 'that comes from the side'. It is the not-so-obvious question that takes a conversation away from expected but unhelpful paths. The grounded questions in my TEDxPlainpalais talk are all sideways questions: not 'What's wrong'? but 'Why did you become a teacher'? [10]

For example, you could ask your team, 'How do we improve retention rates for our customers'? Or you could ask about their own experiences of being consumers: 'Have you ever let a subscription, membership, or coverage lapse? Why?'

Use open and closed questions
The two basic kinds of questions are well known:

Open — Begins with what, why, how, when, or where. These allow for exploration, exposition, and story-telling.

Closed — Begins with have, do, did, are, is, has, have, can, or will. Great for testing clarity: 'Have I understood you'?

Sometimes a closed question works well as a grounded question: 'Was there ever a time …?' 'Did you feel proud …?' Asked out of real interest, they become an invitation to tell a story.

Frame agendas around questions
Try writing your next meeting agenda as one or two succinct grounded questions to invite dialogue. Not 'Project update' but 'Are we back on track yet?' Not 'Marketing' but 'Which market will we choose?'

HOW ONE SCHOOL BEGAN ITS
TRANSFORMATION

Your operation is rated the worst. You're given a budget and deadline to turn it around. You ask 'What's wrong?', 'How do we fix it?', implement a change program, and wonder why it failed. This group did something very different.

I have sketched the story of how the transformation of a school began when some teachers named their own brilliance more richly. Here is the larger story.

Soon after being appointed, the principal was summoned with thirty-nine colleagues to meet the Director-General. He told them their schools were the worst in the state and gave them a budget to 'fix' them within two years. Here is how the principal described what she believed most would do:

'They'll go shopping in the supermarket of educational programs. It's like "Tasmania" (she had been on one of my retreats). They are filling a sheet of cardboard titled "School Transformation" with any and every idea and project the experts recommend. It won't work. When the money runs out, the schools will only be more disheartened'.

We talked about doing it differently. I reminded her of my dad's advice: 'Big doors swing on little hinges'. [11] It only takes two or three well-chosen small things to move something large.

Dad believed these were two people of goodwill, two acts of kindness, or both. In this context I felt we needed two teachers to tell their stories.

She arranged the best two-day offsite she could afford. Instead of an agenda we searched for a grounded 'sideways' question. In the end, we had two:

Day 1: Why did you become a teacher?
Day 2: What do you think about the children?

BIG DOORS SWING ON LITTLE HINGES ... YOU ONLY NEED TWO OR THREE SMALL THINGS ON WHICH THE BIGGER THING CAN TURN.

Imagine the staff. Good teachers bravely teaching in tough conditions. Many losing confidence. Some cynical of the system, the new principal, and me. Think what we might have asked:

— What's wrong?
— How do we fix it?

Either question would drive the conversation into a downward spiral of venting frustration. Instead, when everyone was present, I leaned forward in my chair and asked: 'I'd love to know something: Why did you become a teacher'?

Slowly, they told their stories. Every teacher told a noble story. Why did they become teachers? 'To make a difference'. Every one of them. And they had, and still were. After the last story the room fell quiet. Some smiled, some had tears.

We drew no 'therefores' from any of this. We tried to be present to the richness of the stories. I ended the session as I had begun: 'It's been a privilege to hear your stories. I hope you enjoy the rest of the day reflecting and relaxing'. That was it.

OUR GOAL WAS SIMPLY TO BEGIN TO CHANGE THE MOOD AND OPEN SPACE FOR DIALOGUE.

Imagine how different the session would have been if I had asked, 'What's wrong?' and finished with an action plan. People assume 'transformation' is about finding a solution for every 'problem'. In contrast, we assumed that:

- Transformation begins in people knowing their brilliance.
- People often can't name their brilliance.
- Stories are the key to finding brilliance and engaging each other.
- Making space for stories can stir the courage to bring a conversation to life.

The next day, I asked our second question: 'What do you think and feel about the children?' No slides, lectern, or amplification. Again, they told stories,

laughed, and wept. Sometimes the awful decision must be made to remove a child from school. These teachers knew that but agreed that it always felt like they had failed the child. They wanted every child to succeed.

Again we ended the same way. We drew no 'therefores'. We sat with the questions and the stories we heard. The conversation had begun.

I need to be clear about what we were trying to do. We were not trying to fix these teachers or the school. A couple of grounded questions and some story-telling, no matter how brilliant, won't fix anything. Our goal was simply to begin to change the mood and open space for dialogue. Our hunch was that the teachers might reanimate a conversation about teaching and learning if they saw and felt the dignity and hope in each other's stories.

Over the next year or two, by every educational and social measure, the school began to be transformed. It all began those two days with those two 'sideways' grounded questions, a room full of stories, and the will to stay present. Ten years later the brilliance and pride continues.

'MAYBE IT'S TIME TO FIND A GOOD QUESTION OR TWO'.

LIVING
CONVERSATION

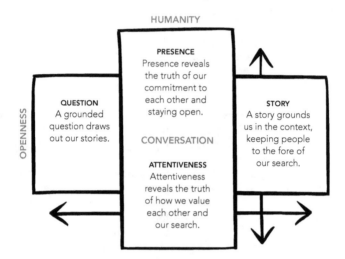

Two axes of conversation

Openness (Question+Story) +
Humanity (Presence+Attentiveness)
= Conversation.

Well, almost. No formula will do
conversation justice. This one tries to
capture two big themes.

Axis of openness. I have emphasised
the role of conversation in how we
know and shape meaning. Grounded
questions and story are the ways we
shift from the closed 'first road' mode
of communication to the open 'second
road' mode of conversation. This is the
mode of searching together and being
open to new meaning. It is this interplay
of grounded questions and stories that
feeds conversation.

Axis of humanity. In *Chapter 1: Wisdom*,
I said presence and attentiveness are
vital to reading life's patterns well.
Presence reveals the truth of my
commitment to the people and the
challenge. Attentiveness reveals the
truth of my valuing of the others and our
search. This is the mode of encountering
and engaging with each other and being
open to each other's brilliance. It is this
interplay of presence and attentiveness
that centres conversation.

Conversation is not so much a process
or event as a disposition toward life.
A disposition to bring life. This is the
role of grounded questions and stories,
presence and attentiveness. These
are ways of knowing that breathe life
into conversations.

Living conversation tips

Frame a grounded question

1. Consider how to bring the human dimension to the fore.
2. Look for a 'sideways' question to draw out stories.
3. Frame questions in plain, direct language.
4. Explore with open questions: When, Where, What, How, Why?
5. Clarify with closed questions: Have, Do, Did, Will, Is, Are, Can?

Draw out stories

1. Listen for management talk that obscures the human dimensions.
2. Invite the stories that have not been told.
3. Look for patterns between the stories.
4. Frame vision as a new chapter/ story that builds respectfully upon others' stories.
5. Frame strategy as an argument for that new chapter/story.

Stay present

1. Channel your authority into 'author-ising' others.
2. Don't contrive, but live your commitment to the people and conversation.
3. Refuse the games of meetings. Being present isn't necessarily being nice.
4. Use simple summarising statements to name the situation with integrity and hope.
5. Hold your commitment through breakdown until new meaning is created.

Be attentive

1. Learn to listen well. It is a mark of character.
2. Listen for language that stifles and weakens.
3. Listen for the stories at the margins.
4. Consider who is too often at the centre or the margins.
5. Keep watch on how you impact the conversation.

Nurture conversation

1. Model presence and attentiveness.
2. Encourage conversations more than meetings.
3. Make the whiteboard a place of creating as well as recording.
4. Respectfully 'call' weak speech and behaviour.
5. Schedule strategic and design conversations.

Master the rhythm of conversation

1. Move between questions and stories.
2. Give room and time for new meaning. Don't force solutions.
3. Expect and encourage iteration so long as it brings fresh perspective.
4. Build pathways from conversation to design.
5. Provide opportunities to reflect on and consolidate learning.

There's no point talking to ...!

Conversation to end an impasse

An infrastructure Operations team met offsite to plan. They were particularly frustrated by internal organisational obstacles. Near the end of the retreat, a familiar scenario was played out. Operations had been waiting between six and eighteen months for several systems that their corporate colleagues in Human Resources had promised. All in all, Operations was waiting for HR to deliver something like 17 projects. The strategy of the VP Operations was to once again berate the VP HR to deliver. There is a wiser strategy, but it requires humility.

The VP Operations might ask if there is a story behind HR's failure to deliver. For a start, no team will deliver on 17 projects (not counting all the ones HR had to deliver to other VPs). No team can! Moreover, Operations did not have the expertise to design the systems themselves. Nor did HR have the contextual knowledge to design good systems on their own. They needed each other: Operations needed well-designed systems; HR needed a design partnership, a realistic number of projects, and some respect.

The VP Operations made a strong call to stop the gossip and blaming. He went after something better. His commitment was tested. After an initial period of suspicion, the two executives began to talk. The conversations were difficult and awkward at first. Unsurprisingly, they broke down.

Both leaders sensed they had to commit to each other, stop throwing things over the wall, and find a way forward. Eventually they did.

This is about more than compromise. This is about respect. This is about holding commitment in the face of breakdown to let new meaning (and relationship) emerge.

At the beginning of this chapter I said: conversation may not yield new meaning — but new meaning will not take hold without conversation. I don't want to be naïve about what conversation can accomplish. There's no magic in simply getting people together.

This is why I emphasise commitment. Breakdown is epistemological — about knowledge and how we know — as much as relational or psychological. If we are after new meaning, deepened commitment is key.

Sustain core conversations

Name and pursue the central idea

At the heart of every group is a conversation that must be maintained. It is the leader's job to name that conversation and to keep it alive.

The Greek poet Archilochus wrote: 'The fox knows many things, but the hedgehog knows one big thing'.[12] It was a playful variation on the One and the Many. The Russian-British philosopher Isaiah Berlin made use of this saying as a metaphor for Leo Tolstoy and his account of the Russian revolution. To Berlin, Tolstoy was a fox who wished to be a hedgehog: he had many theories but he was in search of a great idea that could make sense of the whole period and of his own writing.

In *Good to Great*, Jim Collins drew on this background for his Hedgehog Concept — 'the one big thing, the one big clear idea'.[13] Everything comes from this.

This one big idea needs to animate the conversations that sustain the work of an organisation.

When leaders do not foster a rich environment of conversation a kind of void can appear at the heart of the organisation.

What does this void look like?

- Void in a business — Managers talking more about their products than about their customers.
- Void in a health system — Officers talking more about their protocols than about their patients.
- Void in a school — Teachers talking more about problem kids than teaching and learning.
- Void in a community — People talking more about an event than how to support each other.

A group that has lost its way has lost its core conversation. This conversation does not magically take care of itself. This is the work of leaders.

Think about ...

Reanimate a key conversation

1. How would you name the conversation?
2. Who would be good partners in bringing this conversation alive again?
3. What one simple thing could you do to get the conversation started?

Champion strategic conversations

Structuring an argument for change

Conversation is key to casting a vision and building ownership of it. I see vision as a future story. Strategy is then an argument on behalf of that future story. So setting strategy is about conversations long before it ever becomes about planning.

So what is a strategic conversation, and how can it be shaped?

In our discussion of leadership I went back to the root metaphor of walking together. Interestingly, we use a similar metaphor when we talk about strategy. We talk about needing to get from 'A' to 'B'.

This simple spatial metaphor lends itself to a heuristic and tool: Second Road's AcdB® model for strategic conversation.[14] The heuristic structures an argument for change across four places of thought. (There's a bit of Aristotle behind this one too.) I think of the movement from 'A' to 'B' in terms of crossing a chasm.

'A' is the place of discernment

Where are we? What's so? What are the tensions shaping the current state?

'B' is the place of imagination

Where do we want to be? What's possible? What do we desire?

'C' is the place of invention and judgement

What's missing? What do we need to make? What could span the 'chasm'?

'D' is the place of action

How do we make the 'C'? What is needed to support the 'C'?

Disarmingly simple, the AcdB® model lets us give voice to identity, purpose, agency, and will. But that's hard work. We have to clear away the board table, get rid of our slides and piles of paper, gather around the whiteboard, and start playing — seriously.

Conversation itself is another kind of game ... It is not an exam. It is questioning itself. It is a willingness to follow the question wherever it may go.[15]

DAVID TRACY

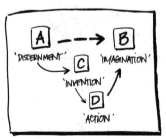

AcdB® Model, Tony Golsby-Smith

Q. # How does conversation relate to leadership and the patterns?

A. Wisdom has a great deal to do with reading life's patterns, especially the patterns of human experience and knowing. One of these patterns is how new understanding arises through conversation. Sure we make meaning in our heads. But it doesn't get traction until we talk about it. Of course clear communication will always be crucial to change. That's how we distribute the meanings we have created. But conversation is where we craft new meaning. This is the work of leading — to name those conversations and keep them healthy.

Building relationship may not increase influence. But no-one increases influence without building relationship.

CHAPTER 5

Influence

To lead is to influence

Leaders unavoidably influence

John Maxwell rightly observes that 'the only measure of our leadership is the influence we have had upon others'.[1] So how do we influence wisely and well?

We engage with others to enable them to change in trust and mood, meaning and action.

We trust relationship, not position, to effect change in hearts and minds.

Influence is a knife-edge. We have all seen abusiveness and manipulation dressed up as leadership. As a young man I saw that in myself and avoided leadership for many years after. But influence needn't be a dirty word. Indeed, there is something deeply human, mature, even noble, about influencing honourably for the good. But it takes us into risky territory.

The moment I think I can see or do something that might help you, I risk imposing my ideas on you, patronising you, or worse. I have to get past this. I need confidence in what I'm doing and why I'm doing it. I can't afford to be paralysed over my motives or fear the mistakes I will inevitably make.

Position, process, and skill all play big roles in influence. But our influence on others can only be as great as our relationships with them. Little relationship; little influence. Both can be grown. And there lies the twist: we cannot and ought not change others, only ourselves. Indeed, if I try to change others, my influence both diminishes and distorts.

There's no avoiding character in this conversation. Leading well, leading wisely, takes strength of character. Quieter and slower change ultimately can be deeper and quicker. But sometimes we don't have time. Sometimes trust must be gained quickly. What follows is such a tale.

THE STORY OF
JOSHUA CHAMBERLAIN

Very often, quieter and slower change is ultimately deeper and quicker. But sometimes we don't have time. Sometimes trust must be gained quickly.

Colonel Joshua Lawrence Chamberlain

The movie *Gettysburg* recounts the American Civil War battle of July 1–3, 1863 near the little town of Gettysburg. An early scene leads into the heroic engagement at Little Round Top on July 2.[2]

Colonel Chamberlain has recently taken command of the 20th Maine regiment, a once proud outfit of 1000 men now less than 300. The scene opens as Chamberlain's crusty old Irish aid brings the ailing colonel some unusual news.

A detail of 120 men of the disbanded 2nd Maine are arriving under guard. Most soldiers enlisted for two years but these men signed for three years. When the regiment disbanded, they thought they could go home. Told they had another year to serve, the 120 refused to fight. Re-assigned to Chamberlain, he is authorised 'to shoot any man who will not do his duty'.

A spiteful captain has marched the men at bayonet point without food in order to 'break them'. When dismissed, the captain makes a pointed speech to Chamberlain within hearing of the men to humiliate and threaten them. Chamberlain refuses the bait, dismisses the guards, and offers the men food and shelter.

Private Buckland identifies himself as the elected spokesman for the mutineers. Chamberlain invites Buckland to his shelter where he learns their grievances. A courier brings orders that the 20th Maine is to move immediately to the forward position, and Chamberlain gathers the men to address them.

A VIVID STUDY OF A LEADER WHO MUST QUICKLY ADD THE CREDIBILITY OF CHARACTER TO HIS FORMAL AUTHORITY.

His new orders give them little time to talk. He acknowledges the situation is ridiculous: 'They tell me I can shoot you. Well, we both know I won't do that. Maybe someone else will, but I won't'. Nor will he ask them to fight without a reason. He sees a noble purpose: 'We are an army out to set other men free'. But like them the war has wearied him: 'We have all seen men die'.

Near the end, Chamberlain becomes self-conscious and apologises for 'preaching'. He offers to give back muskets to those who will fight and to seek a fair trial for those who refuse. Turning to walk away, he pauses: 'Gentlemen, I think if we lose this fight, we lose the war. So if you choose to join us, I'll be personally very grateful'.

Making sense of the story

Various sources affirm the scene is faithful to Chamberlain's words and actions.[3] It is a vivid study of a leader who must quickly add the credibility of character to his formal authority.

Chamberlain carries his authority with dignity and humility. He puts the surly captain in his place not to assert his own superiority but to silence the captain's contempt. The contrast was profound: he dismissed the guards and saw to the men's needs. Here was a fair leader men could trust.

Chamberlain invites Buckland to talk and offers his hand, coffee, and a seat. Sensing he is a man of courage, Chamberlain acknowledges Buckland's experience, anger, and grief. There is truth in his outburst and Chamberlain does not dismiss him or justify himself; neither does he join the ridicule. His humility and humanity show him worthy of his rank.

Walking to address the men Chamberlain remains unsure what to do. Standing below them, he calls them informally to himself. He speaks with courtesy and without deceit.

He acknowledges he can't make them fight. Nor will he shoot them. He will try to secure a fair trial. His account of their circumstances is candid. His rhetoric

rises until he becomes self-conscious and apologises for 'preaching'.

Of the 120 mutineers, 114 men chose that day to fight. Later, in a lull between onslaughts, he appealed again to the six. Three chose to fight; one possibly saved Chamberlain's life. He did his best to ensure a fair trial for the three remaining mutineers. Nothing was said to those of the 117 who survived. Many credit the final heroic bayonet charge led by Chamberlain that day with turning the whole battle.

Chamberlain was wounded six times in the war, left for dead once, and retired a Major General. Chosen to receive the surrender at Appomattox, he stunned both sides by calling his troops to salute the defeated Southerners. He served four terms as Governor of Maine and finally succumbed to his war wounds in 1914. His men loved him to the end.

Chamberlain carried great formal authority but he relied on the informal and relational. His actions enabled a new shared understanding. He did not gain the compliance of 117 men, but their hearts and minds.

'ENGAGING HEARTS AND MINDS'

Real influence is based in relationship.

A useful distinction: Position influences compliance. Character influences hearts and minds.

Two modes of influence

I find it helpful to think of position and character-in-relationship as two modes of influence, each carrying authority: one formal and one informal. Drawing on the authority both of position and of character-in-relationship, a leader names the present and future story.

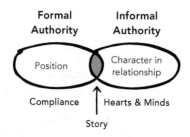

Formal Authority — Informal Authority

Position — Character in relationship

Compliance ↑ Hearts & Minds

Story

Position. The conferred authority of a position can reach as far as what can be written down — whether certain people have done certain things in certain ways to a certain quality at certain times.

Character-in-relationship. When expressed authentically in relationship, the earned authority of character can touch the meanings, large or small, that people inherit and create about themselves and the world.

Story-at-the-intersection. It is part of positional authority to name the present and future. But people do not follow bullet points: they will commit to a credible story told by a person bearing the authority of a worthy character evidenced in relationship.

Our previous story bears eloquent testimony to this dynamic of influence:

First, as Commanding Officer of the regiment, Chamberlain's position carried formal authority and responsibility. The regiment had to take up forward positions and the mutineers had to accompany them. He could not undo the charges, nor revoke his authority to shoot them.

Second, Chamberlain had to bridge the vast gulf between his position and Private Buckland and his peers, whose trust and commitment he sought to win. He revealed his character in the hope of forming relationship. He dismissed the guards, fed the men and met them as far as possible on equal ground.

Third, Chamberlain knew that rank could not make them fight. They had to choose on the basis of a reason they deemed compelling from a leader they deemed fit to follow. Chamberlain tells a story that casts a vision.

Chamberlain had mere hours to influence these men. The authority of his position reached only to what could be written down: 120 prisoners delivered. But the authority of his character formed a fledgling relationship under great strain. His story touched their hearts and minds such that they regained their convictions.

CAVEAT: Many of these men then died. I do not mean to glorify war.

The boundaries of influence

Discern the relationship

Influence depends on the boundaries of relationships. We need to discern the true bounds of different relationships and engage well with people within them.

The leaders of your country have a political and legal relationship with you. Through a wider process, they can set the tax you pay, the content on your television, the side of the road you drive on, and how your nation is represented to the world. But they can't determine whether you pay your taxes, watch TV, drive responsibly, or feel proud of your country.

The influence is real within the bounds of the relationship, but no further. You can seek to secure or remove their influence by participating in the wider process.

Your bosses have a fiduciary and commercial relationship with you. Within the bounds of the law and employment agreements, they can structure your pay, role, and more. They can decide you need to be engaged, empowered, restructured, and 'let go'. But they can't determine whether you are actually engaged or empowered. The influence is real within the bounds of the relationship, but no further. And if you have a grievance, you can seek redress through a union or the courts.

Sue and our children have a familial and intimate relationship with me. We can influence one another in profound ways. It all depends on how we conduct the relationship. If I want compliance in our home, I may insist on that old relic, 'the man of the house'. But what I'm doing is misnaming the relationship as legislator, police, judge, and auditor. And I'll pay for it dearly later on.

I can't determine how our family will turn out. If I want to grow old with a partner and children who love being together, then I need to love them, and choose to be part of their lives in ways that are meaningful and valuable to them.

Power can distort relationship

In politics, business, and family, a person's influence may overstep a relationship with devastating effect. In ancient Rome the empire dominated every facet of human life. A majority of the working population in cities were slaves with no human identity at law. And *pater familias* gave a man power even to death over his household. Underneath it all, the hearts and minds of many seethed. In many places, this hasn't changed.

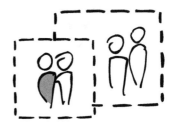

Discern the bounds of relationships.

COMMITMENT AND MEANING
ENABLE INFLUENCE

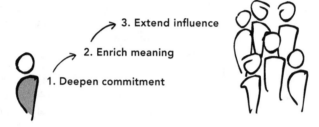

3. Extend influence

2. Enrich meaning

1. Deepen commitment

Commitment is bedrock

Leaders must deepen commitment to extend their influence.

A leader wants her team to change their practice. They know this involves adopting new thinking — new meaning. But they're reading her commitment. Is she commited first to them, or to the outcome?

Commitment must be first to the person, and then to the outcome.

At her best, her influence is barely noticed. For the most part, the ways her team reads her commitment, and whether they are open to change, is all tacit.

Commitment enables meaning

Leaders must help broker meaning before anything will change.

The more our leader's commitment to her team becomes evident, the more they are open to new possibilities. An enriched understanding begins to take hold and with it the prospect of change.

Commitment enables meaning. Meaning enables influence.

You can see the close connection with conversation and naming. As she commits to the team — yes, and the outcome — they become partners in meaning-making.

Building relationship

Check your agenda

You will not establish relationship by seeking to change someone.

A participant in one of my workshops became frustrated with my picture of deepening commitment to enrich meaning to extend influence. It didn't match his experience.

'I'm committed to the organisation, and I'm working to create new meaning. I've written numerous emails and given two presentations', he said, 'but the CEO still doesn't change'.

It was hardly surprising the CEO hadn't changed his mind. This would have to be the most common tactic for 'influencing up', and the least effective.

When I asked if he ever had coffee with the CEO, the answer was immediate and emphatic: 'Of course not!' Why? Because the CEO was two ranks higher and, supposedly, people just don't ask CEOs for coffee. (In my experience, this is a glass ceiling that canny influencers break all the time.)

So I suggested he drop his campaign until he was prepared to establish a meaningful relationship with the CEO. To me that means dropping the agenda to change him and seeking to know him. Where could he start?

Know the person

This is a person you don't know enough. Start with curiosity.

Many people would start by telling everything they've done to get their message across. Instead, I asked if he knew the CEO well. What mattered most to him? How many others were sending emails to influence him? He had little idea. Imagine a different start.

'Thanks for giving me the time. You know I've been sending emails about XYZ. Sorry. It was a dumb thing to do because I don't know you. I was wondering, what's it like to be in your role — apart from getting dumb emails from staff?'

Most CEOs would be sceptical. But if they thought the person was genuine, they'd welcome the conversation. That's the challenge. Not your agenda, but your credibility-in-relationship.

'PERHAPS A CUP OF COFFEE WOULD BE A BETTER PLACE TO START...'

WHEN WE HEAR EACH OTHER

The impact of listening to another and of being listened to well is extraordinary. It might open new realms of respect and partnership.

Working from sweet spots
Influence begins in appreciation, not criticism.

After decades honing her skills as a teacher and deputy principal, a friend finally accepted an invitation to become a principal. The high school was in a high stress, high debt estate where many families struggled to maintain a facade of success to match their somewhat awkwardly pretentious homes.

Previously we had worked together at an inner city high school where we introduced philosophy café for 14 to 15 year olds. That was fun! Under the hand of her then boss, that school had been exemplary for student initiative and achievement. Her new school, however, was markedly different.

Knowing the story of transformation I told in *Chapter 4: Conversation,* she was looking for similar input in helping the staff and students to find and leverage their brilliance.

I led and facilitated several professional development days for the teachers and followed up with mentoring based on their teaching stories. I also met with the elected student leaders to help them think through the influence they hoped to have on their peers. Both initiatives had positive outcomes.

The power of hearing each other
Influence arises within conversation, not communication.

The teachers had noticed the growing maturity of the student leaders and their impact on their peers. The students had likewise noticed changes in the teachers. For my final session that year, I suggested we bring both groups together in conversation.

My process was simple. I invited the students to tell stories of changes they'd seen in themselves and their peers. After a few rich stories, I asked the teachers, 'What was happening for you as you heard these stories?'

In a word, they were moved and said so. Then I asked the students the same question: 'What was happening for you as your teachers spoke just now?' They felt touched by their teachers' humility. I invited the teachers to tell their stories. And so on.

Soon they began to address each other directly rather than through me. They spoke of seeing each other through new eyes. Respect and vulnerability overcame cynicism and wariness. Mutual commitment had been growing tacitly all year but was now named and openly reciprocated. Commitment. Meaning. Influence.

Q. # Does this picture fit your own experience as a CEO?

A. I had to make big calls early to keep us running. At my first budget session, I saw why we'd run so many deficits. Expenditure was set first, and income assumed to match. We needed a new mindset: set income to market analysis, then set expenditure for a surplus. Some cheered; some were aghast. I had the board, CFO and Deans behind me, but I had to convince other executives we could turn the ship around. That meant lots of one on one. People committed bravely to their colleagues and stakeholders. This commitment, and subsequent surplus, created the room to begin a new story.

THE ANCIENT ARTS TO
INVENT AND PERSUADE

Rhetoric. The philosophers hated it and with cause. We too have heard our share of bloated but empty words. Yet words outlive our lives and there is much to be said for words crafted and delivered with artistry and wisdom.

Words outlive our lives

Hopefully two things have come through clearly in this chapter and in the book so far.

First, while formal authority must be embraced and discharged well, I'm putting greater weight on the informal authority that derives from character and is expressed in presence and relationship.

Second, our words carry huge impact. Again, this is why they feature so prominently in the wisdom traditions. Our lives can have significant impact upon others, but our words can carry this influence far beyond us.

From ancient times in many cultures leaders have drawn upon the arts of invention and persuasion known in the West as rhetoric.[4]

On sophists and philosophers

The earliest Greek intellectual provocateurs were as likely to be called 'sophists' as 'philosophers'. Both words derive from *sophos* (wise). Where philosophers sought Truth, sophists would argue any position for a fee.[5]

Socrates had dismissed the sophists and rhetoric as adding persuasion to ignorance.[6] To Plato rhetoric was a 'knack' powerless to uncover the truth.[7] But Aristotle would transform rhetoric.

Speech is a powerful lord ... (whose) effects are almost divine.[8]
PLATO

Aristotle limited logic to 'things that cannot be other than they are'. Human affairs were different. For this, he argued, we need rhetoric's power to integrate 'the science of logic and the ethical branch of politics'.[9] But how?

Rhetoric, Aristotle argued, begins with invention not persuasion. We create something with words. Our primary tool is the heuristic.[10] A heuristic is a mental shortcut for seeing connections.[11] I have used several already. For example, the idea of One and Many helps me read complexity; the image of dualism helps me recognise false splits in our thinking.

The works of Aristotle and his Roman admirers, chiefly Cicero and Quintillian[12], shaped the trivium — grammar, logic, rhetoric — making rhetoric foundational in Western education from Rome to the nineteenth century.

On great orators and speeches

To find a man who in plain terms and without guile speaks his mind with frankness, and neither for the sake of reputation nor for gain … (is) the good fortune of a very lucky city.[13]

DIO CHRYSOSTOM

On occasion a leader's strength of message and oratory has helped turn the tide of history. I think of Henry V at Agincourt (1415), and Elizabeth I facing the Spanish Armada (1588).

More often the impact of great speeches has unfolded in time. I think of the Apology of Socrates (399 BC), Cicero's Catiline Orations (63 BC), Jesus' Sermon on the Mount (c30 AD), Wilberforce's plea to Parliament to abolish the slave trade (1791), the extemporaneous 'Ain't I A Woman? by Sojourner Truth (1851) and Lincoln's Gettysburg Address (1863).

In the last century, I think of 'Ireland Unfree Shall Never Be at Peace' by

Patrick Pearse (1915), Churchill's radio addresses in World War II (1940), Gandhi's 'Quit India' (1942), Kennedy's 'Ask Not' (1961), and Martin Luther King Jnr's 'I Have a Dream' (1963).

The moments were huge and the addresses profound. But their impact only became apparent later.

On moving audiences

There is power where authenticity and rhetoric meet.

Only a handful of the great speeches show formal oratorical brilliance. Many were delivered haltingly by leaders driven more by the weight of need than confidence in their oratory. One only has to think of George V's radio speech to England in 1939 brilliantly portrayed in the movie *The King's Speech*.

Few of us will be the next Nelson Mandela or Aung San Suu Kyi. Our words may never endure like those of Elizabeth I and Abraham Lincoln. Yet our words do and will touch lives. At some point, we will stand before those who look to us and declare the past, the present, and the future.

We must craft an argument that can only offer confidence, not certainty. We must carry the argument with the conviction of character visible in relationship.

Slides full of words don't show great regard for an audience. Nor does unnecessary showmanship. If we can't state an idea simply, we still don't know it well. Perhaps it's time we combined authenticity with the skill of the old rhetorical arts.

'I'M NOT GOING TO ARGUE. THAT'S NOT THE POINT'.

Who we are and how we relate is the basis of our influence.

All it takes is little hinges

A few apt words
A seminal moment, a brilliant speaker, yet we remember a word, a phrase, perhaps a sentence.

Words have enormous impact. Actually, only a few words have enormous impact: 'I have a dream'; 'Ask not what your country can do for you…'; 'Never… was so much owed by so many to so few'.

I learned these aphorisms from my dad. You may know them too. Their origins are obscure:

Big doors swing on little hinges.[14]

Take care in little things.

Faithful in little things, faithful in big things.[15]

Leave things — and people — better than you found them.

The meanings build one upon the another. Big changes come from little things. We all know that. We'd do well to remember it when setting strategies, leading projects and cultural change, and seeking to influence others.

A few apt kindnesses
Nothing influences like an act of kindness.

The sting is in the next two sayings. 'Take care in little things'. 'Faithful in little things, faithful in big things'. They call us away from ego and arrogance.

Who hasn't heard, 'If a thing's worth doing, it's worth doing well'? It's not just about skill. It's the heart. It's regard for the other person.

'If you desire great responsibility', Dad said, 'show yourself ready by doing small things well'. I figured I'd learned that until one day he noticed my reluctance to do something 'beneath' my sense of self-importance. 'Now', he said, 'comes the test. You did small things well; larger things came to you. People look to you. Will your ego disprove their confidence, or will you humble yourself?'

I believe great influence ultimately springs from small things. A few apt words. An act of kindness. An unheralded break with convention. A choice to set aside status. The orientation of our hearts determines whether we will commit to others in ways that make it possible for us to see ourselves and the world differently and to change.

'BIG DOORS SWING ON LITTLE HINGES'.

Influence in social systems

Networks are key
In a social system, networks and communities enable different kinds of influence.

Groups formed along formal reporting lines are communities of practice. People within these communities can improve an existing system incrementally. But to change a community fundamentally, we must find and leverage the 'positive deviants' (see next section) within it.

When it comes to changing a social system itself, we need to look to networks of 'positive deviants' spread throughout communities within the system. The informal authority of these networks maps across the pattern of influence: Deepen commitment > Enrich meaning > Extend influence.

People in networks are 'hinges' on which a system can turn. Their 'small' anomalous yet positive outcomes embody new meaning. Lacking vested interest in the status quo, they are vulnerable to opposition but ultimately more likely to change the system itself.

The 'positive deviants' in a social system will unlock change.

A network needs a sponsor
A sponsor must provide clear intent and protect the network.

A senior leader of a massive public system told me he believed 90 per cent of his job was to keep the system as it was; and 10 per cent was to transform it. How did he effect transformation? First, he earned room for the 10 per cent by being superb at the 90 per cent. Second, he sponsored networks.

NOTE: I am not advocating influence by devious means.

My interest is to understand the human patterns of change. In my experience, deep change of a system more often arises from the committed actions of individuals who form loose networks for action. This is like Kuhn's insight about 'paradigm shifts' in science.

But networks of 'positive deviants' pose risks. They can be so loose they are ineffective. They can lose the larger picture. They can come under suspicion. They can become elitist.

In my experience, sponsorship is vital to sustaining healthy, focused networks for whole system transformation. The sponsor must name the intent and champion those working for change in the face of opposition from those with vested interest in the status quo.

THE POWER OF
POSITIVE DEVIANTS

Jerry Sternin had six months to solve child malnutrition in Vietnam. Impossible. But some children weren't malnourished. Their mothers were 'positive deviants'.[16]

A tacit approach to change

It probably comes as no surprise that I'm somewhat sceptical about transformation programs and change management. I'm certainly for genuine transformations of hearts and minds that help others flourish. But I've rarely seen a program deliver such changes. Change management only seems to manage changes in compliance.

PROGRAMS WON'T DELIVER TRANSFORMATION.

For my part, I've been pursuing ways of leading change that I hope show intelligence, respect, and an earthy realism.

Changing from the inside

You can't bring permanent solutions from outside.

JERRY STERNIN

At a formative stage in my own practice I discovered the story of Jerry Sternin and his advocacy of 'positive deviants'. His own theory built on Marian Zeitlin's work on preventing childhood malnutrition. The conventional change model was to fix problems with outside solutions.

But Zeitlin asked: Why did some children always do better? How could we amplify what their parents were doing? The answer was 'Positive Deviance'.[17]

Sternin knew the problem firsthand: 'The traditional model for social and organizational change doesn't work. It never has. You can't bring permanent solutions in from outside ... We call conventional wisdom about malnutrition "true but useless", or "TBU"'.

In the 1990s almost half the children of Vietnam were malnourished. After inviting Save the Children to help, the Vietnamese government then directed Jerry and Monique Sternin to achieve dramatic change in six months and leave. Sternin was 'certain that the only way to come up with a plan to fight malnutrition was to discover it within the Vietnamese village culture itself'.

Most change programs advise building a team from across the whole system. Sternin calls it the 'dinner party' approach: making sure everyone is on the guest list. That has (some) value when trying to change an entire social system. But working within a community, people need to identify with the same challenges and resources constraints.

Working with local Save the Children staff, they enlisted mothers to 'identify the positive deviants within their villages — the mothers whose children were not malnourished'. We might think the process from here is easy: identify the deviant practices and teach them. But the mothers with well-nourished children were deviants not heroes. They broke conventional wisdom.

I'll let Sternin finish the story:

'Conventional wisdom said no to eating certain kinds of nutritious foods ... The positive deviants were going to rice paddies and collecting tiny shrimps and crabs to mix with the rice ... (and) sweet-potato greens ... low-class food — and mixed them with the rice. They were supplementing the carbohydrates with protein and vitamins. And positive deviants displayed all kinds of caring behaviors... They fed children who had diarrhea, for example, even though conventional wisdom said no to this'.

'Once you find deviant behaviors, don't tell people about them. It's not a transfer of knowledge. It's not about importing best practices from somewhere else ... You enable people to practice a new behavior, not to sit in a class learning about it ... Let other groups develop their own curiosity ... Chip away at conventional wisdom, and (show) in indisputable terms, the results that come with doing things differently'.

The results were dramatic. Malnutrition dropped 65 per cent to 85 per cent in two years. A Harvard School of Public Health study showed that children born after the first changes experienced the same enhanced nutrition. 'The program reached 2.2 million Vietnamese people in 265 villages. Our living university has become a national model for teaching villagers to reduce drastically malnutrition in Vietnam'.

Sense the approach to change

- Recognise the wisdom in others.
- Read patterns, not formulas.
- Deepen attentiveness and presence.
- Expect brilliance in the anomalous.
- Follow as well as you lead.
- Choose relational over abstract.
- Find grounded questions.
- Subvert elitism.
- Subvert unhelpful abstraction.
- Renew core conversations.
- Know that meaning always unfolds.
- Find stories of identity and purpose.
- Expect brilliance in the unlikely.
- Help others name their brilliance.
- Honour craft and community.
- Commit to others before outcomes.
- Choose words that build community.

A guide to positive deviance[18]
[Jerry Sternin's guide to change]
1. Don't presume you have the answer.
2. Don't think of it as a dinner party.
3. Let them do it themselves.
4. Identify conventional wisdom.
5. Identify and analyze the deviants.
6. Let deviants adopt their own deviations.
7. Track results and publicise them.
8. Repeat Steps 1 through 7.

Character shapes influence

A life of influence

It's hard to avoid conflict of interest if you are a voice for both the status quo and for change. So there's no avoiding the question of character. Influence requires integrity, courage, and accountability.

It's certainly possible to engage hearts and minds from a position of formal authority. The issue is whether, and how well, we nurture respect by giving it. No-one is going to engage with us, let alone change their beliefs and mood, just because of our positions. If we act like they should, we will soon be resented and resistance will harden.

Leading change is a tough call. I don't think we can change people — further, I don't think we should try. What we have to do is live and lead in ways that create the relationships and space for people to choose to change. And that's a life's work fashioned and evidenced in a thousand little 'hinges' that may or may not swing 'big doors'.

People continually read and respond to our commitments to them and to the change. Our words and actions either energise or deflate. And we can't always get it right. That takes courage. The courage to put our hands up in the first place. The courage to own up when you get it wrong. The courage to remain in conversations when they break down. The courage to refuse to manipulate. And the courage to open ourselves to scrutiny.

A life modelling change

'Be the change you want to see in the world'. We've all seen this quote from Gandhi — except he never said it.[19] What he did say was: 'If we could change ourselves, the tendencies in the world would also change. As a man changes his own nature, so does the attitude of the world change towards him … We need not wait to see what others do'.[20]

Embody change

We are the prototype of change.
Commit to the change — Offer a clear, argument backed by skin in the game.
Embrace the tension — There's always gains and losses, hopes and limits.
Model new behaviour — Like Sternin's work, change is caught more than taught.

Engage people

We influence as far as our relationships.
Commit to others — before the change. It's a surer path to hearts and to learning.
'Amplify positive deviance'[21] — Get alongside these hinges in communities.
Be present and attentive — Learning takes humility, and humility is shown in presence.

Energise people

We carry the commitment.
Extend kindness — When spirits are flagging, little influences like kindness.
Speak hope — Words shape reality. Conversations unfold new meaning.
Tell the story — Here the formal and the informal embrace. Keep telling the new story.

Q. # How do you see change on a social scale?

A. Does change happen top down or bottom up? Is it led by individuals, small groups, or the masses? There's evidence for each. I think Kuhn's basic idea of paradigm change holds. It also fits 'positive deviancy'. As an historian, it seems leaders of change often had access to education and resources. And there's always a strong relational base. I think social change is likely to come from a group of friends who share an 'elite' background but eschew elitism. They may operate at the margins of convention, but at least one will have the skills and presence to be the public face of change.

Depth of character cannot guarantee that we will hold firm in the face of uncertainty and fear. But no-one holds firm without depth of character.

CHAPTER 6

Character

Character rests on dignity

Grappling with what it means to be human

Character sounds so old-fashioned. Personality is our preoccupation. Yet character is before us every day, chiefly when it is lacking in leaders. We read of bishops who abused children or protected those who did. Of politicians in scandal. Of bankers whose greed wiped out the savings of millions. Of unspeakable brutalities by despots against their own people.

The wisdom traditions looked to character to steady and guide us as we face the unknown, ambiguous, fearful, and seductive:

What sort of person, long term, am I becoming by my decisions?[1] **TOM MORRIS**
The integrity of the upright guides them.[2] **SOLOMON**
You can tell the character of every man when you see how he gives and receives praise.[3] **SENECA**
The institutions of the Ruler are rooted in his own character and conduct.[4] **ZISI**

When Tom Morris asks who we are becoming by our decisions, he asks the question of character. For me, character rests on our shared intrinsic dignity as human beings. No matter what tradition we claim, something resonates in the conviction of the old king that 'we are fearfully and wonderfully made'.[5]

It would be true, and more common, to say that we all have value. But value is susceptible to the idea of 'valuable so long as useful'. Dignity goes deeper. Dignity carries profundity: depth, honour, respect, and gravity. So here's how I'm approaching character in terms of dignity:

1. We each have intrinsic dignity and we share this dignity equally.
2. Character is how we 'carry'—apprehend, express, and extend (to others)—this shared equal dignity through our inner life and relationships.
3. Character is particularly visible in the ways we hold nobility equally with humility.

So we need to look further into dignity before we ask how it helps us understand character.

REFLECTIONS ON
DIGNITY

In classical history dignity stood for rank, and for the status and bearing of one who held high rank. Somewhere we began to speak about the equal shared dignity of all.

Deep dignity and surface dignity

Dignity is notoriously difficult to pin down. It doesn't help that we use the word in several senses. I think there are two main ideas: I call them deep dignity and surface dignity.

ALL HUMAN BEINGS ARE BORN FREE AND EQUAL IN DIGNITY AND RIGHTS.[6]

Deep dignity is that which names in our hearts the intrinsic wonder and worth of our lives. Surface dignity is the visible marks accompanying a person's claim to merited worth. I don't mean to minimise such marks of dignity by calling them 'surface'. Those who occupy public office know well the importance of bearing oneself in a manner that befits the meaning inherent in the role.

Nonetheless, we cherish some sense of a deeper shared dignity. The Universal Declaration of Human Rights affirms that we 'are born free and equal in dignity and rights'. Numerous countries affirm 'the inviolability of human dignity' in their constitutions.

Like wisdom and love, dignity is tough to define. Yet we know it when we see it, and can feel when it is honoured or dishonoured. It is what makes life worth living and grieving. History holds some clues as to why we see it as we do.

From rank to equality

Dignity derives from Latin *dignitas* meaning the status and bearing of those of high rank. Given the hierarchies of classical society, a view like the Universal Declaration was inconceivable. The consistent understanding was surface dignity from Homer to Augustine.

Modern writers appealing to the democratic ideals of classical Athens often overlook these realities. Those in the *demos* were equal (in voting). But the *demos* was exclusively for free born men of significant rank and wealth. That's a long way from 'all human beings are born free and equal in dignity and rights'.

So what happened? Basically, an obscure first century movement brought together an old idea, an unlikely story, and a radical conclusion. First, that humans are the image of God.[7] Second, the story of Jesus of Nazareth, the humble and humiliated king.[8] Third, that relationships could disregard ethnicity, gender, and social rank.[9]

Today — via Augustine, Kant and others — we uphold classical *dignitas* and that all people are 'born free and equal in dignity and rights'.

Character goes beyond rights

Modern affirmations of dignity are made as a basis for rights.[10] Life is unbearable without freedom, so we rightly assert a right to freedom, and against being enslaved or unjustly imprisoned.

But deep dignity lies in those aspects of human dignity that lie beyond justice. Think of love, joy, peace, inspiration, wonder, harmony, delight, awe, solidarity, empathy, creativity, compassion, faithfulness, kindness, and so much more. These are the markers of dignity that guide character.

When people live from such a place they flourish, and others and the world flourish through them. Moreover, most of these experiences are only known in relationship and all are heightened by relationship. Dignity comes to expression through character-in-relationship.

I want to assert the intrinsic dignity of every person no matter their disability or disadvantage, and even in extreme cases of personal corruption. Hitler was not a nothing doing nothing. He wilfully suppressed his true dignity to crush the dignity of others with unspeakable depravities. Hitler did not lack deep dignity: he suppressed and perverted every aspect of it. Tyrants convicted of crimes against humanity share the dignity of the murdered. Without this common ground there can be no case.

Dignity and character can grow

Here again is how I am relating character first to dignity, and then character to nobility and humility:

1. We each have intrinsic dignity. We share this dignity equally.
2. Character is how we 'carry' this shared dignity in and from our inner life and our relationships.
3. Character is made visible in nobility (I have dignity) and humility (you have dignity too).

My friend Anne put it well: 'Maybe character is how we address our responsibility for expressing our intrinsic dignity, and appreciating it equally in others?'

We grow into naming dignity deeply. We make dignity concrete in story and action. And thus character unfolds:

If dignity is in the ways we flourish in relationship, then character is delight, compassion and grieving.

If dignity is difference as much as sameness, then character is caring for the stranger and vulnerable.[11]

If dignity is equal and shared, then character is our response to both praise and ridicule.

If dignity embodies truth, beauty, and goodness, then character is tested in how we face our shame.

A little exercise: Next time you're in a meeting, unobtrusively look at each person. Let yourself appreciate them. Especially those you don't like.

Nobility and humility express character

A powerful combination

Character is made visible in nobility and humility. As Tom Morris says, 'It is the combination of the two that is so powerful'.[12] Indeed, I think it is the interactions between them — the ways we hold them not so much in balance as in tension — that colours so much of what we call character.

Michel de Montaigne said, 'On the highest throne in the world, we still sit only on our own bottom'.[13] A Serbian proverb is a little more prosaic: 'Be humble for you are made of earth; be noble for you are made of stars'. We may hear the echo of an ancient king:

When I consider the heavens, the works of your hands, the moon and the stars which you have set in their places, what is mankind that you are mindful of them … Yet you have made them a little lower than yourself, and crowned them with glory and honour.[14]
DAVID

I am but a speck. I am the pinnacle of creation. This is the paradox of true character: from here we dare to bless the world and do not despise the small acts by which it may come.

The holding of nobility with humility defines character.

Leadership is proven, not taken

When humility tempers nobility, there is restraint upon arrogance and self-interest. When nobility fortifies humility, there is release from the paralysis of self-examination and self-pity.

A great man [or woman] is always willing to be little.[15]
EMERSON

In *Chapter 5: Influence,* I told the story of Colonel Joshua Chamberlain. His rank and orders gave him the power of life and death over the 120 mutineers. No-one could have refuted his authority to treat them harshly.

His bearing removed all doubt as to his authority. But he did not hold himself lofty or aloof. He put aside protocol to hear the men's complaint. He addressed them from their shared story of lost conviction and lost comrades.

Chamberlain was asking these men to trust him and he did not take that lightly. He did not make a show of leadership, nor put himself above his men. Already their Commanding Officer, that day he became their leader.

Chamberlain wasn't a 'heroic leader'. He was more like those 'quiet leaders' that Joseph Badaracco believes are marked by restraint, modesty, and resilience. [16] These are the kind of leaders who, as my friend Gail says, 'offer (dignity) from a place of common decency and humanity'.

A useful distinction: Personality expresses individuality. Character is the substance beneath it.

When we became brands

Personality sums up the unique behavioural and emotional disposition of a person.

Character sums up a person's unique expression of human dignity in inner life and relationship.

Personality is easier to read. Is someone charming, serious, or shy? We notice behavioural and emotional traits in how we present ourselves and respond to others and to circumstances.

Character is harder. How do we assess integrity, resilience, and fairness? These are deep beliefs and commitments based on how we apprehend what it means to be human.

In 1984 Warren Susman described a shift from a 'Culture of Character' to a 'Culture of Personality'.[17] But a further shift was already well underway. When Tom Peters proclaimed 'The Brand called You',[18] personality was morphing into brand. Marketers say we are brands. Some say 'personal branding is a leadership requirement'![19]

We need to know our stories and brilliance. But if our 'look' becomes our value, we veer close to the 'narcissistic traits' and loss of 'a coherent self-identity' of which Anthony Giddens warned.[20]

Not long ago integrity was said to be our most valuable asset. Now some say it is our personal brand. I wonder: if we live like brands, what will we do to character and relationships?

Be known for character

The wisdom traditions scarcely recognise personality. Their interest is character. They might well name as pretentious, if not foolish, what we call a personal brand. Yet these are traditions from other times and we must translate for our own contexts.

Put more trust in nobility of character than in an oath.[21]
SOLON

Character lies 'beneath the surface' of experience. We can deepen or distort it. Personality is how we appear 'on the surface' as it were. I don't mean shallow. Personality matters in how we relate to others; some are glad I've worked on a few changes! Brand lies 'above' experience: I project what I want you to believe.

Can we turn this logic around? What if a leader trusted character to be her 'brand'?

BRAND

PERSONALITY

CHARACTER

DIGNITY

Character lies deeper than personality or brand.

DAUGHTER OF THE KILLING FIELDS
THEARY CHAN SENG

Now President of the Center for Cambodian Civic Education,
Theary Seng lost her parents and other relatives to the brutal
Khmer Rouge led genocide in Cambodia.[22]

A narrow escape
In April 1975 the Khmer Rouge were welcomed into Phnom Penh as heroes. Theary was four years old.

Within days her family was swept up in the tragic exodus that signalled the beginning of the brutal reign of the Khmer Rouge. Her father was murdered soon after. The family escaped to relatives but after two years were discovered and captured.

For five months Theary, now seven, was imprisoned with her mother and youngest brother. The chains would slip off her emaciated ankles. By day she would collect buffalo dung amid the rotting corpses of the killing fields, and empty buckets of human waste.

Waking one morning alone with her four year old brother, she realised her mother had been taken and murdered, one of the estimated 2 to 3 million Cambodians subjected to unspeakable atrocities between April 1975 and January 1979.

In 1979 Theary and her brother narrowly escaped to Thailand. A year later she emigrated to the USA. In 1995 Theary graduated in

international politics, then in law in 2000, and went on to join the New York and American Bar Associations.

Throughout her studies Theary returned frequently to Cambodia to volunteer with labour and human rights groups. In 2004 she returned for good.

Advocate for peace with justice
As well as being President of CIVICUS, Theary contributes to an array of national and international initiatives of extraordinary profile and scope. Featured in countless media, documentaries, and even a feature film, she often speaks internationally on reconciliation and human rights, and to raise consciousness of Cambodia's struggle.

At the heart of Theary's work have been the trials of former Khmer Rouge leaders in the Extraordinary Council in the Courts of Cambodia (ECCC). In 2008 she testified at the pre-trial hearing of Nuon Chea, second only to Pol Pot, and the most senior surviving Khmer Rouge leader.

Justice for Theary is 'legal, social, poetic, restorative, and horizontal'. In the court of public opinion, she believes, 'there is room for forgiveness' that legal courts cannot and must not provide. Through various partnerships, Theary works to build civic and democratic understanding and participation, address poverty, and help Cambodians engage in a globalised world.

I have forgiven him but that does not mean … he need not be tried in the court of law.[23]
THEARY SENG

But Cambodia is not a project for Theary. She labours tirelessly and brilliantly for that same peace with justice for which she longs herself. 'I do not believe the tribunal itself will bring about personal healing. That takes place in the quietness of one's soul'.[24]

A leader for the people
I have no wish to beatify Theary! Character is not the absence of flaws but the manner in which we face them. And Theary does. She reminds me of some ancient words: 'Suffering produces perseverance; perseverance, character; and character, hope'.[25]

Theary has known profound suffering. Her earliest years were shaped by brutality and the loss of her family. She has reason to be bitter but is not. In 2001 she met the man she believes is responsible for the death of her mother. Years later she faced him in court. On both occasions she held herself with great dignity. Her presence brings hope. Her humility invites reconciliation:

'But is there not an ember within me also capable of such barbarity? What if I had been fanned, not by love and mirth, but by the right inflammatory rhetoric, social environment, and time? …Who is this savage, the Khmer Rouge? Is she not I, but only one degree removed at birth?'[26]

Theary labours not only to name injustices, but to help her people rename themselves. No longer only 'subjects' and 'survivors', they must become 'citizens' who know their story and choose dignity.

Now I am a simple citizen of Cambodia.[27]
THEARY SENG

Cambodia now
Westerners may think oppression ended in 1979 when the Vietnamese army and Khmer Rouge defectors captured Phnom Penh. Many Cambodians say oppression only changed its form.

Cambodia remains in turmoil. On July 28, 2013 general elections were held. The opposition Cambodia National Rescue Party (CNRP) claims victory over the ruling party of Prime Minister Hun Sen. The CNRP claims electoral fraud, an allegation supported by human rights groups. Calls for independent investigations have gone unheeded. Military build up is reviving old fears.

Theary loves the land she calls 'a sea of human rights abuses'. Her courage is magnified in her humility.

I mourn when I meet a little girl on the street begging. I see my face in her face. The only difference between us is in our opportunities.[28]
THEARY SENG

Character holds the will

Uncertainty is almost certain
When we do not know what to do, we enter a void.

When the way forward is clear, leading is largely a matter of efficient management. But when the way forward is unclear, charting a course is the work of wisdom: we cannot know the path before we walk it. It's like walking into a void.

First, can we find a way through? There's a saying: 'When times are tough, people look for a leader — and get the wrong one'. I don't know who said it first. Nor this one: 'Never trust a leader without a limp'. Together they make a simple point: Wise leaders have learned the hard way not to advocate populist, simplistic solutions. Nor to minimise the uncertainty, risk, or hardship involved in a course of action.

Second, is our team up to the challenge? Even with the highest regard for them, we can't know whether they will meet the challenge. Many stories of great leadership in gruelling circumstances highlight how a leader had to sustain hope on behalf of groups where many or all had given up. Sir Ernest Shackleton's epic journey in 1917 to rescue the crew of the Endurance after their aborted Antarctic mission immediately comes to mind.[29]

Third, are we up to the challenge? There is actually no way to know. But character will count the most.

Character sustains the will
Our compass needs to be set to human dignity.

At a certain point, our challenge becomes deeply personal — we can't know if we're up to it.

Many speak of a moral compass. I get that. But, as I discuss on page 122 in A Tale of Two Trees, the idea of morality is fraught. First, it so easily becomes abstract. Second, we are always complicit in every stand we take.

This is why I argue that human dignity, not morality, is the basis of character. I do get the need 'to do the right thing'. Absolutely. It's just that it's so easy to become more concerned for principle than people.

I believe dignity is a truer 'compass' than morality, though far harder to read and follow. It's much easier to cite a principle than grapple with showing deep regard for others.

Even more confronting may be the fear of losing face. Unless our sense of identity runs far deeper than our position and status, self-justification and self-protection will colour all we do. Paradoxically, we are able to give our best when we feel free to walk away.

Still, after all this, even depth of character cannot guarantee that we will hold firm in the face of uncertainty and fear. Yet without such character, we never will.

Q. # How does wisdom relate to character?

A.   Wisdom and character are the marks of leaders worthy of followers. Wisdom is not an accumulation of knowledge but springs from a deep orientation of the heart. Wisdom gathers around the intent to live fully and authentically. From here we learn to name ourselves and the world truly and strongly. Wisdom is a wonder at life that feeds a curiosity to learn. It is an intent to know the true, the beautiful, and the good. This is our shared, equal dignity. Character is what emerges from us according to how we apprehend this dignity and extend it to others.

TWO VISIONS OF LIFE
A TALE OF TWO TREES

Have you ever noticed how life, not just I.T., feels binary?
Good/evil. Right/wrong. Included/excluded. An ancient tradition
noticed the same thing.

Life as whole and relational

I love the rawness of how the wisdom traditions portray life.

And they were both naked and felt no shame.[30]
GENESIS

Many of the themes and images of Genesis 1–3 are drawn from ancient Near Eastern mythologies. The originality of Genesis lies in how it transformed them.[31] For example, the assumed dignity of human existence, industry, and relationship was unprecedented. In the parallel traditions humans are generally slaves or playthings of the gods. Nothing there approaches the Genesis 1–2 images of full-orbed and harmonious sexual, creative, and industrious human experience uncomplicated by morality.

Life as fragmented and binary

The narrative takes a dark turn. The plunge into chaos is told in the symbolism of the 'Tree of the Knowledge of Good and Evil' and 'Tree of Life'.[32] The first tree takes centre stage. The central prohibition, and risk, is not knowing evil, but knowing good and evil.

In the middle of the garden were the Tree of Life and the Tree of the Knowledge of Good and Evil.[33]
GENESIS

The irony of the temptation to acquire 'wisdom' is poignant. Once the man and woman eat from the forbidden tree, knowledge becomes fragmented and life chaotic. In the ensuing dialogue, nakedness is a metonymy for an exposure of hearts and minds that is now unbearable. Every relationship, every choice, every way of knowing, and every facet of experience is now fractured, binary, and individualistic:

naked:clothed. dignity:shame.
open:hiding. love:enmity.
affirmation:blame. work:frustration.
harmony:discord. desire:subjection.
gift:possession. included:excluded.
blessing:curse.

Naming two defaults

The power of the greatest myths is their ability to unnerve our sophistication. A good deal of life feels fragmented, binary, and individualistic. Yet life can also be whole, fractal, and relational. [34] In a nod to our digital world, I use 'code' to mark these two typologies as two default ways of life:

<G:E> reflects the Tree of the Knowledge of Good and Evil. Life is fragmented, binary, and individualistic.

<LIFE> reflects the Tree of Life. Life is whole, fractal, and relational.

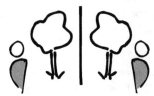

Life often feels so binary. In reality it is whole, fractal and relational.

Take a simple example: getting together with friends. Imagine no-one compared jobs, houses, finances, or holidays. Imagine it didn't matter what we wore or brought. If we end up with three lasagnes, three bottles of Sauvignon Blanc, and no salad, well, we just laugh. Delight displaces performance. That's a glimpse of <LIFE>.

Now reimagine that scene with anxiety at every choice: what we bring, how we dress, who will be there. Comparison brings feelings of inadequacy and arrogance. Status anxiety displaces relationship. That's <G:E>.

Dinner with our friends is a light occasion. Others are life and death. The Khmer Rouge embodied <G:E>. They had so distorted human dignity that rape, torture, and genocide were the new morality. Yet, like Viktor Frankl's observations from Auschwitz and Dachau,[35] <LIFE> was present in every Cambodian act of courage and kindness.

Choosing <LIFE>

We seem wired to judgement, standards, reciprocity, win-lose. Try thinking of economics without the categories of capitalist or socialist markets. Or of a viable commercial enterprise based on altruism. Or a world without IP that cooperated in bringing life-saving medical innovations to market.

For many years I have worked with leaders struggling to integrate strategy and leadership. I help them uncover the fragmentation, binary mindsets, and individualism that unwittingly shape organisations. Naming complicity, contradiction, anomaly, and abstraction is half the work of reaching a breakthrough. The hardest work of all is to frame a strong future story of flourishing.

I'm not suggesting we can avoid <G:E>. Some things must be declared evil. Surely we must feel outrage at the exploitation of women and children. There is a time to take an ethical or moral stance. But there lies the deep problem with <G:E>. Our complicity feeds self-righteousness and drives morality into moralism. We cannot distance ourselves. Perhaps, then, character is about how we face these distortions and sustain the hope of <LIFE>.

The old text has been sadly lost to us through an unfortunate debate. Yet it is startlingly apt: shame, hiding, enmity, blame, frustration, discord, exclusion. These are the impacts of binary mindsets of performance and judgement. They kill strategy, innovation, engagement — and joy. Imagine work where we flourished.

Brokenness

Dignity is not moral goodness

In 2012 I spoke at a conference titled 'Wise Management in Organisational Complexity'. The conference reflects a growing academic and popular appeal to wisdom and use of the traditions. [36] But there is a glaring omission in these appeals.

No-one ever became extremely wicked suddenly.[37]

JUVENAL

The wisdom traditions give great attention to foolishness as well as to wisdom. They see people and the world as broken as well as glorious. All the traditions acknowledge that we learn to be wise not only by watching what is wise and whole, but by facing what is foolish and fragmented. Modern advocates of wisdom, however, rarely address foolishness or brokenness.[38]

It has become axiomatic to assert 'all people are intrinsically good'. Sometimes the meaning is all people have dignity. If so, I heartily concur. But at other times the meaning is moral: all people are morally good. This is the trap of morality I have tried to highlight through the two typologies of life symbolised in the Two Trees.

Dignity is not moral goodness. It is manifestly false to say all people are morally good. Further, it is false to say that anyone only demonstrates moral goodness. But I want to address something even harder.

Leaders are broken people

Every day our media confronts us with images of corruption, violence, and human-engineered horror from every corner of the world. How do we reconcile the maxim 'all are good' with this constant refutation?

Perhaps we ignore what we see. That might work for those cocooned from these horrors. Perhaps what we really mean is 'all (the people I feel good about) are intrinsically good'. The others — terrorists, paedophiles, refugees — are intrinsically evil. If that's what we're saying, tacitly or openly, then we are moralists and elitists.

Who is this savage, the Khmer Rouge? Is she not I, but only one degree removed at birth?[39]

THEARY SENG

The deeper issue is not whether we deny, ignore, obscure, or distance ourselves from brokenness 'out there'. The issue is our own brokenness. Leaders are broken people of dignity leading broken people of dignity. As leaders we are menaces to the degree we don't face our own brokenness.

Dignity isn't positivity. Nor is facing our brokenness negativity. All dignity is dignity-in-brokenness. This is who we are. Character is therefore not about how we transcend (or deny) brokenness, but about how we indwell it. Again, we hold nobility with humility, and humility with nobility.

'I wronged you. Period'.

Another old idea worth reclaiming

Repentance goes to the heart of dignity, and thus of character.

Perhaps it's time to recover the meaning and use of an old word: repentance. Today it's mostly used in religious contexts, but not originally. It's another word that goes to the heart of dignity, of nobility and humility, and thus of character.

In *The Fifth Discipline*[40], Peter Senge speaks of 'metanoia'. This is the classical Greek word for repentance. Senge uses the word to mean 'a change of mind' and the etymology suggests that's a fair translation (*meta* 'after'; *noein* 'to think'). But etymologies rarely match usage.

There are two classic instances of the word in ancient Greek texts. One involves John the Baptiser recorded in the Gospels. The other is the writings of Josephus, a Jewish historian and apologist for Rome after the destruction of Jerusalem in 70 AD.

Working out of the same world view toward very different ends, John and Josephus called their hearers to acknowledge they had misunderstood the times, wrongly interpreted events, and placed their confidence in the wrong leaders. Each called his audience to acknowledge the futility of their current courses of action, to turn around, and to shift allegiance: in short, to repent.

When we repent, we learn

There are times a leader must face the group and name failure. This isn't the time for blame, but to identify with people and share the need to turn around. It's much harder when we have wronged others. It's tough to face our own brokenness: perhaps there was hubris, malice, deceit, intimidation, self-pity, abuse, or injustice.

Saying 'I'm sorry' is self-protection, not repentance. Repentance is a full and open acknowledgement that I have wronged you. Sorrow may well be appropriate. But I'm not the point — you are. Until I acknowledge that, I still don't recognise or honour you.

The point of repentance is relationship. We hope for reconciliation on the basis of putting things to right and honouring dignity. Repentance isn't about beating ourselves up — it's a strong choice to face shame and choose <LIFE>.

Managing relationships
When we've wronged others ...

1. Name it truly and strongly.
2. Don't blame 'the system'.
3. Name your brokenness to yourself.
4. Tell the person you wronged them.
5. Express your desire to act anew.
6. Don't seek forgiveness. Leave it to them.
7. Choose to learn. That's 'turning around'.
8. Choose to grow in character.

Choosing character

Refusing pity

Pity and tears make poetry; but they do not raise ... houses.[41]

HELEN KELLER

An infant sickness left Helen Keller blind and deaf. She is rightly loved for the indomitable spirit by which she overcame profound disability: 'No pessimist ever discovered the secrets of the stars, or sailed to an uncharted land, or opened a new heaven to the human spirit'.[42]

Her political activism was less appreciated: 'I found that poverty drove women to a life of shame that ended in blindness'. [43] Conservative politicians and editors dismissed her socialism as due to her 'limited capacities'. But Keller would not be so patronised:

'So long as I confine my activities to social service and the blind, they compliment me extravagantly ... But when it comes to a discussion of poverty ... that the industrial system under which we live is at the root of much of the physical deafness and blindness in the world — that is a different matter! ... (T)o advocate that all human beings should have leisure and comfort, the decencies and refinements of life, is a Utopian dream, and one who seriously contemplates its realization indeed must be deaf, dumb, and blind'.[44]

HELEN KELLER

Every refusal of pity is a choice for character.

Refusing simplistic answers

In times of distress people expect too much.

RONALD HEIFETZ

In *Leadership Without Easy Answers*, Ronald Heifetz explains the attraction of simplistic solutions in tough times:

'People ... form inappropriate dependencies that isolate their authorities behind a mask of knowing. And then everyone rationalises the dependency ... As a result, doubt, the exchange of ideas, weighing contrary values, collaborative work, the testing of vision against competing views, changing one's mind, seem like unaffordable luxuries. Raise hard questions and one risks getting cut down, even if the questions are important for moving forward'.

Heifetz is not arguing that authority is less important in times of distress:

'(T)he need for leadership from people in authority becomes ever more critical during periods of disequilibrium, when people's urgency for answers increases. Yet that role is played badly if authorities reinforce dependency and delude themselves into thinking that they have the answers ... Feeling pressured to know, they will surely come up with an answer, even if poorly tested, misleading, and wrong'.[45]

Every refusal to rush or fake an answer is a choice for character.

Imagining your end

Make your life extraordinary

Gather ye rosebuds while ye may,
while time is still a-flying.[46].

ROBERT HERRICK

In an early scene in *Dead Poets' Society*, John Keating, the English teacher played by Robin Williams, leads his new students into the foyer where they gather around a wall of photographs of old boys of this exclusive private school.

He asks if they know the poem *To the Virgins to Make Much of Time* by Robert Herrick. They twitter, embarrassed by the title. One of the boys reads the opening lines: 'Gather ye rosebuds while ye may, while time is still a-flying'.

Keating tells them the Latin term for this sentiment is *carpe diem*, 'Seize the day'. Drawing them closer to the photographs, he asks them what they see in the long-dead faces. Did they wait too long to realise their potential? To make a difference? For they are now 'food for worms, boys'.

Moving behind them, he breathes, 'Carpe diem. Carpe diem. Seize the day, boys, seize the day. Make your lives extraordinary!'

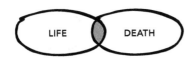

Character is also defined by how we hold together the preciousness and fleetingness of life.

'I will die'

Only by taking my death into myself … does an authentic existence become possible.[47]

WILLIAM BARRETT

Reflecting on the German philosopher Martin Heidegger, William Barrett wrote:

'So long as death remains a fact outside ourselves, we have not yet passed from the proposition 'Men die' to the proposition 'I am to die' … The authentic meaning of death — 'I am to die' — is not an external and public fact within the world, but an internal possibility of my own Being … Only by taking my death into myself, according to Heidegger, does an authentic existence become possible for me … Though terrifying, the taking of death into ourselves is also liberating: it frees us from servitude to the petty cares that threaten to engulf our daily life and thereby opens us to the essential projects by which we can make our lives personally and significantly our own'.[48]

To face the fact of our own death is to peer into a great darkness. I don't mean to be morbid. Or send you into therapy! Yet our mortality is intrinsic to what it means to 'know thyself'. The thought may consume us. Or set us free.

Here, like few other places, we may feel nobility and humility within our own hearts — the preciousness and fleetingness of life. Perhaps character is also how we hold death with life.

Growing in character

Here's what I'm arguing

Character is how we carry our shared human dignity in ourselves and our relationships. I believe we carry this dignity in tension: as nobility with humility, dignity with brokenness, and even life with death.

Character rests on our shared human dignity.

But a deep default works to deaden these life-giving tensions; to reduce them to the false certainty of binary choices. I tagged this default as <G:E> based on the 'knowledge of good and evil'. Here life and character are reduced to morality.

Dignity is not morality. Nor is character. Dignity is the things that make for flourishing: both ours, and the wider world through us. Character is how we apprehend this flourishing and express and extend it to others.

Character is a habit long continued.[49]

PLUTARCH

But we experience this dignity and flourishing within brokenness. We cannot distance ourselves from the brokenness of the world as moralists do. It simply does not square with the witness of our own hearts to being in some way complicit in whatever we might judge in another. Again, character is not morality. A leader's work is not to judge, but to hold out hope.

Character then is not the denial or defeat of brokenness. Rather it is how we carry our shared dignity in the midst of our own inadequacy, our own suffering, and even our own propensity to hurt others. Faced with false and simplistic choices, character chooses <LIFE>.

A few suggestions

1. Guard your integrity and your heart with meaningful accountability.
2. Invite correction from people you can trust to be straight with you.
3. Learn from characters you admire. Notice how they hold the tensions.
4. Grow your curiosity in others and their stories. This sets your compass to dignity.
5. Don't reduce life to binary decisions. Rather ask what makes for flourishing.
6. Face your inadequacies and failings. Don't project them onto others.
7. Keep short accounts with people. Don't let 'mole hills' become 'mountains'.
8. Apologise freely. Don't ask for forgiveness: let them make that call.
9. Come clean quickly when your own talk has ensnared you.
10. Don't say anything about someone you wouldn't say to them.
11. Repay insult with kindness. Be generous.
12. Give credit where it's due. Don't gloat when a competitor falls.
13. Show yourself faithful in small things as well as great.
14. Let others praise you, not you.

Q. **If questionable people succeed, what's the value of character?**

A. Wisdom and character do not guarantee success. The wisdom traditions bluntly acknowledge that fools may succeed. Likewise character does not determine success. Mother Teresa and Steve Jobs achieved extraordinary things and influenced millions. Yet their biographers and colleagues describe them as deeply flawed people. I think we can argue for a myriad of ways that wisdom and character help us avoid pitfalls and leverage possibility. But the larger argument for leading with wisdom and character only works if we challenge what we mean by success. We would need to widen success to what makes for human flourishing. This will not convince all.

PART III

Arts

Story, Brilliance, Promise, and Grace are four arts by which we may lead wisely. Nobody masters them. But we can grow in them our whole lives.

WISDOM AND LEADERSHIP
1 Wisdom
2 Leadership

Why do we need to lead with wisdom?

PATTERNS
3 Naming
4 Conversation
5 Influence
6 Character

ARTS
7 Story
8 Brilliance
9 Promise
10 Grace

How do we lead with wisdom?

APPLYING THE
PATTERNS AND ARTS
11 Leader's Journey
12 Leading One
13 Leading Many

Where must we lead with wisdom?

THE STORY BEHIND ARTS

Wise leaders draw on the old arts

We have already seen how stories shape our identities and thinking, how there's far more to people than we usually recognise, the huge impact of our words, and how small acts of kindness can move hearts and minds. These are the Arts of Story, Brilliance, Promise, and Grace. They express what I have seen in leaders I admire. Not just famous leaders, but people I've worked alongside and even my friends.

In Chapter 7: Story, I look at how we can draw out and honour past and present stories, write a new story, and work with our own stories. Story lies at the heart of our identities, our cultures, our sense of purpose, and even great designs. Story help us subvert abstract ways of thinking and being that suck the life out of people. Story brings clarity.

In Chapter 8: Brilliance, I look at how we can open space for people to name their own brilliance and work from it. I see brilliance not as IQ, but as the ability to shine. The clues lie in our stories. Brilliance helps us subvert the kinds of mediocrity and conformity that stifle innovation. Brilliance brings edge.

In Chapter 9: Promise, I look at how we can speak in ways that are true and strong, and that hold out hope. Our words show how we interpret life. Promise helps us subvert weak interpretations that rob people of the power to act. Promise brings strength of character.

In Chapter 10: Grace, I look at what it takes to treat people with dignity and kindness whatever their rank or status. Grace reframes strength. Far from soft, grace enables us to make tough calls with respect. Grace helps us subvert senseless status and elitism. Grace brings heart.

Drawing out old stories and imagining new ones may not change a culture. But a culture won't change until old stories are honoured and new stories are made.

CHAPTER 7

Story

Story is the stuff of life

Story speaks to all our themes

Stories are how we access the patterns of life. Stories name us. The path of influence through relationship is the path of a new story. Stories show us most clearly the dignity and brilliance of people. Stories have a way of bringing us back to the things that matter most.

At the widest scope, story is our key to culture. More personally, we know ourselves through our stories. Anthony Giddens draws on the crucial role of story in our thinking and in our identity when he speaks of how '(we) integrate events … and sort them into the ongoing "story" about the self'.[1]

By now you won't be surprised to hear that I'm no more inclined to define story than I am wisdom, love, or leadership. We know a story when we hear one, and when we don't. Think of the person who starts to tell a story but then drifts to opinions, ideas, or advice. It starts to sound like a lecture, or sermon, or a slide with bullet points. Stories are great at carrying a message, and that's a key skill for leading well. But I want to look deeper.

At some level, those who lead wisely are those that get that stories are the stuff of life. I think of this as having a 'storied heart and mind'. It means recognising the limits of abstract thinking when it comes to people and complexity. This isn't about being anti-abstract thinking. It's about a disposition that sits well with the open-ended, messy, but rich meanings that come through stories. As my friend Sam says, 'stories retain an element of mystery'.[2]

Leaders are entrusted with stories to make new chapters possible. A wise leader embraces this. This is the art of story.

A useful distinction: Abstractions claim certainty by ignoring people and context. Stories enable clarity by engaging people and context.

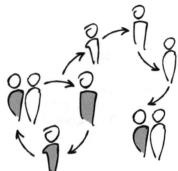

Abstractions make for very neat meanings with people & context safely in boxes.

Stories make for very rich meanings with people & context kept in view.

Abstraction offers neatness

Theories + data — [people + context] = meaning

Abstraction works from the idea that truth lies in the essence of something. Logic leads us to that essence, stripping away everything else as irrelevant. Meaning is meant to be neat.

A power company had wrestled for decades to improve generator reliability. Some fine engineers had put enormous amounts of energy into searching for a breakthrough. Yet, while incremental improvements had been made, the larger problem seemed intractable.

Reliability was seen as a 'problem' to be solved piece by piece with the right method, analysis, and engineering smarts. Those are all essential and the engineers had made gains through the years. But complexity needs insights and ways of knowing that can look at the whole.

Stories offer richness

People + context + memory + emotion + imagination + ideas = meaning

Story works from the idea that truth is inseparable from the messiness of people's experiences, relationships, and contexts. Meaning is rich but rarely neat.

We brought together people from every part of that same power company for a day. Old-timers said it had never happened before. The engineers debated 'best practice'. Then I asked a grounded question: Where have you cracked a similarly intractable problem? Safety! As they told their safety story they gained by analogy a rich meaning of reliability.

Reliability was now viewed as a 'wicked problem' — impossible to 'solve' but amenable to breakthrough by analogy gained through story.

'Storied' thinking

Stories go where abstraction can't

Human beings think in stories.[3]

STEPHEN DENNING

I love ideas and I'm a huge admirer of our ability to think well while thinking abstractly. Without this skill, there'd be no science, medicine, or engineering as we know them. Perhaps I sound like I'm contradicting myself.

Abstraction is only a problem when we use it to push people and context out of mind. When I advocate storied thinking it's not just for the warm human factor. Time and again I've seen stories unlock solutions that experts couldn't crack, even in the most seemingly abstract and technical of contexts and challenges.

Abstract thinking done well can be quite extraordinary, even indispensable. But abstraction works by shutting out people and context. Eventually that cripples our thinking, not only in grappling with obviously 'human' problems, but even in the most technical ones.

So how do we think in stories?

It is true that story-telling reveals meaning without committing the error of defining it.[4]

HANNAH ARENDT

In this critique I am following the twentieth century philosophers Michael Polanyi, John Macmurray, Marjorie Grene, Ludwig Wittgenstein, Hans-Georg Gadamer, and Thomas Kuhn. Each one, in their own ways, highlighted human knowing as personal and relational, as doing as much as thinking, and as contextual and unfolding. And that's what makes a story.

To know anyone or anything, including ourselves, we must wend our way through events, experiences, contexts, emotions, expectations, memories, and relationships, weaving an interpretation that makes sense of it all — or at least enough of it.

For the most part we don't even know we're doing any of this — it's tacit. And whatever we call this thing we do, this way of finding coherence, eventually it comes out as a story.

Stories seem to be at the core of how we think. The best doctors diagnose from the patient's whole story. In my own work, I've lost count how often it is the most unlikely story that brings rich clarity in the midst of confusion and complexity. It's unsurprising really. Lineal modes of thinking don't work well with paradox and contradiction. But stories do. As much as grounded questions lead to stories, stories lead us back to new grounded questions. And it's in this dynamic that we get the kind of conversations where new meaning is shaped.

Stories birth ideas. Stories ground thinking in experience. Stories hold the contradictions of our contexts and so help us make sense of complexity. Stories welcome our humanity.

FAITH, HOPE, AND LOVE AS STORIED
WAYS OF KNOWING

Three big ideas underpin modern approaches to change. Change is good. People are equal. And knowing is more than rational. A marginalised ancient writer helps throw some light on this.

Beyond Aristotle

[For Aristotle] the virtues central to human life were ... unavailable to the poor man.[5]

ALASDAIR MACINTYRE

MacIntyre's *After Virtue*[6] has been seminal for writers applying wisdom to leadership and organisation. Rejecting Nietzsche's radical critique, MacIntyre claims Aristotle's virtues are our only adequate basis for ethics.

But Aristotle's schema was elitist, not egalitarian; geared to the status quo, not transformation; and individualist and rationalist, not geared to how communities find meaning.[7]

A few things about the first century. First, social rank coloured every relationship. Second, Rome's power reached into every corner of life. Third, the ideals of knowledge were abstract, individualised, and elitist. Ideas and virtues that sound egalitarian to us look very different when their dependence upon and support of elitism is understood. This is the background to Paul of Tarsus, whose legacy is grossly distorted without this background understanding.[8]

Several innovations in the history of ideas first appear with Paul. First, his idea of grace inverted the social pyramid. Second, his positive use of 'transformation'. Third, his relational approach to knowing. Each of these innovations was a dramatic departure from classical and Graeco-Roman views of life and society.

Abstract and storied ways we know

The tendency of philosophy to become detached from people often locked (it) into an abstract cycle of debate in general terms, driven more by the sheer rationality of the tradition than by reference to any actual social situation.[9]

EDWIN JUDGE

Paul dismissed philosophy for failing to deliver the certainty and enlightenment it promised. His radicalism came to a head with the elites at Corinth: 'Knowledge puffs up, but love builds up'.[10]

Familiar as 'the wedding poem', 1 Corinthians 13 employs love to address knowledge. It opens with a provocative contrast between love and the philosopher's goal 'to know all things'. It concludes with knowledge.

Paul knew as a child; then an adult. He knows in part; one day in full. While knowledge remains incomplete, Paul says, he knows by faith, hope, and particularly love.[11]

We may hear faith, hope, and love as religious, spiritual, or moral. But they are simple human ways of knowing that turn intellectual elitism on its head.

The making of our contradictions

It's ironic that Paul's innovations were later inverted in the religious and political structures of the classical-Christian alliance that dominated Western thought and society for over 1500 years.

Augustine represents a watershed in the convergence of these two traditions. In Paul's account of faith, hope, and love, Augustine glimpsed a new account of knowledge. The classical starting point had been the autonomous knower working his way toward certainty by reason alone.[12] But, as Augustine put it, 'we believe in order that we might understand'.[13]

The worlds of Plato and Aristotle, Paul and Augustine, came to be entwined. Not as one coherent tradition, but as an unstable yet highly productive hybrid whose clash of ideas continues to enrich us: status and grace; convention and transformation; abstract rationality and relational storied ways of knowing.

These tensions shape every context of leadership and organisational complexity. Wisdom, I believe, lies in exploring these tensions, not in obscuring them.

Faith, hope, love — and story

Faith, hope, and love are sapiential ways of knowing: dispositions that help us read life well. Hope and even love have found their way into corporate discourse.[14] But faith?! Listen to the opening words of the Charter of the United Nations: 'We the peoples of the United Nations … reaffirm faith in fundamental human rights, in the dignity and worth of the human person …'.

Reason can't show us what's worth believing. I love what Eva Illouz says: 'Reason's indefatigable attempts to unmask and track down the fallacies of our beliefs will leave us shivering in the cold, for only beautiful stories — not truth — can console us'.[15]

Stories depend on what is passed down (faith). Stories reveal our longing (hope). And stories come from care (love). But there's no faith > hope > love process. And, as Paul said, love is the key. Badiou agrees: 'love … alone effectuates the unity of thought and action in the world'.[16]

Analysis and plans are vital: But complexity is more than a set of choices. Somewhere we wrestle with things too big to grasp (faith), the serendipity of desire (hope), and the profundity of care (love).

We tend to equate knowing with thinking and thinking with analysis and logic. Yet we know(!) knowing is bigger. Every day we see and exercise faith, hope, and love. Every argument carries convictions, dreams, and desires. To lead with wisdom is to lead with faith, hope, and love.

Story and identity

To know me is to know my story

To be a person is to have a story to tell.[17]

KAREN BLIXEN

You're with a group. To get to know each other, everyone writes three personal interests and shares them. It feels like we know each other. But imagine we tabulated the results: 27 per cent like eating out, 19 per cent like music, 12 per cent play golf, and so on. Perhaps those lists don't say much at all.

But imagine everyone shared a personal anecdote. It wouldn't matter if the story was touching or funny. Just a glimpse reveals us in ways that no list ever could. All it takes is a story.

When you tell me a story, I know you in ways I never did before. But no matter how revealing your story, I don't know you well. Yet even one story gives me a glimpse of the whole. The problem is that I lack the context and familiarity to interpret your story well.

Knowing our stories is deep

We are in part a mystery to ourselves.

So: no story — no me; know story — know me. That's why people say 'we are our stories'.[18] But are we more than our stories?

What do we mean by 'I'm not feeling myself today'? We can't point to a 'self'. Perhaps we (tacitly) mean: 'I'm not feeling like the person I know well

from my stories'. Daniel Dennett uses an analogy of a centre of gravity (COG) to say much the same thing.[19]

COG is a useful abstraction from physics. It sure helps explain riding a bicycle. Perhaps our 'self' is like a storied, human centre of gravity. Quite simply: you start telling your story and you (and others) know whether it's 'in synch' or 'out of whack'.

Now consider this: we can't know ourselves or our stories exhaustively. Our stories feel coherent, but they're fragmentary and changing. So we could feel we're floating helplessly on a sea of stories. Sadly, that happens. But my storied human COG makes it meaningful to describe my 'self' and still be a mystery!

And this helps with another big thing. Our stories straddle what's given (DNA and contexts), what shapes us (contexts and relationships), and how we shape ourselves (interpretations and choices). To borrow my friend Tony's phrase again, we are Readers and Authors of our stories and lives.

'AM I WRITING OR READING MY STORY?' ???

Story and relationship

Exchanging stories

Our narratives are intertwined with those of many others.[20]

ANTHONY RUDD

There's a fascinating ritual to how relationships grow. It's about the giving and receiving of stories.

Imagine we just met. If we didn't get past day-to-day type chatting, then that's as far as the relationship goes. Or you might tell me a story. If that felt okay to both of us, I might tell you a story too. And if that was okay, we might keep swapping stories until time ran out or it didn't feel okay.

We each have a sack of stories. At first we only take ones near the top labelled 'Okay to tell anyone'. Later we might reach those labelled 'Do not share lightly'. This is how friendship forms. Each 'deeper' story shared and heard is an invitation and a test. But even in our closest relationships, we avoid the stories labelled, 'Too much shame to share'.

We barely think about what's happening, but it's profound. It's not just the content of the stories. It's the telling. The presence in listening. The subtly of reading each other. It's all tacit and it's all bound up in story-telling.

And at some point we find we are no longer after the stories. We want to know the other. This is relationship. This is the power of story.

Building memories

To still tell each other the same stories with irreverence and warmth, that's very special.

All parents have hopes for their kids. One day Sue and I named ours: We want our kids to remain dear friends with each other and with us. And it occurred to us that if in times to come we still loved being together, it will be because we never left each other. Not physically, but in memories. And that means having stories.

One day my older friend Jim shared his tradition of special days with his kids. So twice a year, I spent a day one-on-one with each of mine. One was an overnight trip outdoors; one was a day they chose.

Hannah wasn't keen on the outdoors. So one year we drove our station wagon to a national park, cooked dinner on an open fire, and slept in the back of the car. Well, she thought it was a great adventure and talked about it for weeks.

One year Miriam asked to go to a concert and I got tickets to the (free) graduation concert at the Conservatorium of Music. They were fine young musicians but, for Miriam, it was as though I'd taken her to hear the greatest soloists of our time.

Rich stories; rich relationship. If you can keep telling the same stories, with tears and irreverence and warmth, then you have something very special.

Story and culture

Cultures are carried in stories

I can only answer the question, 'What am I to do?' if I can answer the prior question, 'Of what story or stories do I find myself a part?'[21]

ALASDAIR MACINTYRE

We carry identity in the stories we tell and how we tell them. It's as true of groups as of individuals. Stories shape a culture, and the culture shapes its stories.

Old stories and interpretations hold the mind and the heart of a people. Think of the Balkans, Iraq, Rwanda, and the Sudan. Even in the euphoria of overthrowing an oppressive ruler or regime, old hatreds were already organising to destroy each other.

Not that we always know or acknowledge our own stories. The immediacy and vibrancy that many indigenous and 'first people' groups find in their founding stories seems largely missing in Western societies. And in some Western nations — Australia, New Zealand, South Africa, Canada, the USA — the founding stories of the first peoples sit uneasily alongside those of the colonists.

Cultures and their stories are never clean. Yet they persist. We experience this on entering a new workplace. After the formal orientations and introductions, we begin to hear the stories. They may be ambiguous and just plain wrong; but they are the founding stories. We belong not when we've heard them, but when we can tell them.

Leaders are entrusted with stories

We must navigate with care the stories entrusted to us for there to be a new chapter.

Cultures have founding stories and it's usually near impossible and likely disrespectful to try to change them. Yet neither the culture nor its stories are static. In a sense, though they are often resisted, new chapters are always being written. This helps clarify the responsibilities and possibilities of leadership in bringing change.

As leaders we need to remind ourselves that we have been entrusted with the stories of the groups we lead. Most often we have come in after, perhaps long after, the group began. We weren't part of the founding stories. So bringing lasting, welcomed change takes great respect.

Leaders must find and respect the stories. But not all stories are helpful, nor even deeply believed. Some are mere gossip, some are spread with malice. Respect does not mean we have to agree. It means understanding why a person or group holds a story. Stomp on the story and you will most likely stomp inadvertently on some deeply held passion.

We must navigate with care through stories. Honouring the past cannot guarantee we can write a new future. But no-one can change a story without first honouring it.

WHAT HISTORY OFFERS US

More partners in one of the world's major strategy firms have taken the Oxford PPE (philosophy, politics, economics) than any other degree. Knowing the big stories helps us read small ones.

Listening to history

[History] ... is an enquiry about other people, whom we encounter ... [an enquiry] driven by our own curiosity, about ourselves.[22]

EDWIN JUDGE

'We have been experimenting with what ancient history may offer to a modern university'.[23] So concluded Professor Edwin Judge of Macquarie University in his retirement address. Edwin often remarked that history needs no defence, an idea to which he gave extraordinary substance. Hearing the title of his address, 'Ancient Beginnings of the Modern World', I thought he was finally going to give the defence. Instead, he did what he always did; he opened history to us and left us marvelling at the panorama that is human life.

Take six artefacts: statues, masks, coins, and a mosaic; from Egypt to Rome via Afghanistan and Greece. Add notes on: mummies and their DNA, the Egyptian Book of the Dead, the text of an administrator, the seven maxims of the sages of Delphi, school kids' Greek exercises, and a letter by a professor of rhetoric. All from circa 2400 BC to 450 AD.

It sounds like a recipe for the dullest talk you ever heard. What we got was an unforgettable journey through what makes us who we are.

They're like us!

The people of the past are not remote ... It is vital to our future that we understand the world as they and we have made it.[24]

EDWIN JUDGE

When we encounter bones ringed with the pollen of flowers, 'we have crossed the threshold of history, because we can recognise the human sentiment'.[25]

An Egyptian administrator is buried with pomp. An emperor's mother mints coins to secure her son's power. Three millennia apart an Egyptian man and Roman woman were trying to understand and safeguard against the changes in their worlds.

Like us they saw as people of their times. As Edwin shrewdly noted: if 'we cannot live comfortably with the confusing reality we know, we set up explanations of ourselves, or take over the ones other people supply us with'.[26]

So who are we in this story? 'We are all heirs of those who broke with the unified ideal of the classical republic, because they insisted on choosing for themselves how to live'.[27]

Our task is to understand each other in a dialogue across time where 'our human identity is created'.[28]

Q. # How do you find stories that connect with people?

A. Someone gave me two tips for learning to write clearly. First, edit the worst bits of my own writing. Second, read good writing. Both proved helpful. By analogy: look around for the systems and processes that needlessly irritate people. Ask yourself and others, what's the missing 'people bit'? You'll hear stories of how people work intelligently around these systems. Now look at good design (of anything). Why design? Because great designers work from people's experiences. They design from stories. Look at how they do it. All this grows a storied heart and mind. The disposition comes first, then the skill.

Drawing out stories

Finding the primary sources

Sometimes reality is too complex. Stories give it form.[29]

JEAN-LUC GODARD

Historians speak of primary and secondary sources. The best historians work from primary sources; and not just the literature, but mummies, statues, graffiti, coins, and letters.

As a student I worked on a papyri letter of a man appealing for justice against a higher ranking man who refused to return his donkey. It doesn't sound like much. But thinking we know the first century after reading Seneca is like thinking we know sixteenth century England after reading Shakespeare.

Or thinking we know a business when we've read the Quality Standards. My colleague Jim Ireland once dramatically uncovered the poverty of that idea.

A huge manufacturer had been through TQM and the engineers insisted the plant be run precisely to standard operating procedures. When the operators did so, spoiling and breakdowns increased.

Jim then discovered the crews ran the machines by ear. As this discretion was removed, the problems increased. Jim devised a storied solution: his team and the operators co-designed a way to train people to operate by the procedures *and* by hearing; the operators became the trainers.

Jim found the primary sources. The operators responsibly followed the standards, but nothing matched the subtlety of their listening.

Entering their world

[Such] leaders comfortably inhabit the spaces between fields … they are connectors of fields of knowledge.[30]

ALISTAIR MANT

Jim finds stories by entering others' worlds. There he reads the patterns of life. He doesn't expect stories to present themselves. It's like listening to machines. You get an ear for what experts ignore.

You notice someone in a boardroom, executive, or lunchroom conversation. They begin a story that others don't find interesting. You hear life in it, while everyone else sounds like 'Tasmania'. Ask them: 'I'm intrigued. Could you take us back to that story?' Or you hear an 'odd' idea: 'Can you flesh out that idea for me with an example or story?'

A story can signal itself in many ways: a frustrated sigh, a personal anecdote, or even a rough diagram of stick figures and arrows. Drawing out stories means sitting present with people, okay with complexity, not rushing to solve or fix, respecting that those present hold the knowledge and the stories.

Two maxims: Stories are to leading, as numbers are to managing. Questions are to leading, as answers are to managing.

A STORIED APPROACH TO
CHANGE

Can you invent a story in which you can be competitive, world-class people? That's an act of committed imagination ... Value is not produced by hard work. Value is produced by a story. Value lies in creating a new possibility.[31]

FERNANDO FLORES

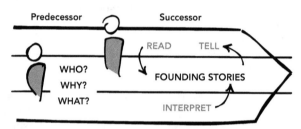

Promoted or invited, you're entrusted.
Each leader helps write a chapter in an ongoing story.

Know the story

Nothing changes without respect.

A list of storied things that have been helpful to me as an adviser and as a CEO. Many I learned the hard way:

1. Wait. There's no need to start with vision and mission.
2. Recognise that you've been entrusted with the stories of the group.
3. Learn the founding stories and how to tell them.
4. Understand how those stories sustain the culture.
5. Understand the limits of founding stories — understanding is the key, not critique.
6. Understand that people do, and don't, want a new chapter.
7. Be curious about your people. Let yourself feel their beliefs (faith), longings (hope), and passion (love).

Renew and retell the story

Nothing changes without a dream.

1. Begin to name a vision as a story. Take your time with it.
2. Build it respectfully, congruently, and believably on the older stories.
3. Test it against strategic concerns and operating realities.
4. Tell the story in ways that invite others to edit, improvise, and enrich it.
5. Draw the story in rough sketches and models. Yes, literally.
6. Use everyday language, not jargon.
7. Widen the story-telling.
8. Wonder together at what's possible.
9. Allow others to test it against convictions held by the group.
10. Don't release until you sense desire gathering around it.
11. Tell it. Tell it. Tell it.
12. Don't be afraid to revise.
13. Ask: 'How will ... be remembered?

Stories unlock value

Bluffed by vision and mission
It's too easy to hide behind 'world's best' and 'excellence'.

I had been talking with the CEO of a global business that specialised in large-scale building projects. At the time they were in negotiations with a major health care organisation to build a hospital complex.

The CEO had recently spent time away with his senior team. He asked for my feedback on the key slide that arranged Areas of Excellence and highest level KPIs around the revised Vision, Mission, and Values statements.

As such slides go, it wasn't bad. It had all the 'stretch goal' and 'game-changing' words and ideals. But something in it didn't ring true to me.

'Those are laudable values, aims, and objectives', I said. 'But if we were to delete your logo and substitute that of, say, a company that makes tin cans, would we need to change any of the other details?'

He was understandably defensive.' Of course. We are very different businesses — we manage huge physical infrastructure projects, they manufacture ...'

I interrupted him. 'Yes, your businesses are different. But I'm asking about what's on this slide. What is there in this statement that is unique to your business. "World's leading ... best

practice ... excellence ... high value to stakeholders ... innovative" — these words apply to anyone and everyone'.

Unlocking the story and value
How many of your team have heard you tell these stories?

We talked on. I didn't have answers, just a hunch that there was more to this man and company than what I saw on the slide.

I took a different tack. 'Imagine', I said, 'I'm the head of the hospital group you're pitching. I want the best to build our new hospital. So why, when there are capable cheaper options, would I choose you? Convince me'.

Slow at first, what he told me was a revelation. With deep passion, he expounded his philosophy of people, communities, and the built environment. 'Imagine ... Imagine ...', he said, followed each time with a story of patients being cared for, or hospital staff working well, because of clever, very 'human' design and construction choices. I was fascinated so I asked:

'How many of your team have heard you tell these stories?' None.

His senior team had gone away to talk about the future of the company, but had never asked the grounded questions or told the stories that would have opened and enriched the central conversation.

ABRAHAM LINCOLN'S
GETTYSBURG ADDRESS

The Gettysburg Address is one of the classic examples of story-telling in a crisis to galvanise hearts and minds.

Background

It was November 19, 1863. The American Civil War would rage another two years. The occasion was the dedication of the cemetery of those who had died in the bloody Battle of Gettysburg.

Speaking first, Edward Everett had recounted the three-day battle. Lincoln knew he must gain the hearts and minds of his fractured people. And he couldn't take another two hours.

THE BRAVE MEN, LIVING AND DEAD, WHO STRUGGLED HERE, HAVE CONSECRATED IT, FAR ABOVE OUR POOR POWER TO ADD OR DETRACT.

The partisan audience expected Lincoln to dwell on Northern victory, to take the high moral ground on slavery, and to base his address on the Constitution. But Lincoln honoured all who had fallen, he did not mention slavery directly, and he looked beyond the Constitution to the Declaration of Independence from the English.

Lincoln was powerfully positioning the call to move beyond the current impasses — he achieved this without mentioning them.

The address

Four score and seven years ago our fathers brought forth on this continent, a new nation, conceived in Liberty, and dedicated to the proposition that all men are created equal. Now we are engaged in a great civil war, testing whether that nation, or any nation so conceived and so dedicated, can long endure. We are met on a great battlefield of that war. We have come to dedicate a portion of that field, as a final resting place for those who here gave their lives that that nation might live. It is altogether fitting and proper that we should do this. But, in a larger sense, we can not dedicate — we can not consecrate — we can not hallow — this ground. The brave men, living and dead, who struggled here, have consecrated it, far above our poor power to add or detract. The world will little note, nor long remember, what we say here, but it can never forget what they did here. It is for us the living, rather, to be dedicated here to the unfinished work which they who fought here have thus far so nobly advanced. It is rather for us to be here dedicated to the great task remaining before us — that from these honoured dead we take increased devotion to that cause for which they gave the last full measure of devotion — that we here highly resolve that these dead shall not have died in vain — that this nation, under God, shall have a new birth of freedom — and that government of the people, by the people, for the people, shall not perish from the earth.

Lincoln's brilliance

Lincoln's triumph was his interpretation of the founding stories.

This far removed in history Lincoln's words loom as one of the great speeches of all time, hugely influential in shaping the nation. But Lincoln had not even been invited. Many only realised he was speaking as he finished and he seemed to have little impact on the crowd. The speech only gained notoriety after being published; even then it was dismissed by many.[32]

Lincoln knew there was more at stake than the survival of the USA. The world was looking on. The Enlightenment had promised the end of the hold of church and monarchy over the lives and consciences of men and women. But in France democracy had turned to bloodshed and the American experiment was going the same way. This is why Lincoln concluded 'that government of the people ... shall not perish from the *earth*'.

Lincoln's triumph was his interpretation of the founding stories. There he found a way to tell the old story that made a new story possible — a story of mature nationhood.

'NO ONE'S GOING TO REMEMBER WHAT I SAY!'

Working with the story

Our word 'topic' derives from the Greek *topos* for place. For Aristotle, the topics were places of thought. Lincoln's speech ranged across four places[33]:

Past and present: 'Four score...' 'Now engaged ...' 'We are met here ...' 'We cannot dedicate ...'
Future: 'shall not perish from the earth'
Hypothesis: 'great remaining task ...', 'government of the people, by the people, for the people ...'
Action: 'we here highly resolve ...'

Lincoln's speech beautifully illustrates the idea of a vision as a future story built upon the past and the present. It tells a new story in which the people may flourish. His hypothesis — military victory to establish democracy — was clear (though not unproblematic).

Still a great model

The Executive of a government owned and operated railway went away for a few days to regroup. Though several years distant, the memories of two disasters hung heavily upon them. I found myself asking a grounded question: What would happen if the city's rail system fell over for a month? The scenarios were dramatic. I could only reply, 'Well, every day you stop it'.

Later, partly for fun, I asked each Executive to write and deliver his or her own 'Gettysburg Address' — a vision for the railway system they longed to deliver. It began playfully enough but we ended with twelve rich declarations of excellence and integrity for the sake of others. It was a tough audience but they were moved.

A storied approach to strategy

Structuring an argument for change
Resourceful leaders are looking beyond their traditional instruments of strategy and adopting the inspired tools of conceptualisation, conversation, and co-creation.[34]
TONY GOLSBY-SMITH

An Australian Aboriginal proverb says, 'Those who lose dreaming are lost'. This is not talking about the future. At least not initially. The dreaming are the founding stories. Without these no-one can find direction. But to retain the dreaming is to continue to dream of stories yet unknown.

A vision is a future story built upon the past and the present. It tells a new story in which people flourish through a richer sense of identity and purpose and things they will make and do for others. A strategy then is an argument for that story, not a guess at the future.

Tony Golsby-Smith, CEO of Second Road argues that 'a successful business strategy is a robust blend of imagination and a dynamic collaborative rhythm activated by clear, cohered intent'.[35] This is genuine strategic conversation.

Leadership is about walking together. In strategy we talk about needing to get from 'A' to 'B'. This simple spatial metaphor lent itself to a brilliant heuristic and tool created by Tony Golsby-Smith. It is the AcdB® model for strategic conversation, which uniquely integrates rhetoric and design.[36]

Like Aristotle, and Lincoln, the AcdB® heuristic structures an argument for change across four places of thought.

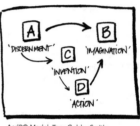

AcdB® Model, Tony Golsby-Smith

'A' is the place of discernment
Where are we? What's so? What are the tensions shaping the current state?

'B' is the place of imagination
Where do we want to be? What's possible? What do we desire?

'C' is the place of invention
What's missing? What do we need to make?

'D' is the place of action
How do we make the 'C'? What is needed to support the 'C'?

The great strength of a heuristic or model like AcdB® is its simplicity and how it can give voice to identity, purpose, agency, and will. It is quite simply a means of moving people from readers to authors. But that's hard work. We have to change our meetings. Clear the board table and get rid of the slides. And turn that whiteboard from a tool of recording to a tool of making.

Images of a storied heart and mind

One weird old prophet

As a postgrad student I took a paper on Comparative Ancient Near Eastern (ANE) literature. For the paper, I picked the Israelite prophet Ezekiel, one of the weirder characters in ANE culture and literature.

I started with his highly mythical funeral dirge for the King of Tyre (28:11–19). It includes a riot of traditions from Eden, mythical beasts, a cherub, and priestly garments, to the great world mountain! The rhetorical effect is to build up the king for a massive fall.

There are four oracles against Tyre, inside seven chapters of oracles against ANE nations, using the themes of hubris and the oppression of Israel. It's a Who's Who of ANE bad guys. Except, the oracle was set in Babylon in the sixth century BC where Israel was in exile. Tyre wasn't an issue.

At that time Israel likened their situation to being back in 'Egypt', the scene of their nation-defining captivity and Exodus. Well, Zeke's oracles end with Egypt humiliated and Israel on an exodus through the desert to what looks like Eden 2.0.

But there's more. Alongside the prophet's apocalyptic vision, he seems to have been developing an anthropology almost universal in scope. In his mind the whole world is being drawn into a back to Eden story. That weird prophet had a storied heart and mind.

The wisdom of janitors

In a favourite TED talk, Barry Schwartz asks what it means to be wise, why we don't value it, and what hospital janitors can teach us.[37]

A janitor's job description, Schwartz notes, has nothing involving people. The job might 'as well be done in a mortuary as in a hospital'. But in three short stories, Schwartz shows that the work of janitors is relational to the core.

Good janitors don't just notice dirty floors. They notice people: an exhausted family in a waiting area; a grieving father keeping a bedside vigil. They attend to people. They adjust their work in aid of healing and grieving.

Good janitors exercise intuition, attentiveness, presence, and care, as much as skill with a mop. Think how a managerial mindset might value their work: 'efficiency' doesn't value attentiveness and judgement.

A storied heart and mind sees through this abstraction. To recall an idea from Chapter 5: Influence, these janitors are 'positive deviants'. They work at the human edge of the system where, by working beyond or even against the system's job descriptions, they actually enable the system to deliver its true purpose — the healing and care of patients.

Those janitors, and Barry Schwartz, have storied hearts and minds.

AND THEN WE SPEAK

'For in Calormen, story-telling (whether the stories are true or made up) is a thing you're taught, just as English boys and girls are taught essay-writing. The difference is that people want to hear the stories, whereas I never heard of anyone who wanted to read the essays'.[38]

Be present

Presence, not charisma, brings respect.

Great leaders in history, both well-known and less-known, have been storytellers. As you plan and get ready:

1. Choose stories that will feed core conversations.
2. Choose stories that touch the heart and mind.
3. Choose sincerity over impact.
4. Go for shorter. Lincoln had 271 words.
5. Ask yourself why you are telling this story. Someone else will ask you.
6. Again, know the point.
7. Assess the impact of the story you tell and how you tell it.
8. Make it as true and as strong as possible.
9. Paint pictures with words.
10. Use strong visuals or none. No text based slides.
11. Rehearse. Start with friends. Move on to tougher critics.
12. Remove distractions if you can. No clutter. No phones. More light on you, less on audience.

Tell it like you were there

A good story doesn't need to be forced.

Add simplicity and focus to authenticity. Drop the extras and stay in the story. As you speak:

1. Be there in the moment. You're a story-teller not a lecturer.
2. Speak without notes. It's a story not a lecture.
3. Connect personally. 'I had no idea what to do …'.
4. Drop all 'abouting'. 'I'm going to tell a story and then …'. Don't talk about telling the story — tell it!
5. Go straight into the story. 'I have never felt so proud as the day …'. Not 'I want to tell you about a time …'.
6. Tell the story 'first hand' even if it's third person. 'Fifty teachers sat in a circle …'. Not 'A group of teachers went away …'.
7. Dramatise a little IF it's natural for you. If not, don't.
8. Take the listener with you.
9. Turn thank-yous into conversations by asking what the person found helpful.

Q. # What does the art of story offer leaders?

A. Story is a window into all of leadership. Your commitment and presence depends in part on being comfortable with yourself: that means sitting well with your own story. Every person you lead has a story: that's worth remembering before reacting. Now story is a powerful way to convey an idea, but it's also at the heart of how we think. Nothing will show you the context like the stories. They will show you where abstract thinking gets in the way. Story offers you clarity and insight about yourself, your people, and context. Story is a way of knowing that deepens character.

Everyone has brilliance but few know well what it is. Our stories hold the clues.

CHAPTER 8

Brilliance

We all shine somewhere

When what we do matches who we are

For the second time writing this book I turned to those connected to me on Facebook. This time I asked about their perceptions of brilliance:

Brilliance is not intelligence, but giftedness used with purpose and passion. GREG
Brilliance outshines brightness! ROLAND
Brilliance is not about outshining others, but enabling others to shine. BRUWER
Brilliance animates — it breathes life into people, things and situations. JP
Brilliance is inner value, not recognised worth. DAZ
Brilliance does not seek to undermine others. GAIL
Brilliance arises in our being and becoming, not in our doing or DNA. DAVID
Brilliance — a quality of character, not a description of one's gifts. JOE
Brilliance is where what you do and who you are lights up other people's lives! RICHARD

Three themes came out quickly and clearly: brilliance is more than intellect, it has a connection to character, and it is most apparent and profound when other-centred. Turns out that's a pretty good summary — though better said — of what I want to argue about brilliance.

It may seem that I'm heading toward drawing a fine distinction between inherent skill and motive behind the skill. Neither I nor my friends, I think, would want to deny or dismiss cleverness, talent, or skill per se. Nor suggest that brilliance only exists with altruism. The artist or athlete may be a narcissist, but I can still admire his or her skill and benefit from it.

Likewise I can appreciate the entrepreneurship of an otherwise self-absorbed leader. But even great skill if coupled with self-interest does not make for leading well over the long run. Brilliance shines when coupled with character and wisdom.

How then do we come to know our own brilliance, and help others know theirs, so that we may shine together? This is the Art of Brilliance.

A useful distinction: Brilliance is ability, heart, and mind expressed uniquely. Conformity shrinks each.

More than ability

Yes, I have mixed my categories. Like chalk and cheese, brilliance and conformity are certainly not antonyms, just two things that don't go together well. But the reason I have juxtaposed them is not hard to see: conformity is the common expectation and context that stifles brilliance.

Conformity — Is when ability and heart are sublimated to a fearful or stifling expectation and abstract objective.

Brilliance — Is when ability and heart are uniquely expressed and freely given that others may flourish.

At one level, brilliance is the unique way we express an ability. The ability itself may or may not be unique. Quite likely other people do something very similar. The brilliance, the way we shine, comes from the unique ways our stories, hearts, and minds shape how we express this ability. But I think there's one more dimension: our brilliance shines brightest when we express it that others may shine.

Conformity stifles brilliance.

That's me!

So brilliance is the capacity to shine. It's more than intellect, it has a connection to character, and it's most apparent and profound when other-centred.

Another way to think about brilliance is the times we feel the 'Sweet Spot' and we can say 'That's Me!'

Sweet spot is a sporting idea. It's a spot on a club. When you strike the ball there with perfect position and timing the ball flies true. In popular use we transfer the image from the golf club, to the shot, to the golfer, and to the joy the golfer feels. The sweet spot sums up the experience, the passion, and the goal. Another way to describe it is to think of moments when we can say 'That's me!'

I always said I didn't have what it took to be a CEO and certainly not in the context of leading a turnaround. My reluctance was about my less developed skills and experience: financials, operations, stakeholders, and fundraising. I ended up able to do them all well enough. But would I seek a role as a COO? No, it's not me. Thankfully I had great colleagues who excelled at the things I didn't. But casting a vision, reimagining programs, or nurturing students and faculty who were open to change — that's me!

No-one only does what they like — not in a team. Finding 'that's me!' isn't self-indulgence, though it could be. It's bringing our best to others.

Everyone can shine

Remembering others' brilliance

I'm not talking Einstein or Picasso, one-in-a-million brilliance here. Nor a kind of top-of-the-class brilliance won after years of study and effort. Study there may be, effort very likely, but brilliance can be something much simpler and more human — something we can hope to find in everyone. If, like me, you struggled to see it in yourself, you may nonetheless have recognised it in others. Perhaps especially in those who impacted you for the better.

Overall, school wasn't a positive experience for me. Yet a couple of teachers stand out for their belief and their kindness, and their skill. Maybe you were fortunate to have had such teachers too. When I think about them, and the many other fine teachers I have met in later life, I'm struck by their absolute uniqueness. Though all brilliant, each teaches differently.

Brilliance is not polished.

HENOCH

One teacher may have made the world of literature come alive by story-telling. Another may have given the sense that we weren't learning chemistry at all — we were learning about life. Still another might have forged lasting creative relationships among classmates, such that they taught one another far more than the syllabus could. Or a philosopher who enthralled with the story of thought. Each one unique, each one brilliant. Like Michelle in my earlier story.

Brilliance rests on dignity

Like character, brilliance derives from dignity not pragmatism. When I say that brilliance is universal, that everyone can shine, I don't mean it as a motivational slogan. I'm not saying: 'C'mon people, just believe and you can shine!' I'm saying we do shine, even if, as my friend Rebecca says, 'brilliance is shining with a gentle glow — not with a blinding light'. Or even if we don't see it all.

We are brilliant because we have dignity, even in our brokenness. But like all our knowing, we are never fully aware of our brilliance. How we see our brilliance depends on how we read our stories. I think the brilliance comes out anyway, but we may neither notice what we've done nor sense its significance.

I wonder sometimes if this blindness to everyday brilliance has something to do with the modern profusion and confusion of celebrity. Today, sociologist Joseph Epstein argues, 'one can become a celebrity with scarcely any pretense to talent or achievement whatsoever'. One only needs careful promotion and a great deal of luck.[1]

True brilliance may well bring and deserve celebrity. Hopefully we can celebrate with such people. But brilliance is all around us. It's a friend or colleague who walks humbly with another to help them regain hope or clarity. It's the supervisor who stands up for her team in the face of a demeaning executive.

[NOT SO]
EVERYDAY BRILLIANCE

We find brilliance in all the classic areas of skill: artistic, sporting, professional, administrative, academic, entrepreneurial, and so on. But our brilliance as leaders, managers, parents, and friends is perhaps less obvious. Here are some examples. As you read: (1) think about some people you admire, then (2) think about yourself.

- Sketching an idea
- Listening well
- Reading people well
- Naming core conversations
- Making things happen
- Noticing the unnoticed
- Making calls with grace
- Noticing patterns
- Asking grounded questions
- Refusing shallowness
- Lightening hearts
- Suspending judgement
- Daring to question
- Mapping a conversation
- Putting people at ease
- Creating safe spaces
- Being vulnerable helpfully
- Speaking an apt word
- Looking past the obvious
- Discerning purpose
- Being hospitable
- Holding the details
- Holding the big picture

- Negotiating lasting deals
- Bridging interests
- Connecting people
- Desiring truth
- Making an argument
- Bridging disciplines
- Asking tough questions
- Daring to dream
- Speaking truth with care
- Assessing risk
- Paying attention
- Believing the best
- Staying present
- Critiquing fairly
- Delighting in others
- Linking people and ideas
- Refusing to give up
- Embracing tensions
- Reading widely
- Honouring stories
- Finding learning in failure
- Imagining a new story
- Not ignoring 'elephants'
- Forgiving, not escalating
- Drawing out ideas

- Nurturing brilliance
- Holding hope
- Perceiving deceit
- Simplifying complexity
- Reasoning soundly
- Wondering what may be
- Leading from the middle
- Backing a hunch
- Walking with the sad
- Loving well
- Detecting nonsense
- Sharpening an argument
- Thinking metaphorically
- Creating room for people
- Reading complexity
- Unmasking abstraction
- Humanising information
- Diagnosing a problem
- Seeing analogies
- Believing in others
- Honouring culture
- Leading from the front
- Translating ideas
- Humanising systems
- Restoring heart

Our stories hold the clues

Learning to pay attention
Why did you become a teacher?

In the next section I'm going to introduce a simple exercise to help you name your own brilliance. But before we go there, I want to pause at the key idea behind the exercise. You won't be surprised to hear me say that the clues to our brilliance lie in our stories. And like the way relationships form around hearing the other person's stories, so we come to know ourselves in part by hearing our own stories.

But there lies the problem. When I asked those school teachers why they became teachers, the hard part was not saying 'to make a difference'. That's the standard answer most teachers give. The hard part was getting the stories that showed what that meant. In other words, the moments when they knew they had made a difference. They knew them, but never talked about them, and rarely even thought about them.

My point then, as it is now, was not to make anyone feel good. If that happens, it's a bonus. My purpose is to forge awareness of what we have done so that, seeing its significance, we learn not only to repeat this brilliance but to deepen it. That means learning to pay attention to those moments we may rarely have considered significant.

Knowing our own stories may not make us wise leaders. But I doubt we can be without knowing them.

Every moment is a clue
When have you felt 'alive'?

It's a darn good thing we don't think about brilliance all the time. We'd be insufferable! You've probably met someone like that at an event where you couldn't slip away. Brilliance doesn't need ego. Ego is fine, except it gets in the way of growing.

The moments that reveal brilliance may not be spectacular. Teachers have classic stories of this. A young adult stops them in the street and thanks them for 'changing my life'. The teacher smiles and thanks them, but can't remember the year, class, or conversation.

Someone has seen significance in something you did that you didn't see then, or now. Other stories are clearer to us. We took a risk. We cancelled something to give someone time. We voiced a question that seemed so out of whack with the general discussion. These are the moments we need to recall.

If our lives unfold in our stories, then we can expect brilliance to mature. In the exercise that follows, when you have recalled enough moments, I'll ask you to look for themes. Somewhere you will glimpse in your experience as a child the seeds of something you do well now. The link is what you need to name and attend to: for each glimpse is a doorway to more.

AN EXERCISE TO
MAP YOUR BRILLIANCE

The clues lie in our stories. This simple but searching exercise helps you find your significant moments and consider what they say about you.

The process

I have done this exercise myself and led many people through it. Set aside a morning or afternoon to get the most out of it. You can get great value out of doing only Steps 1, 2, and 5. But the walk and talk in Steps 3 and 4 adds great depth. The process is:

1. Map your significant moments.
2. Look for connections.
3. Walk and share what you saw.
4. Talk over the experience.
5. Journal the experience and insights.

1. Map your significant moments

Do this step on your own. Use a large sheet of paper (butcher's paper or A3). Write small with a pen, not a marker. Write in small chunks, more like a map than a letter (see my diagram). Use just enough words to capture the moment. Arrange things in chronological order.

Some people say it helps to divide the paper into big periods in your life like ages, places you lived, relationships, vocations — whatever feels like it might work for you. So what do you write?

You are after moments that stand out to you. Note: they must be events, not things you like. Making lists is a waste of time. For example: don't write that you like fishing; think of a specific time you went fishing that's significant to you. Yes, this is much harder to do. Remember: the clues are in your stories.

Some moments may be ones you feel proud about. Or happy. Or amused. Some may be moments when others appreciated you. Find events whose memory lifts your spirits. Yet some may be hard moments. I don't want to send you into therapy, but sometimes our deepest changes came through hard moments.

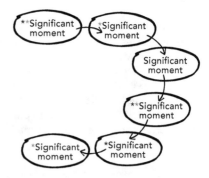

Map the significant moments in your story and look for the connections that lead to insight.

2. Look for connections

Again, do this step on your own. When you feel you've got enough to work with, it's time to stand back from the details and look for the connections. There are two parts to this step.

First, look for common elements in different moments. A childhood moment and a professional moment might reveal similar convictions, skills, or ways of thinking. That's the kind of thing you're looking for. Put an asterisk of the same colour on those moments and any others that feel similar. Use different colours for different themes. Some moments will fit two or more themes.

Second, name the themes. Don't judge what comes to mind. Those first words are often intuitive. Write them down. When you're ready, write a single sentence for each theme. I use sentences like these: 'I am one who …' or 'I am a … who …'. Remember Michelle's story: 'I am a teacher who paints with children'. Make your words strong and true. Each sentence is the beginning of naming some aspect of your brilliance.

3. Walk and share what you saw

Arrange a time and place to meet someone you trust who also did Steps 1 and 2. I can't stress too much how walking enriches this whole process. If the weather is bad, find somewhere to sit and look in the same direction, just like you were walking.

4. Talk over the experience

Find a comfortable place, grab a drink, and let the conversation go wherever it feels comfortable and helpful.

5. Journal what you see

Do this step on your own. In light of Steps 3 and 4, revisit how you named your themes. These are glimpses of your brilliance: make each sentence strong and true. The whole idea is to help you bring your best to others. It's not about putting yourself into a box.

Doing this with a group

First, the picky stuff. When you break for Step 1, some members will turn on phones or hang around talking. At Step 3, someone will want to give advice. Each behaviour is avoidance. It comes from fear and robs someone, certainly themselves, of a chance to reflect and grow. Point this out up front: then it's their choice.

Second, include a group debrief. What was it like mapping your moments? Finding themes? Telling your story? Listening? Being listened to? People might also just want to be quiet.

Third, consider planning over the coming weeks for every member to walk and talk with every other member. There are two benefits. First, getting to know each other well. Second, your story and brilliance will become clearer the more you tell it.

Please respect these principles

1. No-one should feel forced to do any part of this exercise.
2. No-one should feel forced to talk with anyone.
3. No-one should share more than they feel good about sharing.
4. No-one should repeat what someone told them without permission.

Unpacking the exercise

A word on connections

I'm always asked what I mean in Step 2 by seeing connections and themes, and what to write in the sentences. I've done this exercise many times so let me answer with a personal example.

One time I linked three very different events. Moment (1): The look of astonishment on a woman's face on a canyon trip I led. Finishing her abseil down a waterfall into a dark pool in a mountain crevice, her eyes shone as she turned and saw the beauty of a place unlike anything she'd ever experienced. Moment (2): Watching 'lights going on' in the eyes of students, like a wave around the room, as I taught a class on the history of ideas. Moment (3): Sitting on a plane smiling after a week consulting to the head of a federal initiative. On that last day I suggested we go for a walk and that walk led him to a breakthrough.

So what's the link? I wrote two sentences using words that others had said to me but I'd never appreciated before. Sentence (1): I take people to places they might never go, so that they might go to places I might never go'. Sentence (2): 'I am a teacher who opens windows and doors'. Both names still help shape my thoughts and choices.

What if I can't find brilliance?

You're not alone. But just because it's hard to see the richness in your life, doesn't mean it's not there. If you've suffered greatly, it can be hard to see past surviving to who you have and will become. Or if you feel your life has been uneventful, it can be hard to realise the depth of the things that you may call 'small'.

Finding brilliance tips

How can you help yourself see your significant moments?

1. Talk to friends. Sometimes we need someone else to help us see. Tell them about your struggle with the exercise. Ask them: Where have you seen me shine? When have I been helpful to you or someone else? What did I do?
2. Re-read the list of '[Not so] everyday brilliance'.
3. Find everyday things that jog your memory. Photos, music, places, and foods can trigger memories. (Note: I'm mindful this can also be painful. Don't go there if it's too hard. Be kind to yourself. Seek help if you need it.)

Finally, kindness opens the door to brilliance. As clichéd as it may sound, you may need to show yourself a little grace, especially if you more normally focus on inadequacies. If so, the time has come to speak and walk into the darkness of wondering what better things lie within.

Q. # How big is this issue of brilliance?

A. It's huge because conformity is huge. From the start of school, every word we wrote was examined. We learned to second guess the teacher because what he or she thought was right. Teachers wanted verbatim replies, not better questions. We learned to 'fill things up', whether sheets of cardboard or word limits. We started out different, creative, and curious without even knowing we were. Slowly we were tamed. I work with people who long to grow as thinkers and leaders, yet they struggle if I don't give them the answers. We can't lead anyone into their brilliance if we haven't or won't face our own.

INTRODUCING THE BrQ©™®
BRILLIANCE QUOTIENT

Okay, I'm joking. But there's something here worth thinking about.

A whole lot of Qs!

After IQ (Intellectual Quotient) came EQ (Emotional Quotient). Soon there was SQ (Spiritual Quotient). I think it was 1999 when I first thought about WQ (Wisdom Quotient)! I know, it's naff, and I just couldn't do it. Well, several people did do it.[2]

So I searched for other Qs — and IQ, EQ, SQ, and WQ are not even the half of it. Here are the Qs I've found:

AQ Adversity Quotient
AQ Appearance Quotient
BQ Behavior Quotient
BQ Body Quotient
CIQ Contextual Intelligence Quotient
CQ Communication Quotient
CQ Creativity Quotient
DQ Daring Quotient
DQ Desire Quotient
EQ Emotional Quotient
EQ Environmental Quotient
FQ Financial Quotient
FQ Follower Quotient
GLQ Global Leadership Quotient
HQ Handling Quotient
HQ Health Quotient
IQ Intelligence Quotient
KQ Knowledge Quotient
LQ Leadership Quotient
MQ Management Quotient
MQ Mental Quotient
MQ Moral Quotient
PQ People Quotient
PQ Practical Quotient
RQ Reality Quotient
RQ Relational Quotient[3]

SQ Situation Quotient
SQ Spiritual Quotient
WQ Will Quotient
WQ Wisdom Quotient
XQ Experience Quotient

I swear I didn't make up any of them.

So, introducing ... BrQ©™®!

Since I missed out on WQ, and BQ, I'm going to grab BrQ©™®. You guessed it — the Brilliance Quotient™! Okay, I'm joking. But think of the T-Shirts!

You (only) get what you measure

I'm not saying there's no value, even wisdom, in some of the things written under these Qs. The work by Howard Gardner on Multiple Intelligences[4] and the various studies of Emotional Intelligence (EQ)[5] have been timely and important challenges to the myths about IQ.[6]

The problem is three-fold. First, the litany of Qs dumbs down the enquiry and conversation. Second, what we measure blinds us to what we can't measure. The reality is always bigger than questionnaires and formulas.[7] Wisdom is just too profoundly human to reduce to measurement. We may as well try to measure dignity. Or brilliance. Third, we measure to control. That is the deepest problem. At that point we stand on the edge of running counter to everything we want to understand and embrace.

Brilliant by design

Design is wisdom in making
When brilliance comes together well in organisations, the process is more like what designers do, than how committees work.

The design process is intellectual, social, and physical. Design channels our urge for change into a process of making something new. The process is thoughtfully simple and grounded in experience. Think of what guides good architects, graphic designers, or product designers:

Story: Good architects don't start with a list of features. They start with your story of home.

User: Good designers enter the experiences of whoever will use what is designed.

Iterative and provisional: Good designers test ideas. They come back, revise, let go, and move on.

Get physical fast: Designers sketch from the first interactions. They express ideas physically to get concrete.

Useful-useable-desirable: A good design serves a real purpose. Can it be used effectively and efficiently? Is it more desirable to use than not?

Create a small design team
A shared methodology and a small cross disciplinary team works best in a collaborative process. Each team member has the opportunity to enrich the project with their brilliance and expertise.

Sponsorship: The sponsor authorises the team and approves the final design. He or she must sustain focus on the intent and clear any institutional hurdles.

Conversation: The team needs to consult widely by conversations, not committees.

Facilitation: Design facilitation isn't about recording, but giving shape to ideas. Great facilitators move the work from talking to making.

Design room: A dedicated space amenable to iterative, informal, and tactile processes.

Leading design
This mode of thinking and working takes more than a smart process. It takes leadership:

It takes … courage to … embrace the people we are designing for … It takes truth to … not reduc(e) people to abstract labels, such as 'consumers', 'users' … It takes common sense to source our designs from the people who will use them in the end. It takes a sense of discovery to … step into other people's lives and see from their points of view … It takes vision to imagine … the profound possibilities available to us.[8]
LAURALEE ALBEN

Unlikely brilliance

Temple Grandin: Seeing like cattle

Professor Temple Grandin of Animal Science at Colorado State University has revolutionised the humane treatment of livestock. But her PhD, professorship, patents, and publications give little indication of her brilliance.

Temple's parents were advised to institutionalise her. Today she is widely regarded as the world's 'most accomplished and well-known adult with autism'.[9] Temple 'thinks in pictures', but with a fascinating twist: a brilliant nexus between thinking visually and deep empathy with animals. Her first breakthrough in livestock handling design came when she literally, against advice, got in with the cattle to see the world as they do.

Her brilliance as a designer stems from serendipitous discovery as a child of what calmed her. Like an autistic child, cattle, for her, are intelligent creatures surrounded by ignorant others unable to see or feel what they do. Her brilliance is an extraordinary knowing and an ability to translate this to human and non-human alike.

Until her book, *Emergence: Labeled Autistic*, autism was regarded as a life sentence.[10] People with autism were assumed to have little capacity to reflect on their ways of knowing. In Temple's story of 'groping her way from the far side of darkness', and the many who followed, a window has opened on a world few understood.[11]

May Lemke: Unlocked by love

Leslie Lemke is a savant with an inexplicable musical gift. In 1952 Leslie was born severely disabled and doctors had to remove his eyes soon after. Given for adoption, the hospital despaired of finding a home until his 'last chance', May Lemke, a nurse who had raised five children of her own.[12]

For seven years May forced him to eat until Leslie learned to swallow. She sang with her face against his; she spoke to him constantly; she played piano to him; all despite no response. After he stood on his own at twelve, May would walk with Leslie strapped to her body. At fifteen, he walked on his own.

A year later, May and her husband Joe heard music in the middle of the night. Thinking they'd left the TV playing, May came downstairs to find Leslie playing Tchaikovsky's Piano Concerto No. 1. He had never played the piano before and first heard the tune that night. Today, Leslie is still virtually speechless and emotionless — until he plays and sings.

Leslie's brilliance is extraordinary. I'm equally astounded by May. Neuroscience suggests that love establishes neocortical connections between people. If so, then perhaps May's love unlocked Leslie.[13] Perhaps May's love also released her own brilliance — that curious mixture of devotion, stubbornness, tactility, and deep reading — in which Leslie found his own. Here we see brilliance in the wonder of knowing as we are known.

A timely word can release brilliance

Brilliance waits to be unlocked

Life is pregnant with brilliance. I'd like to think I've given clients some great solutions and ways forward. And I'm sure I have. But more often the breakthroughs come from them. What I have done is help them to see and to name.

Let me illustrate from stories I've already told. Michelle and her colleagues already taught brilliantly; sometimes. They already had great stories about why they became teachers and what they felt about the kids. But they hadn't noticed and they hadn't told each other. So long as those stories remained locked away, so did the larger possibilities they could bring.

The power company staff already had a great story of breakthrough in what they had achieved with safety. They already had intuitions into generator reliability more profound than their analyses. But in twenty years they had never convened in the same room, never told their stories, named their intuitions, or noticed the analogy.

Neither of these breakthroughs were sparked by new technology or even a new idea. They rarely are. Albert Szent-Gyrgyi once said that '(c)reativity is seeing what everybody else has seen and thinking what nobody has thought'.[14] This is what we're doing in noticing the everyday brilliance lying in people's stories and ways of knowing — we are bringing together what has never been brought together.

A word in season

There's no sure way to anticipate every facet of brilliance in ourselves or others. What we can do, to go back to wisdom, is grow the presence and attentiveness to notice more readily what we otherwise might not. But it may take more than presence to unlock brilliance.

Often brilliance waits for a word spoken in season. If you have completed the exercise 'Map your brilliance' — or when you do — look back over the moments you mapped. Quite likely you will see times when something new was opened when someone spoke what they noticed in you or wondered about you.

I'm deeply grateful for many such moments. Like when my friend challenged me to take seriously my work on leadership: 'You've found your island … It's Wisdom! It's Naming! It's the Arts! Now drop anchor, burn your boat, and build your new world!' Without that word, you wouldn't be reading this one. Thanks Terry!

Start with your own experience. Can you recall someone speaking something good they noticed in you? Most likely it was spoken with integrity and care. You can clearly distinguish such a word from one that's manipulative or patronising. Maybe now you can see a time when you've spoken such a word to another. If so, then you know what it is to speak a word in season. Such a word doesn't come from trying to fix someone. Rather, it arises from deep regard.

A WILDLY GENERALISED
HISTORY OF BRILLIANCE

Many of our most cherished ideas took a long time coming.
Like the idea that everyone has brilliance.

How we found brilliance

Until the twentieth century it was uncommon to speak of people as brilliant irrespective of their social rank or status, or education. The story of brilliance is one of huge transformations in how we view ourselves: from elitism to the democratisation of human dignity and inspiration; and from dualism to the dignity of everyday life.

How large is the capacity of man, if we should stand upon particulars![15]

AUGUSTINE

Ancient Greek and Roman writers associated brilliance with the unpredictable presence of the Muses, daemons, and Genius. Yet such inspiration could leave one, as Homer said, 'witless and helpless'.[16] And, like most of the gods' benefits, the gift almost invariably went to those of the highest social standing. Brilliance was neither inherent nor equal.

For equality we look to democracy in ancient Athens. We are inspired but disappointed. The assembly (demos) at the heart of democracy consisted of free born men of sufficient rank, land, and wealth. Our idea of equality would

have appalled Pericles and Aristotle. Likewise the value we see in everyday life.

For a thousand years the human body was a common social metaphor. A group was like a body; their leader the head. Paul of Tarsus turned this image on … its head. When the head is simply part of the body, then foot, hand, ear, and eye equally depend on the other. Paul then added another innovation. Each member of the body was gifted in service of the others and these were intrinsic to personal and social transformation.[17]

These innovations might have died soon after. But Paul's ideas morphed with society, and society morphed with the gifts. The result was a powerful but volatile synthesis of contradictions: reason and inspiration; democracy and inequality; hierarchy and service; and the Cities of God and Man.

Classical philosophy had bequeathed a model of the cosmos as coherent and amenable to understanding. This was enough for geometry and mathematics. But science needed more. In 529, philosopher John Philoponus refuted the classical account of a rational, eternal cosmos and advocated a created cosmos that gave a theoretical basis for empirical enquiry and experimentation. Science and crafts were gifts to be embraced.

Over the next thousand years, in contexts often racked by the horror of plague, war, and inquisition, a succession of Renaissances and Reformations, as diverse and dependent as Europe itself, yielded extraordinary figures and changes. Da Vinci. Botticelli. Michelangelo. Machiavelli. Newton. Locke. And so many more. Innovations and inventions in art, music, architecture, manufacturing, agriculture, medicine, jurisprudence, and science not only opened new horizons within the world, but within the hearts and minds of people. Explorers returned from unimaginable places with tales of unimaginable brilliance.

The fresco on the walls of the Council Room in the Town Hall of Siena portrays the changing mood. Lorenzetti's *Allegory of Good and Bad Government* (1339) is a powerful testimony to the new expectation. Church and empire have receded. Combined classical and Christian virtues enable the constructive contribution of the whole of society. Though not yet democracy, the elements of liberty, participation, and gifting are unmistakable.

Old and new drew battle lines. After Pope Innocent III wrote *On the Misery of the Human Condition,* Manetti (1452) gave voice to 'the genius of man ... the unique and extraordinary ability of the human mind'.[18] When della Mirandola wrote his *Oration on the Dignity of Man* (1486) he argued from reason, not tradition. Though steeped in classical ideals, something original was happening — an extension of that unruly synthesis of Plato, Aristotle, and Paul. The mood was still elitist but the trajectory was toward enlightenment and participation.

After Gutenberg's printing press, ideas travelled fast and increasingly in the vernacular. Luther followed Erasmus in his use of Hebrew and Greek manuscripts and more nuanced approaches to text. The idea that one could interpret texts for oneself was a breakthrough as profound as the scientific method.

In 1664 Pierre Bayle launched a journal, *The New Republic of Letters*. It lent its name to a movement marked by reading and conversation. At the heart of this Republic of Letters, Peter Miller writes, was an idea of 'community ... based upon neither family, religion, ethnicity nor political affiliation'.[19] In cafés and debating societies, Renaissance and Enlightenment ideas came within reach of people.

The American *Declaration of Independence* (1776), the French *Declaration of the Rights of Man and of the Citizen* (1789), and the American *Bill of Rights* (1791) trumpeted the dignity and freedom of humanity. Yet it took decades, even centuries for the emancipation of slaves, and the enfranchisement of women and indigenous peoples.

Each theme is intelligible only in its social and historical context. Each gave rise to a more nuanced idea. Such is the history of brilliance.

FINDING
BRILLIANCE IN CRAFT

The term 'knowledge work' has always grated for me.
It's assumed that it doesn't apply to people who work with
their hands. Not so in this tale.

The knowledge work of craft

Sometimes the term 'knowledge worker' is just ignorant and patronising. For sixty years my father-in-law George built houses. I laboured for him on occasion. I always admired how he held a house in his head and built it straight and true with little reference to the plans he'd drawn. That's certainly a deep knowing and certainly brilliance.

Matthew Crawford is a motorcycle mechanic with a PhD in philosophy. His book *Shop Class as Soulcraft* is 'an inquiry into the value of work'. I think of it as a study of brilliance in the world of fixing things.

At one point Crawford draws on the tale of a motorcycle repair misadventure from that old favourite, *Zen and the Art of Motorcycle Maintenance* by Robert Pirsig. After seizing his engine at high speed, Pirsig decided to avoid repairing it himself and took his beloved motorcycle to the repair shop:

'The shop was a different scene from the ones I remembered. The mechanics, who had once all seemed like ancient veterans, now looked like children. A radio was going full blast and they were clowning around and talking and seemed not to notice me. When one of them finally came over he barely listened to the piston slap before saying, 'Oh yeah. Tappets'.[20]

As Crawford summarises Pirsig's tale, 'Three overhauls, some haphazard misdiagnoses, and a lot of bad faith later, the narrator picks up his bike from the shop for the final time':

'[N]ow there really was a tappet noise. They hadn't adjusted them. I pointed this out and the kid came with an open-end adjustable wrench, set wrong, and swiftly rounded both of the sheet-aluminum tappet covers, ruining both of them. "I hope we've got some more of those in stock", he said. I nodded.

I often find manual work more engaging intellectually.[21]
MATTHEW CRAWFORD

'He brought out a hammer and cold chisel and started to pound them loose. The chisel punched through the aluminum cover and I could see he was pounding the chisel right into the engine head. On the next blow he missed the chisel completely and struck the head with the hammer.

'I found the cause of the seizures a few weeks later, waiting to happen again. It was a little twenty-five-cent pin in the internal oil-delivery system that had been sheared and was preventing oil from reaching the head at high speeds.

'... Why did they butcher it so?... They sat down to do a job and they performed it like chimpanzees. Nothing personal in it ... But the biggest clue seemed to be their expressions. They were hard to explain. Good-natured, friendly, easygoing — and uninvolved. They were like spectators. You had the feeling they had just wandered in there themselves and somebody had handed them a wrench. There was no identification with the job. No saying, "I am a mechanic"'.[22]

Drawing on Pirsig's tale, Crawford makes a powerful point about attentiveness, knowing, and craft. Like Polanyi, he recognises that all knowing is personal and relational. One cannot know well from a distance. This is as true for the mechanic as for the scientist or philosopher.

'"Nothing personal in it." Here is a paradox. On the one hand, to be a good mechanic seems to require personal commitment: I am a mechanic. On the other hand, what it means to be a good mechanic is that you have a keen sense that you answer to something that is the opposite of personal or idiosyncratic; something universal. In Pirsig's story, there is an underlying fact: a sheared-off pin has blocked an oil gallery, resulting in oil starvation to the head and excessive heat, causing the seizures. This is the Truth, and it is the same for everyone'.

This Truth is not obvious to everyone. It doesn't come from a manual or a course. Crawford summarises a good deal of what we have seen about wisdom. Deep knowledge takes presence and attentiveness on behalf of the motorcycle, owner, and guild of mechanics. The whole motorcycle must somehow be present to the mechanic. This is not a dispassionate knowing.

'Pirsig's mechanic is, in the original sense of the term, an idiot. Indeed, he exemplifies the truth about idiocy, which is that it is at once an ethical and a cognitive failure. The Greek idios means "private," and an idiotes means a private person, as opposed to a person in their public role — for example, that of motorcycle mechanic. Pirsig's mechanic is idiotic because he fails to grasp his public role, which entails, or should, a relation of active concern to others, and to the machine. He is not involved. It is not his problem. Because he is an idiot'.[23]

Crawford contrasts this mechanic to the craftsmen he has known. Through years of listening to motors and the stories of riders, and of riding their own bikes, these mechanics have come to 'know' myriad problems in myriad bikes. They don't rush to diagnosis. They take time to listen. Their questions come from curiosity about machines and riders and life. They are moved by a machine that delights its owner.

This knowledge is not purely mechanical. It is personal. It is relational. It is story-based. It is the mechanic's brilliance to know how to indwell this story of desire in machine and rider and road.

MAPPING REPUTATION

Mapping three factors of reputation: Competence gets us in the game. Integrity keeps us there. Brilliance gives us the edge.

We start at competence and integrity Reputation maps well across the heuristic of One and Many.

Competence in the One. Any teacher or mechanic needs to be able to do what every other similar professional can do. Businesses too: every airline or law firm needs to be able to deliver the expected. This gets us in the game. And as expertise and expectation grows, so we have to keep growing.

Brilliance in the Many. If we only do what any other mechanic or lawyer can do, or do it the same way, the only differential will be price. For some businesses that may seem okay but it rarely lasts. What sets us apart is doing something unique, or uniquely.

Integrity bridges competence and brilliance. The way we conduct ourselves, in both competence and brilliance, must uphold all reasonable standards of professional conduct. Our reputation is the way we embody competence and brilliance with integrity.

Brilliance gives edge

In my experience, competency rates most highly in strategy. First, areas of competence are acquired, merged, or divested. Second, cost-cutting moves against brilliance first, and places a strain on integrity.

But competitive edge comes through engagement and innovation. This is the Holy Grail of management: a workforce who feel motivated to work, who bring their best to their work, who help to improve products and ways of working, and who imagine and design new products and ways. Each is the domain of brilliance.

In *Chapter 4: Conversation,* I made a case for engagement being an outcome of leaders respecting craft and community, and sponsoring conversation and co-design. Brilliance can certainly be out-of-the-box and leaders need to stay open to this coming from even the most unlikely sources. But it should be evident by now that brilliance is more readily found in the sense of craft that people hold within a community dedicated to that craft.

Engagement is contrived, if not a sham, unless it derives from valuing the brilliance of people and giving them room to express and deepen it. Innovation can come from nowhere else. So here is a way to name the brilliance of the best leaders: they believe brilliance is in others, they draw it out respectfully, and they create the contexts for conversations and co-design that make the new possible. Such ways of drawing alongside colleagues gives meaningful shape to agency.

Q. # How do I nurture brilliance in others?

A.   Most people have no way of answering a question about their brilliance. So don't ask. Just listen. Build trust. In time they will tell stories. Listen. Make your questions grounded. Ask them how they got into whatever you have noticed matters to them. Listen for what it means to them. When the rapport is strong, and you believe your hunch is good and clear, share what you have noticed that sparks admiration for the way they work. When it's clear they have found something that draws their attention, help them name it, but don't do it for them. Share your own story where it helps.

Speaking truly and strongly may not subvert self-defeating words and perspectives. But they are never subverted until someone speaks truly and strongly.

CHAPTER 9

Promise

A strong and true word of hope

We speak to nurture strength

A considered and genuine word of comfort for a friend in pain or grief is a beautiful thing. Often of course we just need someone to sit silently with us. But when it's time to speak, an apt and uncontrived word can restore heart and hope. Sadly, we don't always speak this way.

A respectful and strong word of challenge for a group undermining themselves with deceit and platitudes is a powerful thing. Such a thing should never be done lightly, nor without a relationship that can bear the risk. But when it's time to speak, a constructive and uncompromised word can rekindle integrity and heart. Again, sadly, we don't always speak this way.

At our best, we do. But it's hard. There's a fine line between comfort and platitude. What sounds like a concerned challenge might in truth be disingenuous moralising. A strong word might only be abuse thinly disguised. A reassuring homily about how 'we're all doing our best and somehow we'll get through this together' might be a load of patronising codswallop.

Sometimes a gentle word is toxic, and a hard word full of grace. One word tears down; another builds up. We know the difference. We can discern a true word.

I love this old word promise. Maybe it's because my wife Sue used the word when she helped me name a gift I had seen many times in the leaders I admired most. Promise gathers together integrity and hope. I imagine you've seen it too. In a tough situation, it is so important to hear from someone we trust. And when those words, uncontrived and unaffected, renew our hearts and hopes, well, that is something else again. That is the Art of Promise.

A useful distinction: A promise speaks truth with hope. A platitude is a banal wish.

More than comfort

Promise has two related meanings. First, to speak in a way that others can take us at our word. It's like a declaration or vow. That is the common meaning. But there is an older second meaning: to speak in a way that holds out hope. We speak of an athlete who shows great promise, and clouds that hold promise of rain. Promise in this sense is an expectation of something good. It is a world away from platitudes.[1]

A **platitude** offers wishfulness and trite advice.

A **promise** enables hope and strength of character.

The difference is in many ways about our willingness to face present reality and future possibility. A platitude avoids and reduces the truth. It employs empty wishes to wave away impending challenges. A promise faces and embodies the truth. It holds out measured hope to meet impending challenges.

The strength of facing reality

The first responsibility of a leader is to define reality, and the last is to say thank you.[2]

MAX DE PREE

Platitudes are appealing, especially when we've heard something awkward, confusing, or confronting. A friend says he has made a mess of a relationship. We hush his admission with a platitude about it 'takes two to tango'. With one banal comment we make ourselves feel better, and avoid the terror of entering silence and confusion with our friend.

Business is bedevilled by platitudes. An executive thoughtfully challenges the assumptions behind a strategy. Colleagues dismiss her questioning with platitudes about 'world's best practice'. With one smug but empty comment we reassure ourselves that we are clever, and mask our reluctance for real, strategic conversation.

Platitudes placate, avoid, patronise, and dumb down. They sound profound or original but are banal and trite. They feed self-deceit and cowardice. Promises engage, commit, dignify, and make accountability concrete. They feed truth and courage.

We've all seen strong words side-stepped and weak words pass unchallenged. These are huge opportunities lost. Although finding clarity is a cognitive task, meetings rarely meander for lack of intellect.

We fail to create clarity to the degree we fail to challenge weak and self-defeating behaviours, words, and interpretations. This will not stop until someone speaks truly and strongly.

A caveat: I'm not suggesting constant vigilance of every word we and others speak. I couldn't live like that. Just a mindfulness and commitment to speak.

Words that kill strategic capacity

Executives behaving badly

A long time ago I was asked to facilitate a strategy review for the executive of the Australasian region of a huge and iconic global corporation. To say I was overawed comes nowhere near it. But over the next two days, I witnessed some of the worst executive behaviour I've ever seen.

On day one, I discovered that 'facilitator' meant an MC who wrote things down. There was no conversation to facilitate. Men, all men, sat behind paper piles watching a parade of overhead projector slides. I don't think anyone could name the strategy. But the biggest learning was still to come.

At the end of the day they retired for drinks. The alcohol flowed freely. Keen to shed formality, the CEO egged the team to say what they thought of him and where they were headed. As drunkenness took hold, they did. By the end of dinner, the 'conversation' was defamatory, obscene, brutal, and foolish. They knew they had gone too far but were long past restraint.

Next morning, shame and fear drove the one question in everyone's minds: 'What the %$#& did I say last night?!!' The CEO began awkwardly with an old platitude: 'It's good to get things off the chest'. Actually, it wasn't good. The whole debacle was dishonest and immature. There was no big picture. And no-one showed the courage to face what had happened. This is what stops learning.

What stops learning?

First, dishonesty. Many had misgivings about the abstract view of the world on the slides. But no-one spoke up. It's cowardly to need alcohol to tell the truth. The whole day meandered for lack of honesty.

Second, no big picture. The executives knew their separate roles, but had no grasp of their true level of work as a team. They remained isolated by factional interests.

Third, lack of rigour. No-one questioned the analysis. The planning was a guessing game. No-one framed an argument for the whole enterprise. There was little insight into the complexity of their environment.

Fourth, immaturity. The drunken tell-all did not clear the air. It was a schoolboy brawl. And me? I knew enough not to join the revelry, but not enough to help them grow. Not then.

Clarity comes when we challenge weak and self-defeating behaviours, words, and interpretations. A leader must speak truly and strongly.

'WAIT! THAT'S NOT REALITY. LET'S UNPACK THESE ASSUMPTIONS'.

How words can limit life

Words that limit a life

An ox is bound with ropes and a person with words.[3]

ITALIAN PROVERB

Think of a person you could fairly say has sadly limited their life. Perhaps a sibling, parent, teacher, friend, or colleague. What phrases do you hear them say that epitomise their self-limitation? Perhaps these:

It's not fair. I wish. If only … There's not enough time. I can't wait for the weekend. It can't be done. It doesn't matter. Who cares? Poor me. I can't afford it. It's alright for you. I'm scared. How would you know? You don't know what it's like. It sucks!

What do such words create in people? It limits them; it boxes them in. It becomes their reality. It builds a wall around them. Every phrase puts 'another brick in the wall'.

Words that limit groups

Who sits on the floor is not afraid of a fall.[4]

CZECH PROVERB

What do you hear in your communities and workplaces? In the media? What words reveal the prevailing powerless interpretations of our times?

They'll never let us. The unions will never let us do that. Management will never let us. Politicians are useless. It's too hard. We can't do anything without money. It's not our problem. It's those refugees. It's those liberals. It's those conservatives. Let's go back to the good old days. Someone else will do it. We need a leader.

Words show how we view life

The beginning of wisdom is to call things by their right names.[5]

CHINESE PROVERB

Beneath those words lie interpretations of life: 'Life is about me. Life is unfair. Life is done to me. Life is about getting what you can. Life sucks unless you get a lucky break. Life owes me'. This language sucks hope out of people, and justifies passivity and irresponsibility.

But this can change. Not easily, I grant, but it can change. And this is key work for leaders. When we begin to name things as neither more nor less than they are, but truly and strongly, weak interpretations begin to lose their power.

We have all heard, 'There's no leadership'. Sometimes it's true. But sometimes it's just an excuse for passivity; a code for 'We can't do anything till we get a (better) leader (we like)'. We must speak into this. Not by judging, but by reminding people of their strength.

A teacher once told me, 'I'd rather have the resources, but I could teach brilliantly in a tin shed'. Her interpretation of herself was true. Her words and her work matched. Nothing changes till someone speaks truly and strongly.

Calling false and weak behaviour

Descending into weakness

Executive groups lift their performance significantly when they learn to speak boldly, truthfully, and respectfully to one another. Sometimes this means first speaking into their own self-defeating behaviours.

I was facilitating a strategy retreat for a vice president and his team. The previous day had ended with some rich insights for their division. The VP had agreed to modify the presentation slides overnight for his CEO but had run out of time and said he would do so at the morning coffee break.

Early into the morning session the team began a spirited conversation about leadership. At about the same time, the VP, who was sitting just to the side of me, had half turned away from the group, opened his laptop and begun working on the slides, occasionally turning back as if he were part of the conversation.

The further the conversation went, the more intensely it focused on the group's desire for strong leadership, and the more the VP shifted away to work on his slides. Every eye in the group flicked between the VP and me. I let the tension build, giving room for the VP to get the point. He didn't.

Aside: It is a hard call to know when to let a group run in chaos and when to pull it in. I try to let the relationship guide me.

Speaking into darkness

After a few more minutes it was time to call the VP on his behaviour.

'The team is grappling with the need for authentic leadership. This is probably a conversation you want to be part of. Would you like to join us?' The air froze.

The VP closed his laptop, turned, apologised, and joined the group. The response was as I expected: smug looks on many in the group. This was the moment of learning. My issue was no longer with the VP but with the group. It was time to call their behaviour.

'This is what it takes to lead well', I said slowly. 'I addressed him respectfully over not being present with us. To his credit, he apologised and changed his behaviour. He's not the problem now. You are. Why did you wait for me to say something? You resented his behaviour; why didn't you call it? In truth, you were afraid. But you're better than that. So choose.

'You've seen what it means to speak into another's life. Now I'm speaking into yours. You will not move forward unless you speak the truth boldly and respectfully from now on. If you will, you have no idea of what you will become capable.'

Calling behaviour, even with a strong outcome like this, cannot guarantee a deep and lasting shift. But the shifts won't come without such moments.

Promise strengthens interpretation

Words draw from deep beliefs

All speech in some way reveals the ways we read life and the commitments we hold. If we listen attentively, words become like portals into the layers of meaning we are continually crafting.

At the surface we may sense the anxieties and hopes of the speaker. A little deeper, we glimpse a level of assumptions, as though we heard them say, 'I am anxious or hopeful because I believe this can or can't happen'. Deeper still is the larger world of our basic interpretations: 'Life is...' exciting, unfair, out of control, a sandpit for design, or whatever.

Words draw up from a long way down.

Words may strengthen or weaken

In *Chapter 3: Naming* I told the story of Fernando Flores who was gaoled and tortured by Pinochet's regime. Flores now works with leaders where he draws on this experience and his philosophical reflections on how his words shaped his experience.[6]

Flores argues that '(m)ost people speak without intention; they simply say whatever comes to mind'. We don't appreciate how deeply entrenched we may become in patterns of self-defeating interpretations. Thus when many leaders do come to 'talk about changing their thinking ... they have no idea what that is, let alone how to do it'.[7]

Every strand of our knowledge is part of a rich yet subtly changing tapestry of understanding. We always know in and for a context, and in and for relationships. As David Tracy puts it, '(w)hether we know it or not, to be human is to be a skilled interpreter'.[8]

Flores nails the street value of Tracy's insight: 'We don't realize how much we create reality through language. If we say life is hard, it will be hard. If, on the other hand, we make commitments to our colleagues to improve our productivity, we also improve our mood, and as a result, clarity and happiness will increase'.[9] You can hear Flores' urgency:

We aren't aware of the amount of self-deception that we collect in our personalities ... The key is to stop producing interpretations which have no power ... Speak with intention and your actions take on new purpose. Speak with power and you act with power.[10]

FERNANDO FLORES

What a powerful statement of the work of leaders: to challenge self-deception and neutralise powerless interpretations. And to model richer, truer ways of speaking with intent.

WHAT DO YOU SEE?

We can map stories of management teams on the Reader-Author distinction.[11] Your stories are different. What do you see?

Inwardly-focused readers

Small termites collapse the roof.[12]
ETHIOPIAN PROVERB

Group think and group speak. The managers share an unease about where things are going. Outwardly, they affirm the directions.
☐ NEVER SEE ☐ TOO MUCH

Unwillingness to confront. A manager assures all is well with a project. It isn't, and everyone knows. He is thanked for his report.
☐ NEVER SEE ☐ TOO MUCH

Lack of presence and courtesy. In a meeting: Managers do other work. Text. Take calls. Talk to neighbours. Keep heads down.
☐ NEVER SEE ☐ TOO MUCH

Email wars. CC is used to brag, or to ridicule ('look who knows now!'). BCC is used to go behind backs.
☐ NEVER SEE ☐ TOO MUCH

No-one is content. It's a small way to think and work, but we feel powerless to change it. What drives this? Fear drives dishonesty. Dishonesty reinforces immaturity. Everything is dumbed down.

I mean no blame. Nor would I pretend to be immune. And I know speaking up is hard.

Outwardly-focused authors

As iron sharpens iron, so one person sharpens another.[13]
SOLOMON

A sandpit to play. Time is made for design thinking. A grounded question starts it. Imagination is valued and nurtured.
☐ SEE OFTEN ☐ TOO RARELY

Confidence to think differently. Members commit to keeping focus. Thus they can trust a colleague arguing an unusual idea.
☐ SEE OFTEN ☐ TOO RARELY

Conversations build up. Leaders model purposeful speech. Members speak for themselves. Asking 'on behalf of' enriches discussion.
☐ SEE OFTEN ☐ TOO RARELY

Agreement to call weak language and behaviour. Leaders model truthful, self-reflective speech. Offenses are addressed.
☐ SEE OFTEN ☐ TOO RARELY

Everyone is energised, or challenged. It is an expansive and empowered way to think and work. What drives this? Respect drives honesty. Honesty deepens maturity. How do you begin the shift? I'd pick two hinges: a grounded question for an agenda, and time building a relationship.

CLARITY AND RESPECT IN
STRAIGHT TALK

Good managers may find themselves at cross purposes. No-one
wants it that way. But few know where or how to start anew.

Finding common ground

An infrastructure Group acquired a
very different kind of company. After
several years it was still unprofitable.
There was high turnover among the
managers and a Group change team
had been installed. Safety was chosen
as a lever to drive change and the
audit rated the safety performance of
the company the worst in the Group.
The company managers resented
and resisted this assessment.
Relationships were strained.

I was asked to help. After holding
one-on-one interviews with each
executive and sitting in on their team
meetings, I took the group off-site for
three days. Whenever I do this, my
aim is simple:

First, I want the team to feel the
weight of their lack of coherence and
clarity about strategy and leadership.
Second, I want them to achieve even
a small breakthrough by facing truth
together well. Third, I want them to
understand how this happened and to
commit to working together this way.

We began with some input on
leadership and working together.
Time for personal reflection, walks
with colleagues, and open discussion

afforded opportunities to recall
stories of the best of the company
and themselves. When there seemed
sufficient awareness of the weight of
what they faced, and enough (though
still little) openness to looking at
themselves as part of the problem, it
was time to venture to a harder place.

THIS SET THE AFTERNOON'S WORK
— TO SIT WITH THE CONFUSION
UNTIL THERE WAS OWNERSHIP
AND AN OPENNESS TO WORKING
TOGETHER.

Stunned by lack of clarity

In preparation for the retreat I had
created a map of their current strategic
thinking. My primary source for this was
what I had heard in the interviews and
team meetings, not the various company
and Group strategy documents. I used
Tony Golsby-Smith's AcdB® model.[14]
What I showed them drew a stunned
response. In truth, far more than I had
anticipated.

Their reading of the current situation (the
'A') was clichéd, defeated, and unsubtle.
They had no 'B' — no articulated future
state. Understandably, therefore, there
was no hypothesis for change (no 'C').
And, predictably, they had a long list
of action items (the 'D') that lacked

coherence or argument. At first they thought I was joking — that I would produce the 'B' and 'C' out of a hat.

I reminded them that this is what I heard from them individually and collectively — not what I thought they could do. My summary highlighted not only a lack of strategic clarity, but a willingness to do things they had little conviction would make any difference.

This set the afternoon's work — to sit with the confusion until there was ownership and an openness to working together.

On the brink

The mood at dinner was positive. They were keen to congratulate themselves on a new found sense of working together. But to me, the masks were still firmly in place. They had not yet tested this new rapport. I didn't have to wait long.

The key operational manager and Group safety officer were seated opposite each other and the conversation turned to safety. Late in the evening their banter grew more pointed and awkward. The rest of the group shifted their attention to the pair, making remarks in equal measure helpful and incendiary.

The further it went, the more the pair dug in to their respective positions. And the more the rest of the group turned to enjoying the spectacle. Occasionally there were awkward glances toward me as if I should rescue the situation. I had no inclination to do any such thing.

Finally the manager asked, 'If we're so bad at safety, how come your

own auditors could not believe our faultless electrical safety record in an environment with far greater risk than anything in the Group? As he told their stories, the manager's mood shifted from frustration to pride. And the executive moved to face him. The possibility of new understanding and respect was palpable.

Creating new meaning

Next morning the group believed they had turned a corner. Their mood and words had changed. They had weathered breakdown. But had there been any real shift in interpretations and commitments? I was encouraged and told them so. But they needed to test their understanding. And the way into that, as always, was through story.

To help them, I offered some reflections. Until the manager told his story, he and the executive had sat askance and barely made eye contact. The group were basically side-line critics. But when the manager began to tell his story, the pair faced each other and gave eye contact. The mood of the group became constructive. 'So', I said, 'what was happening for you?' Again, they reflected, walked, and talked together.

The next day and a half were more candid and effective. The new respect and meaning they had forged that morning opened the way for some original thinking and strong united calls. They had lacked respect because they didn't know each other's stories. They lacked clarity because they spoke around and behind each other. They lacked hope because they had no idea what they could do together. Now they did.

ENABLING ROBUST MEETINGS

First, think 'conversation' not meeting. Second, find a grounded question. Third, speak with integrity and hope.

Relationally robust ...

A human being is hasty by nature.[15]
QURAN

Impatience and passivity is an odd mixture but common enough in organisational meetings. I think both may come from the same place: fear.

To choose to be present, commit to each other ahead, and be willing to call behaviour — starting with our own — is to begin to push back fear. Of what? Of losing face and thus of shame.

John Ralston Saul names another fear: '(T)here is indeed a fear of words, particularly words as a force of imagination, and thus as a method of change, rather than as slogans ... '[16]

When we lose our fear to speak truly and strongly — without platitude or formula — remarkable things can happen.

Intellectually robust ...

The way we come at every question is structural, managerial.[17]
JOHN RALSTON SAUL

We have shrunk reason: maybe not always, but often. Saul's argument is that we have privileged a narrowed view of rationality over a wider array of human qualities. And that this is particularly evident in organisations and politics.

Intellectual rigour does not come by ramping up this narrow rationality. If knowing is bigger than thinking — and if we know in and for relationships — then being relationally robust is the prerequisite to being intellectually robust.

Where does thinking robustly start? Humility creates openness. We become ready to learn, to entertain the unusual, analogous, and metaphorical. We chase the question, hear stories, and challenge assumptions. We meet in truth and hope.

'FIRST, THIS IS A CONVERSATION — NOT A MEETING'.

'SECOND, WE NEED A GROUNDED QUESTION'.

Q. # Why change the ways executives talk?

A. I have a hunch. I can't prove it and don't know of any research. Maybe it's a PhD for someone. Negatively: I suspect engagement programs are often sponsored by executive teams whose own interactions model powerless speech and interpretations. I suspect they project their own lack of engagement onto the business. Positively: I can't think of an executive team, functioning powerfully through truthful speech and relationships, that has needed to run an engagement program. I could make similar cases for how well the respective teams and businesses do strategy and innovation. If I'm at all right, I think it warrants some emphasis.

A MODEL FOR SPEAKING
LIFE INTO STRATEGY

Genuine strategic conversations are hard work and rare.
But they can soar. How?

AcdB® once more

Earlier I introduced the AcdB® model developed by Tony Golsby-Smith.[18] The model also helps explain the street value of Promise.

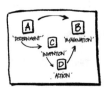

AcdB® Model,
Tony Golsby-Smith

Our words and the ways we speak will determine whether a strategic conversation flounders or flourishes. Will our words be inward-looking and self-defeating? Or will our words look beyond us and create possibility?

'A': From banalities to insights

What can happen: The 'A' is the Present and calls for Discernment. But the conversation can be defensive or just shallow. Groups report back with near identical lists of abstract descriptions of favourite problems. Every item is explained. At the end we know only what we already knew.

In ABCD language, half an 'A' is likely to produce 'Ds' that anyone could have written down at the start of the day. This is neither a conversation, nor strategic.

How to shift this: Most insights come through hard conversations and reflections in which we see ourselves anew. This means naming the anomalies, contradictions, paradoxes, and tensions. Like these: 'We slashed costs by cutting staff, but lost our knowledge base'. 'We talk integration of safety and reliability, but make trade-offs'. Frame a handful of such starkly worded tensions. The greater the 'ouch', the greater the potential for an insight.

THE CONVERSATION QUICKLY REVEALS LEVELS OF PRESENCE AND RESPECT. ALSO COMFORT WITH AMBIGUITY AND COMPLEXITY. I USE WALK-AND-TALKS IN GROUPS OF TWOS AND THREES THROUGHOUT THE WHOLE PROCESS.

'B': From platitudes to promises

What can happen: The 'B' is the Future and calls for Imagination. Conversation easily becomes waffly, loses energy, and retreats to platitudes. Groups report back with slogans about being 'world's best', 'excellent', and the like. The future may sound like little more than the absence of today's problems.

Until there is a story, there is no vision. Until there is an argument for that story, there is no strategy.

How to shift this: If your 'A' has little 'ouch' or urgency, you're unlikely to craft a strong 'B'. If necessary loop back to 'A' and ask: What have we avoided talking about, and why? Here are two questions I sometimes suggest for a walk and talk. One: 'What story do you want to create?' If that's a bridge too far, start with: 'How do you want to look back on this time?' Two: 'What would you tell your children about the future you want?'

IT TAKES RESPECT TO FACE AMBIGUITY AND COMPLEXITY TOGETHER WITH COURAGE AND IMAGINE A FUTURE STORY. THE STRONGER THAT STORY, THE GREATER THE POTENTIAL FOR A BREAKTHROUGH INSIGHT.

'C': From imitation to invention

What can happen: The 'C' is the Hypothesis for Change and calls for Invention. Conversation at 'A' is hard because self-interest works against candour. At 'B', a problem-solution mindset works against imagination. At 'C', our education works against thinking well. We were taught to give back the answers we had been given. But the task now is like telling the teacher you're going to find a better question. Participants often want to bypass 'C' and rush to 'D'.

How to shift this: Crafting a strong 'B' and 'C' requires vulnerability. The fear is that I/we lack imagination and ideas. So I set either of two questions for a walk and talk. First, 'When have you faced an intractable problem, or unreachable opportunity, and now feel proud about what you achieved? Second, 'What one big thing feels like

it's still missing that you would back as a catalyst to deep change?'

If you hold a strong hypothesis, don't pretend you don't. Nonetheless hold open genuine space for your team to dialogue. The mode is challenging: You're asking people to swap thinking like a committee for thinking like designers.

'D': From check lists to design

What can happen: 'D' is What Next and calls for Action. Conversation easily loses depth here and resorts to quick fixes. Groups report back with lists of actions that ignore the deep tensions in 'A', the desired story in 'B', or the choice to create something new in 'C'. Someone may wait till now to drop their 'sure-fire' solution, revealing they were never present. People may retreat to silos. And if there are still naysayers, they will speak now.

How to shift this: You can't wait until now to address disengagement, nor leave it to the facilitator. The walks offer an opportunity. If your partner is present and open, engage the set task. If he or she isn't, stay with them. Don't judge. I take the high ground of ignorance: 'Peter, it's probably just me. I know you care about XYZ, and put significant thought into OPQ. I feel like you're not here. I don't want to judge. If something's going on for you, I'm happy to listen'. It's an invitation for a story. Very often I come away with new respect and they begin to engage. No guarantees.

Ask yourself: What will you gain if your team is engaged? What will it cost you if they're not?

REFLECTIONS ON THE IDEA OF
TRANSFORMATION

Change. Progress. Transformation. The words are everywhere.
Where did they come from and what do we mean by them?

Transformation needs promise
Business leaders talk a lot about things not staying the way they are. Mostly, the talk is positive and it ranges across a spectrum of impact: Change. Improvement. Shift. Progress. Revitalisation. Renewal. Turnaround. Revolution. Transformation. We probably hear at least a few of these words in every meeting and presentation.

TRANSFORMATION HAPPENS LESS OFTEN THAN WE CLAIM.

I'm going to use three words to express this continuum: Change. Progress. Transformation. Change and transformation are used quite commonly in organisations. Progress perhaps less so. Improvement is the more common word. I'm using Change > Progress > Transformation so I can ground our challenges in a bigger story: the history of people asking how to make the world better. Throughout Western history at least, progress and (less so) transformation have been the key words.

So how does this relate to the Art of Promise? As our contexts become more ambiguous, so people become less certain. When we map the

relationship between ambiguity and uncertainty, we start to see the necessity of hope. The greater the ambiguity and uncertainty, the more people need a true and strong hope. And thus the need to speak with promise.

The harder it is to be confident, the more people need hope. So we need to speak with promise.

I'm viewing change and progress, transformation and hope in terms of how we live and work together:

1. Change is common and frequent. It's good that not everything changes. Some changes just have to happen. But not all change means progress.

2. Progress is subjective and less common. Usually we mean extensive changes that enable us to improve life. But not all progress involves transformation.

3. Transformation probably happens less often than we claim. Usually we mean deep changes in our identity, purpose, mood, and reputation for the better.
4. Hope is our inner engine of intentional change. It touches belief, expectation, anticipation, and will — the things that help us take one more step. And as our actions move from change to progress to transformation, the more we draw on hope.

Transformation in history

With obscene haste and generalisation I pass over 2500 years of Western thought. At first glance, Greece and Rome seemed to lack an idea of progress.[19] Since Hesiod (8th BC), ideas of a past Golden Age made history a regress or endless cycle.[20] Yet Xenophanes (6th BC) and Lucretius (1st BC) saw humans shaping history.[21] Moralists like Plutarch (1st AD) preached individual progress within conformity to nature and convention. And the oddball stories of Ovid (1st BC) and Apuleius' (2nd AD) Metamorphoses aren't what we call transformation.

At the height of Roman power, Paul of Tarsus (1stC) raised the dangerous idea that someone might 'no longer conform to the schemas of the age' — rank, empire, religion, economy — 'but be transformed by the renewing of their mind'.[22] When the Visigoths sacked Rome in 401, the dream of Rome transforming the world lay in ruins. In response, Augustine (5thC) brilliantly synthesised the two traditions in a world history that assumed a unified humanity. His phrase, 'the education of the human race',[23] would reappear in the Enlightenment.

This hybrid of Plato, Aristotle, Paul and Augustine, via Arabia, enabled the great achievements of medieval and renaissance periods. Classical society censured change and Paul's innovations went underground. Later, Joachim of Fiore (12thC) imagined an end to hierarchy, but powerful patrons sustained the humanism of the renaissance and Reformation (13th–16thC). The French Revolutions (18thC) moved tyranny from monarch to mob to emperor and back, crying 'Liberté, Egalité, Fraternité'. Emancipation was slow; suffrage slower. Echoing these contradictions we hear the towering voices of Voltaire, Condorcet, and Jefferson in the American Declaration of Independence (1776), the French Declaration of the Rights of Man and of the Citizen (1789), and the American Bill of Rights (1791).

Transforming in contradictions

Industrialisation, emancipation, suffrage, wars, Cold War, sexual revolution, consumerism, environmentalism, and terrorism have dramatically transformed us. Progress has ended tyranny, and justified it. We have medicines and weapons previously unimaginable.

We have been transformed, and left confused. We are heirs of brilliant contradictions. We fear change yet we idolise it and try to accelerate it. No leader can make transformation happen. It's a by-product, not a goal. It follows the renewal of hearts and minds. When enough people name reality differently — truly, strongly, and with hope — then transformation may follow. Of course we may never see such change. That we can promise.

Ripple of hope

Challenging with hope

In June 1966, almost three years after his brother President John F Kennedy was assassinated, Senator Robert F Kennedy visited South Africa for five days. [24] He was the first white international politician to visit during official Apartheid.

Kennedy was smeared with making the trip for political gain.[25] Certainly he would have calculated the benefits and risks.[26] But his speeches and writing confirm his courage and nobility. Exactly two years later he too was assassinated.

Across five short addresses the sense of common occasion rings clear: he mentioned change or progress fifty-three times. The focus of this change was equally clear: he mentioned freedom or liberty thirty-nine times; justice seventeen times; hope thirteen times; and equality and dignity. Likewise the means of change: he commended courage twelve times; and appealed for dialogue that could restore heart and minimise violence. His most famous lines are these:

Each time a man stands up for an ideal, or acts to improve the lot of others, or strikes out against injustice, he sends forth a tiny ripple of hope, and crossing each other from a million different centers of energy and daring those ripples build a current which can sweep down the mightiest walls of oppression and resistance.[27]

ROBERT F KENNEDY

Framing hope

Kennedy did not presume to know or judge. He drew strong analogies between the countries: the hopes of European forebears; the abuse of first peoples and slaves; the bonds of allies in three wars. Talk of war prompted one of his most pointed statements. Many viewed Africans as savages unfit for self-governance. But, Kennedy proclaimed 'it was not black men' who committed the great atrocities of the twentieth century. Closing his last address, Kennedy came to leadership:

(It is) easier to follow blindly than to lead with … the impregnable skepticism of the free spirit, untouchable by guns or police, which feeds the whirlwind of change and hope and progress in every land and time.[28]

ROBERT F KENNEDY

The documentary, *RFK in the Land of Apartheid*, frames RFK's visit in post-Apartheid South Africa. In 1966 Kennedy met the extraordinary leader, Chief Albert Luthuli. In 2009, his daughter Congresswoman Dr. Albertina Luthuli played at a joyous thought: 'I'm sure if my father and Robert Kennedy were together now in the new South Africa — I can't even express … !

That joy shone in the young black men who today bear Kennedy's name. One man said: 'He gave me this name maybe because he wanted me to live like a king'. Perhaps he did.

Q. # How do you relate hope to leading?

A. I have long admired Vaclav Havel, the Czech writer, poet, dissident, and politician. Havel called hope 'an orientation of the heart'. He believed it's only when we realise that everything we do will pass away, that we can discern which of our actions may be truly significant. 'Only this awareness ... can breathe any greatness into an action'. So hope is 'not the conviction that something will turn out well, but the certainty that something makes sense, regardless of how it turns out'.[29] The proof of hope is significance and meaning, not success. Such, I think, is the 'orientation of the heart' of one who would lead wisely.

Disheartened people may rebuff all offers of kindness and dignity. But nothing is more likely to help them find new heart.

CHAPTER 10

Grace

Grace is the 'yes' of life

Grace welcomes us home

My aim in *Lead with Wisdom* has been to make a case that leadership needs wisdom, and that wisdom enriches leadership. This is not the 'new thing' on leadership. Wisdom is an old theme. What I'm arguing can't be proved and I'm not trying to prove it. I can only point to the things we hold dear about life and each other, and ask what ways of being and leading sit well alongside them and help us all to flourish.

There's lots of ways to lead and not all are wise. And of all the ways that one could lead wisely, not all will succeed. In fact, that's the bitter pill of bringing wisdom into the conversation. Most of the time when we talk about leadership we want to know how to succeed. But wisdom can't guarantee success. Wisdom isn't even about success — unless, of course, we redefine what success is.

For me, grace is the 'yes' I hear in life and that I choose to give back. All the Patterns and the Arts affirm deep beliefs about people and life. I think it's those underlying beliefs that create the rich synergies between naming, character, brilliance, story, and conversation, and the rest. Somehow grace both leads me to the other Patterns and Arts, and is where I always return. Maybe grace is part of character. I'm okay with that. It's never been that important to me to categorise things. But somehow grace seems prior.

What then is grace? I think we can speak of grace as the deep disposition to believe in human dignity and to treat everyone accordingly without thought to status or merit. I think life calls us to live fully and deeply out of thankfulness and wonder as those who have been welcomed home.

Grace is a radical idea

Grace challenges us deeply

The traditional definition of grace is 'unmerited favour'. Two things may immediately come to mind. First, grace is only a religious idea. 'Unmerited favour' is of course the standard theological definition of grace. Second, talk of 'unmerited favour' or unmerited kindness can sound patronising or worse. Who am I, or you, or anybody to speak of anyone else as not meriting our favour?! Wait; not just patronising, it sounds arrogant. But...

Grace turns out to be an extraordinarily beautiful, affirming, and strong idea. Not only is grace the antithesis of an arrogant and patronising spirit, it subverts both. Grace is perhaps *the* radical idea for understanding ourselves individually as in community.

Any wise account of what it is to be human, both theoretically and empirically, must give equal weight to our dignity and brokenness. More than give an account of each, I think it needs to integrate dignity and brokenness. No idea does this like grace. But it's the way it integrates them. Grace celebrates our true dignity. But grace also exposes and subverts everything to which we might cling that is unworthy of that dignity.

This is more than theoretical. Grace provokes me relationally, existentially, and very practically. I am challenged to face my dignity and my brokenness on behalf of seeing others flourish.

Grace meets us as we are

Grace. It's such an old-fashioned word. The particular thing about grace is that it's about extending kindness and generosity without any regard to rank or position, either theirs or our own. There may be all kinds of reasons why we are disposed to look up to one person, and down on another, but grace ignores it all. We are people of dignity no matter our rank in the world. Grace meets us here. But there's another dimension.

Grace accepts this dignity and extends kindness and compassion especially when it can rightly be said that they, or we, have no merit or claim upon this kindness. Such as when we have been wronged, or we have wronged someone else. Grace faces the world with eyes wide open yet refuses to judge.

Grace fosters heart and community. It chooses for the flourishing of all.

Grace is like welcoming the stranger to our family, or the estranged child as though he'd never left. Rembrandt captured it exquisitely in his *The Return of the Prodigal Son* (1669). 'This whole work is dominated by the idea of the victory of love, goodness and charity. The event is treated as the highest act of human wisdom and spiritual nobility, and it takes place in absolute silence and stillness'.[1] Looking beyond the main characters, the eyes of the bystanders are revealing. Grace welcomes all, but not all welcome grace.

A useful distinction: Grace subverts status

Status makes life binary

In *Chapter 6: Character,* I told A Tale of Two Trees. There I drew attention to a deep binary disposition in the ways we know and engage with life: good/evil, left/right, in/out, acceptable/unacceptable, and so on. The story turns on the 'knowledge of good and evil'. I used the symbol <G:E> to characterise this binary mode. And I used <LIFE> to characterise where we choose ways that lead to flourishing.

Performance is the modern word that comes to mind for <G:E>. I'm not talking about the appropriate sense of fulfilling responsibility. I'm talking about that mode of being caught up in measuring and judging ourselves and one another. That disposition sets us up for needing to be on top. And to gather to ourselves the things that make us feel we have performed and succeeded. That's status.

Most of this is likely to be tacit. Images of perfection go hand-in-hand with performance. All this comes out somewhere. One is fantasising about prestige, that magical place when we have all the status we want. It's a short step from there to power. You're only useful to me if you help me gain more status. In the end, status makes life binary—you have it, or you don't.

Status fosters envy and strife. It chooses the self-interest of the few. Grace fosters community. It chooses the flourishing of the many.

Grace makes life whole

Self-interest fuels status. It turns healthy competition into the desire to beat the other down, and strife when we don't. Status feeds on power too. The desire to control the other turns to anger when we can't. Self-interest doesn't like vulnerability. We judge, we try to fix others, and we feel shame whether it works or not. The toxic mix of self-interest and status desires to diminish the other, and leaves us with envy when we can't.

Status comes at the expense of others and fosters envy, strife, and alienation. Leaders are as susceptible as anyone. People look to us. We have authority that carries power. We have expectations and standards. We want the world to know what we've done. None of this is 'wrong'. It just needs grace if it's going to help anyone flourish.

This is the disposition of leaders who foster heart and community. We see one another with equal shared dignity. Every step toward brilliance is a step toward being whole. Grace makes life whole.

'SORRY, I COULDN'T SEE YOU BEHIND ALL THAT WEALTH AND STATUS'.

A further distinction: Rank is responsibility. Status is self-interest.

Rank is not status

There is a great misperception about grace: that it's soft. I don't think grace stands opposed to authority, power, or expectation. I think it reframes them. Authority can be reframed in terms of trust. Power in terms of agency. Expectation in terms of creating space for brilliance. Nor does grace undercut rank, only the way some hold it. The problem there is status not rank.

In classical society rank was a social (and usually legal) position which carried responsibilities and obligations to others, especially to those of other ranks.[2] Status, on the other hand, was the prestige of a rank without its obligations. Ambition was generally applauded and *philotimia*, the love of ambition, was prized as a virtue.[3] And where this ambition flourished, status tended to convert itself into rank.[4] Rank becomes fossilised status!

Travelling in Turkey, Greece, or Italy today, you can't miss old stone honorific inscriptions. There's even graffiti. These map the evolution of the social order across hundreds of years.

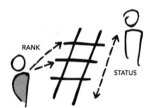

Rank is fossilised status. It's snakes and ladders!

Grace subverts status, not rank

Far from dismissing rank, grace enables us to hold it well by being clear-minded that it is responsibility before privilege. But grace is savage against status. Think of how status distorted rank in some of the spectacular corporate collapses of the 1990s and 2000s.

Grace subverts status by turning the social ladder on its side and lifting up all.

Grace respects rank but subverts status.

Grace teaches us to see rank as an entrusted responsibility that carries a claim to respect of which we must show ourselves worthy. It enables us to hold rank with dignity when discharging its responsibilities. And it teaches us to stand shoulder-to-shoulder as equals with everyone as regards their humanity.

Every position of leadership is a context in which we can show the power of grace to renew heart and build community. Where there are self-defeating behaviours, they are sustained by cynicism, gossip, blame, and guilt. Grace enables us to walk a human line: to stand with people, but apart from these behaviours, without superiority or rudeness. It is here that a leader begins to restore heart and build community.

Grace reframes strength

Grace is strength that is fair

Nothing undermines heart like injustice, real or perceived. And nothing restores heart like grace. Sometimes it only takes the simplest act to address a wrong and renew hearts.

I heard a great example of this in a talk by a former army officer who had taken command of a squadron in the lead-up to war. Although they were an elite group of soldiers, morale seemed low. He spoke about his options. He could get tough, or he could get friendly. But he had another approach.

Every structured community, he explained, has one or more conventions which serve no purpose other than to make a few people feel superior and the rest inferior. He had learned to find that convention and do away with it.

Boots. The troops grumbled most about there being two kinds of boots — one for officers and one for the rest. His solution was brilliantly simple and fair. He announced that from that time any

soldier of any rank could have either type of boot. Each soldier and officer was to choose the style they prefered. You can probably guess what happened. Very few changed their boots. And morale began to turn around. It was a simple act of grace, subverting a nonsensical convention, and establishing him as a decisive and fair leader.

Grace is strength that is deep

As wisdom leads us to reframe success, so grace leads us to reframe strength. Leading with grace is a question of character. But that's not how we have popularly or even historically understood strength. For millennia strength has been associated with physical power, great courage, force of oratory, the honour of rank, and the ability to make one's will prevail. And there's a time for each.

Self-interest distorts strength to be strength *over* others. Grace transforms strength to be strength *for* others. Grace is strength to lift up others. Humility, care, integrity, compassion, and empathy were viewed in classical times as weaknesses. Grace makes them strengths.

Deep roots are not reached by the frost.[5]
JRR TOLKIEN

The more we lead from grace, the less we need to assert ourselves. The more we lead from grace, the less we try to control others.

From 'strength' that holds others down to 'strength' that lifts others up.

A TALE OF THE
HARMONY OF GRACE

The Swedish movie *As it is in Heaven*, beautifully portrays grace in many dimensions. At its heart is the fear of grace of those who cling to law.[6]

Grace versus law

Daniel Daréus (Michael Nyqvist) is a violin prodigy who became a renowned conductor. Following a career-ending heart attack he returns to the town of his troubled childhood in far northern Sweden and tries to assume anonymity. Succumbing to insistent invitations to hear the church choir, and the charms of Lena (Frida Hallgren), Daniel reluctantly agrees to lead them. The scene is set for an epic but wholly one-sided struggle with the dominating and interfering pastor Stig (Niklas Falk).

Daniel's odd methods begin to win the admiration and affection of many in the choir. They glimpse hope. But as grace becomes vivid, brokenness is unleashed. Every step toward their own hearts and brilliance becomes a step away from the convention, austerity, and moralism of the pastor. It is also a step into their own dysfunction. Interference becomes accusation, slander, and violence. The lack of performance from the choir, and the suspicion of immorality, drive Stig further into hypocrisy and isolation. The more Daniel sets aside the ego of a lifetime of professional renown, the more he finds freedom and grace.

The finale is set up by one act of courage, and three acts of shame. When the angelic voiced Gabriella (Helen Sjöholm) finds the courage to leave her abusive husband Connie (Per Morberg), the cowered choir and village finally draw the line to choose grace over moralism and violence. As Stig loses control over his wife Inger (Ingela Olsson), and the town, his impending breakdown is finally triggered in a plot to kill Daniel that he cannot fulfil. And in his rage at Gabriella and the town, Connie finds Daniel and beats him almost to death. It is then that both realise Connie is the bully from Daniel's childhood. And Arne (Lennart Jähkel) enters the choir in an Austrian singing competition for his own ambitions as much as the good of the choir.

[I wanted] to create music that will open a person's heart.
FROM *AS IT IS IN HEAVEN*

On the day of the competition, the choir is ready on stage but Daniel is nowhere to be seen. Rushing back to the concert he suffers another heart attack, and stumbling into a restroom, he collapses and hits his head savagely. Helplessly slumped on the floor, he hears from the loudspeaker above him the murmuring of the competitors and audience as they await the turn of his choir who of course are waiting for him.

All is chaotic on stage until the one of least 'merit', the one so often shunned before, the young autistic Tore (André Sjöberg) in his anxiety emits a single sustained sound. At first they seek to hush him. But Gabriella and then Lena glimpse the moment. It will not and cannot now be a performance. It can only be music. It can only be friendship. The whole choir gathers around this single note from Tore and bring the most joyous, free renditions of their hearts, which in turn captivates every other choir at the festival and the audience.

No-one speaks. There is no score. There is no melody. A community is formed among competitors and listeners alike as they indwell that one note augmenting it with harmony and possibility. Life stands still in this one note and all join. All become present. Performance is eclipsed. Expectation evaporates. Merit has no place. Rank means nothing. Status is banished. It is a poignant illustration that we cannot know what meaning will be created when we are drawn by the wonder of what might be if only we stay open.

Still listening on the floor of the restroom as his heart nears the end, Daniel smiles to himself and then dies, having reached his life's goal 'to create music that will open a person's heart'.[7] He has opened theirs; and they have opened his. In a final scene reminiscent of the Roman Elysian Fields, Daniel the man wades through the long grasses of fields by the town as Daniel the young boy runs into his arms.

The story is a rich reading of life. The title of course alludes to the Lord's prayer: 'Your kingdom come, your will be done, on earth as it is in heaven'.[8] Therein is the irony and beauty of the story. The pastor represents this kingdom on earth but does not know its grace. He preaches it, or rather distorts it, and clings to his life terrified of being known by his wife or anyone else. Daniel is devoid of religion and of dubious morality in the eyes of Stig and Siv. As his own merit is stripped away, so is his self-protection until he knows as he is known. There he comes to know grace through his most reluctant giving of grace to those whom he had judged without merit.

Two leaders. One is terrified to lose his leadership. One is reluctant to lead. One knows only <G:E>. One comes to know <LIFE>. One isolates himself as he fragments the lives of others. One realises his life's longing as he enables wholeness in the lives of others. Of such are our choices.

Sometimes a single note from the 'least' is all we need.

GRACE:
HOW TO USE THE ARTS

The Arts work together. Your stories are different from mine.
What do you see in the diagram below?

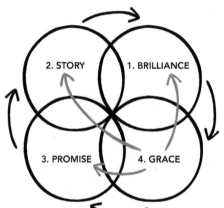

The diagram makes two simple points:
1. The Arts all work together
2. Grace has a certain priority

1. Brilliance is often the focus

Imagine a conversation with your team about brilliance. One approaches you later not sure where his brilliance lies but wanting to know and grow. He feels sufficient rapport and trust with you.

2. Story shows what's there

The clues are in his story. If you agree it seems appropriate, you might use the exercise 'Map Your Brilliance' from *Chapter 8: Brilliance* (see page 160). Think about whether you, or a colleague, or a friend should be the partner. Personally I'd want to start more informally. Grab a coffee and perhaps ask, 'I don't really know your job. What are the moments that make it good?'

3. Promise is ready to speak

Do you hear self-defeating language and interpretations? Only speak into his life as far as he welcomes. If he looks blocked, and recognises it, suggest what sound to you like self-defeating beliefs. This needs sensitivity.

4. Grace is why we do it

Grace sits behind all this. Why give this man your time? I believe people have dignity. I assume there's always brilliance. To hear his story, is to honour him. You don't have to agree with how he interprets his life. You're not there to judge, but to help him throw light on his own life. But why do any of this? Because he, like all of us, is worth it.

Q. # How can you have grace in tough situations?

A. Leo Tolstoy once said, 'It is a mistake to think that there are times when you can safely address a person without love'.[9] When I was CEO, I faced the wrench of closing eight campuses and reducing staff by half. The buck was clearly with me to make the call. But how do you do it? Apart from a few I couldn't reach, I gave the news face to face. I also had to address stakeholders with vision and hope. That put me under scrutiny. As leaders we must absorb misunderstanding and blame, and keep extending dignity and kindness even with the worst news. I didn't find that soft, or easy.

EXPLORING THE PRACTICAL INSIGHTS OF
GRACE IN BUSINESS

Grace is the bedrock of strong choices to act on and with dignity. But is grace practical?

I'm asked this question often. First, I can't think of anything more likely to restore heart to people. Second, I think grace is an unseen assumption in doing business well. Without grace: strategy may be lifeless; innovation may be stifled; and engagement may be a nonsense.

Strategy gains insight

Wisdom throws light on strategy. Negatively, wisdom helps us avoid false splits and unhelpful abstractions in the ways we read ourselves and our strategic and operating contexts. Positively, we can read vision as a future story and strategy as an argument for that story.

Strategy is traditionally owned by finance, planning, and analysis. The approach is somewhat generic: 'We are a — building, energy, aviation — company seeking maximum market share and return on investment for shareholders'. The options are usually mergers, acquisitions, divestments and cost cutting. In many cases that may be justified.

But the traditional approaches rarely address 'organic growth' — how to improve the company's position by doing new things with what

they already have. Organic growth requires insights. And insights require vulnerability. We need to face what impedes us and engage those whose experiences we have never drawn upon. That's the mindset of grace.

Grace helps shift the strategic process from analysis to argument. That often means burrowing into our understanding with fresh questions. In the words of TS Eliot, we learn to look for 'the wisdom we have lost in knowledge … (and) the knowledge we have lost in information'.[10] The greater the 'ouch', the greater the potential for insight. In my experience, many of these insights may lie with people we otherwise overlook because of their lower rank or status, merit or achievement. We might now approach them as experts and authors in their worlds.

Innovation gains agency

Wisdom also throws light on innovation. Often imagining and creating what hasn't been made or tried before starts in renaming. Conversations that forge new understanding will lead to innovation. And when people attend to their brilliance they often not only do better work, but create new ways of working. Grace is crucial to these moves toward innovation in one all important sense.

Innovation requires us to let go the desire for certainty. There is understandable fear in trusting people and human processes outside of our expectations. Some fear is about failure. Some fear is about losing control if we authorise and release agency. As people shift from passive readers to active authors of their worlds, innovation — and non-conformity — follows.

Design is key to being deliberate about innovation. Design is a way of knowing and being that is open, provisional, iterative, grounded, playful, and ready to fail. No-one designs by committee or at a distance. Design honours user experience and insights first; technical and design expertise second. None of this happens without leaders who will back unlikely people.

Engagement gains credibility

The big question with engagement is: engage in what and to what end? Initiatives for engagement usually go hand-in-hand with major system changes, or bigger changes like a merger and/or restructure. With system changes, engagement usually means compliance. With mergers and restructures, engagement usually means … compliance. This time with descriptions of 'best practice culture' — effectively, how people should feel, think, believe, and act. The test is often whether they can repeat the descriptions. It's like school.

You've probably heard something like this: 'I've been working here 15 years. I've seen three CEOs and more restructures than that. This latest CEO seems okay, but he and his change program will come and go like the others. I'll still be doing my job — if I have one'. This is usually taken as evidence of a problem.

But this is not an obstacle to overcome. It is an insight to explore. Stories like this are entry points to the craft and community that keep the organisation running. The only things that stand between leaders and these rich insights are assumptions, prejudice, and ego. Humility is where we begin. Appreciation and thankfulness open the way to real engagement. Grace is not a soft option.

A grounded exercise

Imagine two dinners

1. In the first, you have invited the most senior people in your organisation and those most likely to be promoted to senior ranks. Here's your question for the guests: What overall strategy do you believe we should adopt for the organisation?

2. In the second, you have invited people from high and low and everywhere in between: people you find fascinating for whatever reason. And here's your question for these guests: If you had six months to hear what our people and customers say we do best, what do you think you would learn?

What do you imagine each conversation being like? And what do you think might emerge from each conversation?

Let it go

A man who chose grace — twice

Love … keeps no record of wrongs.[11]

PAUL OF TARSUS

Paul's words may seem a platitude to us, but not to his first-century audience in Corinth. The litigiousness of modern societies, even the USA, does not match ancient cities like Corinth. A man could only bring a suit against a peer or a man of lower rank. The point of the system was not damages but to humiliate an opponent and further one's own standing with patrons. It was paramount to 'keep a record of wrongs'. A friend of mine refused to do this to me — twice.

It's gut-wrenching to lose your job. It's also gut-wrenching to take jobs away from people. I know both. Twice, I made the same person redundant. At college I inherited a problem of too many campuses, programs, and staff. Ron was a valued faculty member in a program I shut down. I followed due process but it was my first time running a restructure. My leadership was clumsy. Some time later Ron won a different position and delivered great service. Then, a year later, I had to restructure again and Ron's second role was one of those to go. Ron kept no record of wrongs. Rather he showed me remarkable grace — twice.

My turn to choose

There's more to the story. Ron and his wife were among the first to extend hospitality to us. Later when we bought a home, they arrived with a beautiful meal that we shared with great mirth amidst the boxes. Being made redundant twice gave Ron ample reason to feel bitter. There were times he could have embarrassed me. Instead, he defended me. Though he loved what he did, Ron did not base his identity on it. He was carried by a deep-seated thankfulness.

Years later I felt wronged by a process and decision. No-one suggested I'd done anything wrong — quite the opposite. But the glowing endorsements of my contribution only made the decision more difficult. People expressed dismay. Some urged me to take action. I'll admit I was hurt and bewildered enough to think about it.

Then I remembered Ron. He hadn't judged me, nor kept a record of wrongs. I looked again at those who had taken the call against me. They're good people; some are friends. Thinking about their process and decision, I knew I'd run poor ones myself. I could fixate on that one decision, or I could remember great years working with common heart. I could justify myself, or I could follow Ron down his path of grace and choose to keep no record of wrongs.

It would be too easy to be facile about forgiveness or letting things go. I certainly do no want to go there. I know only too well how hard it is. There are times to confront and work through betrayal. But I know this: the world is not transformed by keeping a record of wrongs, but by grace.

When rights are not enough

The limits of rights

Let me be clear. I'm not saying it's wrong to seek redress. The wrongs you have experienced may make my choice to 'let it go' seem puerile. I don't know your circumstance. It's not my place to advise whether to seek redress. We make our own calls. So what am I suggesting?

Simply: We can't address the wrongs of the world, nor of our lives, nor solve their problems, without grace. The complexity of our lives, personal and social, and our complicity in their brokenness, condemns us to frustration and hypocrisy if we demand an eye for an eye. Peace comes by reconciliation not legislation. Somewhere, we choose to absorb hurt rather than repay it.

Historically we emphasised responsibility to king, church, or God. In recent years we asserted rights — and rightly so. But a stand-off follows. Women have rights: unborn have rights. Citizens have rights: refugees have rights. Owners have rights: workers have rights. Rich have rights: poor have rights. So we look again to responsibilities for balance. We each have rights *and* responsibilities.

Right responsible relationship

Noel Pearson is an indigenous Australian, a lawyer, and a tireless advocate for his peoples. His views alienate people across the political spectrum. His argument, anchored in experience, seems hard to refute: A massive gap — social, educational, economical, health — exists between indigenous Australia and the rest. Welfare has created dependence and undermined responsibility. Indigenous Australia must become free of welfare. But ending welfare too soon will kill people. In Pearson's opinion, the campaigns of the 'welfare industry' have proven patronising and destructive. He memorably calls for 'the right to be responsible'.[12]

Grace enables us to address the wrongs and to absorb the hurt, rather than repay it. The right to be responsible is grounded in relationships.

The right to be responsible assumes relationship. And relationship is shaped by common hopes for truth, beauty, and goodness, or it is nothing. It means we address wrongs where they can and should be; and absorb wrongs where they can't.

I have stood with those seeking justice and would do so again. But we can't flourish by an eye for an eye. Heather Warren says: 'The life of grace is fundamentally others-oriented — social and connectional … As such, it might be a key, or even essential, to the growth of a genuinely multicultural society'.[13] I suggest grace is vital in every society, family, and relationship.

PEERING INTO THE PUZZLE OF
GRACE UPON GRACE

Grace is bigger than we are. I have emphasised our disposition to
extend grace to others. But this begins in our own experience
of grace.

Knowing grace

Grace is a commitment and choice to
treat others according to our shared
equal dignity irrespective of status,
merit, or brokenness. Our dignity and
brokenness might seem irreconcilable
if not for the link of grace's kindness,
forgiveness, and welcome.

Grace holds together dignity and brokenness.

Grace embraces us before we
embrace grace. This is the dimension
so beautifully portrayed in the song
'Grace' by U2.[14] Grace is bigger
than we are. Grace infuses the world
with goodness and beauty. Grace is
the stubborn 'yes' of life to dignity and
beauty and hope. It is why we fight
to save a life and why a newborn's
smile moves us deeper than the most
majestic alps.

Accounting for grace

I'm conscious of making big
assumptions here: about what it
means to be human, about how we
know, and a lot more. Every view of
life wrestles with deep, wondrous,
and hard things. For me any liveable
account of life has to:

- Echo the resounding 'yes' of life.
- Hold in tension, unity, and diversity.
- Reconcile dignity and brokenness.
- Privilege the relational.
- Thrill to the mutuality of nature.
- Feel how language permeates life.
- Tell a story about stories.
- Prompt thankfulness, joy, and love.
- Stir me to resist what violates us.

For me, grace holds this together. But
my view of life doesn't easily fit any
philosophical, religious, spiritual, or
scientific tradition. I'm mindful we all
see this our own way. And some views of
life leave little or no place for grace. This
is particularly so of scientific views that
depend on materialist and rationalist
philosophies. Without wanting to
judge, I need to wade a little into these
views. Caution: a short excursion in
philosophy follows!

Resisting grace

Materialism holds that reality is matter
and energy: nothing else is needed
to explain reality. Rationalism holds
that human reason (in various forms
of logic) is sufficient to describe reality
exhaustively. Together materialism and
rationalism offer a promise of certainty.

But there are problems. It can be argued that this isn't true to science's own methods and discoveries; that it involves a logical fallacy; and that it's not terribly liveable.

Take the table I'm writing on. It makes perfect sense according to classical (Newtonian) physics. But at the quantum level, it makes no sense at all. Down there the table is both particle and wave. Physicists have to hold both the wave/particle contradiction and the Newton/quantum contradiction. It's a paradox, and I'm fine with that; lots of life is paradoxical. But rationalism doesn't welcome paradox. Plus physicists don't build theories by adding Copernicus + Galileo + Newton + Einstein + Heisenberg + Schrödinger. Theories are overthrown as much as built upon.

Philosophers of science long ago abandoned ideas of science as certain, neutral, and objective.[15] Science works within tradition, presuppositions, and hopes. The materialism-rationalism package rests not on reason but on belief.

We can't step outside reason to argue for reason. The standard definition of knowledge is 'a properly justified true belief'.[16] That little word on the end is the problem. Logically, belief is prior to reason. We use reason because we believe it works and we can't conceive of doing anything else. That's the kind of circular reasoning that's only supposed to happen for, well, 'believers'. It seems we all believe — or we couldn't think!

Knowing is bigger and more richly human than just reasoning. The biological philosopher Humberto Maturana provocatively put love at the centre of intelligence: 'The only emotion that expands intelligence is love ... Love is visionary'.[17] I think love is the greatest form of knowing. It's relationship not reason that makes life work. And it's humility that makes knowing possible. Bless his socks, dear old Socrates was right! I need to acknowledge that I don't know.

Welcoming grace

Any liveable view of life has to hold dignity and brokenness together. To see only brokenness is to condemn ourselves to despair and to ignore the extraordinary ways our lives bring beauty to each other. To see only dignity is to condemn ourselves to an illusion that ignores the brutality and distortions of which every one of us is capable if not complicit.

Since the 1990s Sue and I adopted the 'Rwandan test' for life views — particularly for very positive Western views. We ask ourselves how well a view of life would work for people in, as it was then, war-torn Rwanda. There's very often a glaring mismatch.

I can't explain evil, but nor will I explain it away. What I do know is that nothing addresses evil, and my own brokenness, like grace. In the embrace and welcome of the 'yes' of life I find hope for transformation.

Work it out backwards

Start with leaders you've observed:
• Whom do you admire?
• How do you want to lead?
• What life-view will guide you?
• How does grace figure in that?

Growing in grace

Plan for grace — a nice irony!
- Name a troubling person or group.
- Consider their story.
- Name a wrong to be righted.
- Name a hurt to be respected.
- Name a perspective to be heard.
- Name a needless status distinction.
- Name a meaningful kindness
  to offer.
- Commit to doing it.
- Assess the effect.
- Continue to lead with grace.

Growing into grace
In *Chapter 1: Wisdom* I quoted from some friends who answered my question about presence and attentiveness. Their insights speak well to grace. Here they are again edited for our present interest:

Be thankful. Let stillness settle in you.
TARA

Give. Attentiveness, encounter, vulnerability, gratitude, and curiosity are most present in the moment of giving and gift.
JOHN

Tell yourself your own story as a story of grace in brokenness. Think of the fracturing forces that shaped it. What are you now able to face that you could not before?
DAVID

Listen deeply. Attentiveness and presence is not dissociation. It is the courage to be vulnerable.
EMMA

Create some life practices. Reflect on your day: what brought consolation and desolation?
BELINDA

Look to the people you admire for their grace.
ME

Reflection
Seeing the Patterns and Arts in the light of Grace
- Where and when have you seen kindness and thoughtfulness shift people and cultures?
- Did grace resonate for you? Why or why not?
- What might it offer the way you understand yourself and your leadership?
- Which Pattern or Art caught your attention and your imagination?
- What do you see in the other Patterns and Arts when you view them through your favourite?

Nobility of spirit is the great ideal. It is the realisation of true freedom, and there can be no democracy, no free world, without this moral foundation. Whitman's masterpiece, his whole vision, is exactly about this: life as a quest for truth, love, beauty, goodness, and freedom; life as the art of becoming human through the cultivation of the human soul. All this is expressed by 'nobility of spirit': the incarnation of human dignity.[18]
ROB RIEMEN

Q. # What final thought can you leave us?

A. *Lead with Wisdom* does not offer a set of steps to leadership wisdom or success. The Patterns and Arts are ways of seeing. In this last chapter I tried to present Grace as more than the fourth Art to Story, Brilliance, and Promise. I wanted it to feel a bit like a window on the other Arts. Even on the Patterns of Naming, Conversation, Influence, and Character, and the larger questions of Leadership and Wisdom. I encourage you to see the Patterns and Arts not like a stepped process or independent ideas. Put them together. Try seeing one in terms of the other. There's more there than I've seen.

PART IV

Applying the Patterns and Arts

In the end, what matters most is what happens in our lives and in the lives of those whom we are privileged to serve. Often the deepest learning is closest to home.

WISDOM AND LEADERSHIP
1 Wisdom
2 Leadership

Why do we need to lead with wisdom?

PATTERNS
3 Naming
4 Conversation
5 Influence
6 Character

ARTS
7 Story
8 Brilliance
9 Promise
10 Grace

How do we lead with wisdom?

APPLYING THE
PATTERNS AND ARTS
11 Leader's Journey
12 Leading One
13 Leading Many

Where must we lead with wisdom?

THE STORY BEHIND APPLICATION

Wise leaders know their stories

We come now to how to work well with the Patterns and Arts. Each chapter tells a single story. Together they chronicle how the ideas of *Lead with Wisdom* came together for me. None of the stories is a success story. But that's not what wisdom is about.

In Chapter 11: Leader's Journey, I take you inside my own story. Here's a sample: chronic illness, little schooling, truck driver, married, three wonderful kids now adults, and following my nose and heart into the strangest of things — writing, speaking, and advising on leadership. It's just my story. Yours is different and yours is the point. I've told my story to encourage you to tell yours.

In Chapter 12: Leading One, I take you into the story I share with my son Luke. He's almost 30 now, married, and about to become a dad and a lawyer. No-one could have imagined any of this when the heartaches began. Luke finishes the story with his own account of what it meant to him along the way, and now.

In Chapter 13: Leading Many, I take you into a little known ancient story. It's not unknown because the man is unknown, but because of how the story is traditionally told. The man is Saul of Tarsus aka Paul the apostle. My university studies began in theology but how they approached questions never worked for me. In the mid 1990s I had the privilege of studying under one of the world's finest ancient historians. My doctoral research read Paul not as a theologian or biblical scholar would read him, but as an historian of ideas. Sometimes I ask retreat participants if they'd like to hear about the man who was arguably the architect and leader of one of the greatest shifts in Western thought. This is the story I tell.

Leaders help people create a new social reality: a new story. But to lead others into a new story, you must first know your own story.

CHAPTER 11

Leader's Journey

We need to know our stories

And help others find theirs

Wise leadership always comes back to the person. You. Me. Us. It cannot come from a book — not even this one! We do not lead from principles or techniques but from who we are.

That which your fathers have bequeathed to you, earn it anew if you would possess it.[1]
GOETHE

Our stories are more than the sum of our experiences. The ways we tell the story are as significant as the events themselves.

We recall what we find significant, even if we don't know why. Associating one event with another gives us the beginning of a coherent tale. Telling and retelling the tale, we sense and interpret how things have worked together to make us who we are, and to bring us to this moment. From here we anticipate and dream more to come.

Leadership needs self-knowledge. More than once I have seen the devastating effect of a leader who seemed, or pretended, to have no idea of their impact upon others. That's one reason to know your story.

Bigger still, to lead wisely is to help others find their stories, their identity, their brilliance. I can't and shouldn't do that, if I don't or won't know my own story. It is difficult, even confronting, work. I cannot ask another to do what I won't do myself.

Here then is my story…

THIS IS

MARK'S STORY

The themes of *Lead with Wisdom* might make more sense after reading my story. That could be interpreted many ways.
Feel free!

In 1980, newly married, Sue and I grabbed an opportunity for graduate study in the USA. When I failed my first exam in philosophy a window opened in a most unexpected way.

It was the way I'd failed the exam that earned me an invitation to my professor's office. I had completed less than half the exam because I'd scribbled all over it, in the margins, between the lines, and on the back telling the professor what I thought of his 'stupid' short-answer section while I argued for multiple answers to the multiple choices!'

Instead of railing at me, the professor asked me a simple question: 'Mark, why did you come here?' That afternoon he coaxed from me the fragments of my life and I began to hear my story for the first time. This is what I told him:

As a child I had chronic asthma and was covered in eczema. Adrenalin injections kept me alive. Sometimes I'd be fine for days or weeks. But more nights than I care to remember were the same. Mum would patiently bandage my body with coal tar ointment, lint, and bandages cut from my dad's old undershirts. At the end she would tie mittens on my hands to try to stop me scratching.

I'LL FIGHT WITH YOU. IF YOU DON'T KILL THIS, I THINK IT WILL KILL YOU.

Throughout it all I would focus on a spot on the far wall. I'd push my back against the bedhead to relieve my diaphragm. An asthma attack means you can't get air out, but it feels like you can't get air in. My chest would heave, head pound, nausea come in waves, throwing up would feel like drowning, and my skin would ache and crawl. Until I fell asleep I'd focus on a single task: to breathe.

Night after night I escaped the only way I knew how: I'd lose myself in thought. Years later I was struck by William Barrett's reflections on death and meaning in *Irrational Man*. He argued we're not truly alive until we pass from the general statement 'we will die' to the specific statement 'I will die'. I knew what he meant: I'd faced that more than once as a boy.

One day we heard that another boy with asthma had died. Mum came into my room, sat on my bed, and said to me:

'Mark, you know you are just as sick as that poor boy who died today. I don't know what else to do to help you, but if you'll fight, I'll fight with you. If you don't kill this, I think it will kill you'. I was perhaps ten or eleven. Who knows how these things happen, but I think that night I chose to fight.

A good deal of my fighting was at school. Not physical fights — though I was bullied often. My fight was to understand. It was more than the subjects at school; I wanted to understand life and my own mind. At home sick I'd sit and think. Back at school everyone had moved on. There was little interest in the questions I asked night after night.

Scoring near the bottom of the school in the trial high-school exams woke me up. I crammed and made it into university. Three weeks after starting, I left. I worked as a labourer and truck driver. Later someone convinced me I should study. Four years and three institutions later I had my first degree — and went back to driving trucks.

Now I was halfway around the world in a professor's office because I felt stupid doing his exam and had reacted with anger. Feeling confused and exposed, I did what I always did: I fought.

I WAS CONFUSED AND I FELT EXPOSED. SO I DID WHAT I ALWAYS DID: I FOUGHT.

'Mark, why did you come here?' All I could tell him was that I wanted to think and read and question. Maybe I wanted to stop fighting and learn; if I did, I didn't know how. But I was about to learn.

A handful of remarkable teachers became my friends and mentors. They helped me understand how I learn. They let me chase my questions and create dialogues between the disciplines and with them. At times they let me follow an unofficial curriculum.

Always they pushed me. Always they modelled the responsibilities of scholarship. Their friendship and belief in me, together with Sue and my friends, began to bring clarity to a naming that would still take years to unfold.

Near the end, my favourite professor, a bear of a man with a mind, heart, and laugh to match, drew me aside. 'Follow your heart, Mark', he gently counselled. He saw two paths before me. On one path I'd take up a PhD offer, teach, research, publish, and work toward a professorship. A known and honourable path.

But there was another path, he suggested, unknown and uncertain. It could mean no platforms other than what I created. But I'd be free to pursue what lay in my heart. He urged me to learn to speak from the rawness of life as much as from scholarship. 'Both paths are before you', he said: 'I hope you follow your heart'.

We did. With our new daughter Miriam, Sue and I headed home to Australia with half a dream but no place to go. We could never have predicted what would follow.

With two wonderful friends, we founded a community. I learned to lead from the heart there by watching them. I fell into a partnership with a local university. The philosophy of their experiential

THIS IS MARK'S STORY

program had confused and alienated most students and quite a few staff. I ran workshops to help the school understand their own experiment.

Our home was alive with the conversations of people working for change. Our kids grew up thinking it was normal for students to board with us, or to find people staying over for conversation or care.

After a few years as a publishing editor, I joined my friend Tony in his new business. We were puzzled by the ways smart people sometimes produced confused presentations and documents. A hunch took shape: perhaps if we brought clarity to their documents, they'd invite us upstream into their thinking. And they did.

In 1992 I hit the wall, not for the first time, but certainly the worst. I was long acquainted with Churchill's 'black dog' of depression but nothing like the lows of the next three years. Perhaps ironically, this was also when I completed my PhD in the history of ideas: an enquiry into the roots of modern leadership complexities, particularly in the legacies of the classical period. It was a long way from the kind of narrow dissertation I might have written a decade earlier at a European university. And it was also the beginning of my professional focus on leadership.

Looking back I can smile at the irony. I was researching the legacies of an ancient innovator who had inverted classical ideals of leadership. At the heart of this revolution were this man's frank self-disclosures of weakness and

his refusals of status. (I tell his story in *Chapter 13: Leading Many.*) And I was writing about him in the midst of my own breakdown! I had no idea that in a year or two I would be earning my living talking about leadership.

Known for facilitating strategy and design work, clients began to change the brief. Increasingly they engaged me to partner them and their executives on the changes *they* needed to embrace first as a group before they could lead wider change. I was reluctant to own the word 'leadership' given the clichés and formulas that are too often associated with it. But the language was unavoidable and I began to take note of what they were saying. I made the call to stop taking facilitation gigs and concentrate on putting my ideas in a form I could share with others.

I invited some friends to spend a weekend together so I could trial a client leadership retreat that I would lead two weeks later. On the Saturday night we went for dinner and to discuss the day.

A single statement brought me undone: 'It's not you'. Ouch! They nailed me. I wrote all night stripping out the ideas that were not mine or not where I wanted to take them. It was rough, they said, but now it did sound like me. Two weeks later at the end of that first client retreat, the business leaders echoed the verdict of my friends: it was rough, but good.

A couple of years later one of those leaders would help me find greater clarity. Working together on his organisation, Terry had watched me chop and change my ideas. One night over dinner he called me on this behaviour. Among his many interests he raced yachts; thus the metaphor:

'Mark, when are you going to stop sailing from one island to another?' he said, exasperated with me. 'I've seen you do it twice in the time I've known you. You find an island, stay a while, find something wrong, and sail off. How many times have you reinvented your leadership material? You've found your island! It's Wisdom! Naming! The Arts! Now burn your boat and build your new world'. He was right and I did.

Through the next few years a theme had surfaced a few times: would I take on a CEO role. As I've already recounted, I tended to dismiss the idea with a lame reading and naming of myself. Sometime after I had been challenged quite hard about this, and opened myself to the idea, I was approached by the Chairman of a tertiary college in Aotearoa New Zealand. It was an old and venerable institution but another world to me in more ways than geography. Still, a very persuasive Chairman sold me the hope of being part of a far-reaching turnaround in vision and influence.

The board gave me a simple but wide-ranging brief: to 'bring the institution into the twenty-first century'. And although the college had a proud history, fine people, and a strong balance sheet, it was struggling.

We operated ten campuses, each with a board that operated (largely) autonomously; especially that of the main campus. An issue could be debated and deferred across four levels of governance with some people sitting on three or even four of those groups.

Financially it had been running in the red for years. Each campus operated to different Charts of Account, often on different software.

Student numbers were roughly half what they'd been five years before; staff had doubled. Few staff had contracts. There was an unwieldy number of courses from Certificate level to research Masters degrees and each qualification required extensive administration and auditing.

THE CULTURAL CHALLENGE WAS TO HONOUR THE PAST, LET GO OF WHAT WAS HOLDING THE COLLEGE BACK, AND TOGETHER WRITE A NEW CHAPTER.

The greater issue was vision. The college had been founded in 1922 by entrepreneur and philanthropist Robert Laidlaw and pastor and theologian Joseph Kemp. Laidlaw's vision was for men and women of character and faith serving across New Zealand society. Kemp's vision was for missionaries and his vision had prevailed.

Yet for almost thirty years before I arrived the majority of students did not come to train for missions or church related vocations but to return to roles in commerce, schools, academia, politics, and welfare. In a sense they were coming for a modern restatement of Laidlaw's vision.

To me this was the central strategic challenge: What would this college

THIS IS MARK'S STORY

need to become if it was outstanding in equipping people to live and serve in both spheres?

The cultural challenge was to honour the past, let go what was holding the college back, and together write a new chapter.

I was heartened to see my ideas on leadership hold true. I was humbled to have to learn them all over again. I learned more about the art of grace than anything — through the grace of others toward me!

We had to close eight campuses and most programs. Half the original staff lost their jobs. Governance was brought back to a single national board. We recruited four senior leaders to inject new vision and conversation.

We put all faculty on contracts with higher pay, lighter teaching loads, better study leave provisions (for most), less administration, and gave real support for those finishing PhDs. The only way we could achieve this fairly under NZ employment law was to require everyone to reapply for their jobs. No-one lost a job. That's not to say this process, or any other, was always run as well as it might have been. More than once, I said or wrote too much, too soon, too insensitively.

One Friday the Executive reached consensus on how we would launch our largest restructure. Over the weekend I received emails from each executive urging me to slow down with the changes. I fumed at what I deemed to be a lack of courage. But by Sunday

night, having read the emails over and over, I knew they were right. They hadn't pulled back from the changes. They just had a clearer grasp of the impacts and timing. Sometimes it's wiser to follow than lead.

Like any CEO I wrote strategy papers for the board. But I wanted staff to write the key milestone documents once we were well underway with change. Calling a group of them together, I made known what I'd been mandated to do, my own priorities, and left the writing to them.

The faculty wrote an Accord committing them to a development path that cleared the way for many of the biggest changes. Later the whole staff wrote a vision and mission statement. Each department added their own statement of what it would take to realise the vision. The processes were difficult but crucial and rewarding.

One of my fondest memories is the night we relaunched the college as Laidlaw College. The team had already delivered outstanding changes: we ran every budget to surplus; we put in place a transition program from ten to two campuses; we completed a friendly acquisition of another college; we initiated a joint venture that almost doubled the balance sheet; and we earned top marks on a vital accreditation audit. The staff achieved all this during a time of unprecedented upheaval for everyone.

At the end of the ceremony, a long-standing member of faculty, a gentle and humble man, said, 'Mark, I've never felt prouder to be part of this college'.

We need to make sense of our stories

Looking back at my time at the college, I not only had to grapple with the ambiguities and tensions of the context, but I had to enter into them. I had to honour a story that I could only ever know secondhand; I also had to name and challenge some legacies.

I needed to encourage all, but invest deliberately in those who were open to change. I needed to value what each person brought, but also name what was missing and find those who could provide it. I needed consensus wherever possible, but I was responsible to deliver sweeping change. I could not move fast, but I could not wait for all.

And while I needed and wanted support to keep moving forward, I had to make hard calls and face disapproval, sometimes resentment, without self-justification. I failed often.

Looking further back I see my ambivalence about being a leader. As a young man I had seen distortions of leadership and that I could go that way. Yet each time I distanced myself from leadership I was walking away from part of who I am.

Seeing the big picture has always been part of my story.

I have spoken often in this book about brilliance. Again, I don't mean IQ, but the ability of everyone to shine. I suspect the unique ways we learn have a lot to do with the unique ways we shine. Perhaps this helps make sense of my 'fighting'. I was not only fighting to learn but fighting to find out what I had.

Growing up, I knew I thought differently from most other kids — and the teachers. Now I'd say that I thought in big pictures. I mulled over ideas I could seldom articulate. For a long time I named myself as odd. Now I see the strengths in the ways I learn.

I count myself extraordinarily blessed with people who have believed in me: from my family to professors to a friend starting a business to clients to the chairman of a college — none more so than Sue and our three children.

And one more thing: joy. I am glad for who I have become through the tough times. I have loved seeing lights in people's eyes when I teach, seeing people discover their brilliance, and working alongside so many who have enriched the humanity of schools, corporations, and communities.

Your story may be similar or very different. The key is to know your story.

LOOK FOR THE PATTERNS AND THE ARTS

As you read my story and the reflections, perhaps you recalled some of the patterns and arts we have discussed. Here are a few links I have made:

Wisdom — the challenge of attentiveness and presence.

Someone once told me I was a brilliant listener ... for a few minutes. I have always struggled with being present though I think I now see some growth. But I'm struck with the kindness and gift of people who stayed present to me. They held me in a place to learn.

Leadership — knowing when to lead and when to follow.

The college executive (rightly) challenging me on the timing of the restructure was significant for me. I had to learn to follow as much as I had to learn to lead.

Naming — the power of words and of choosing which to leave and which to grow into.

'Odd', 'dropout', and 'not CEO material' were names I had to let go. The ways I used those words robbed me of the power to grow. 'Scholar', 'leader', and 'elder' were names I had to grow into. The ways others first used those names opened up the room for me to grow into them.

Conversation — the meaning that unfolds in a myriad of conversations.

The whole chapter is in there. My ways of knowing were tacit and visceral as much as rational. Conversations unlocked new meaning for me, frequently on the other side of breakdown. Like: My mum the night the boy died. The professors. Sue refusing to let me disappear into my head during the black years. The yachtsman who damn near burnt my boat for me.

Influence — the impact of belief.

I can't think of a single person who influenced the course of my life because of their position. True, our lives would not have touched without them being parents, professors, bosses, clients, and chairmen. But their influence was relational. They walked with me and side-by-side I found new meaning and the courage to choose.

Character — the power of love.

The men and women who shaped my life did not view me as a project or problem. They cared. The suggestion to walk away from a PhD scholarship was outrageous. It was his character and his commitment to me that made me listen. Time and again I needed to realise that the key question for my staff was not whether the strategy was clever, or even sensible, but could I be trusted.

Story — in telling the story we come to know it.

After I told my story to the professor, I went home and relayed our conversation to Sue. I would start each piece with 'as you know...' and she would reply 'no I don't'. In telling the story we came to know each other. In time the themes changed for the telling is shaped by the context in which we tell it. Likewise it was the telling and retelling of the college's story by those new and old to it that opened the way for a new chapter.

Brilliance — the clues are in the fragments of our stories.

They may not look like much. Remembering long nights as a child. A choice to fight. Knowing I knew in my gut what a book was saying about death and meaning. Taking fledgling steps to bring into dialogue the academic disciplines I was learning. Reciprocating strength with my kaumatua and the weight of a cloak.

Promise — the impact of a 'word in season'.

We need to let others speak truly and strongly into our own lives as well as learn to do the same: Like a friend who tells me to burn my boat. Like another friend who says he loves me too much to think that I know what's good for me in my blackest times. And like Sue telling me a hundred times not to sell myself short.

Grace — the gift of dignity and kindness.

I have said before that Grace is the root of all the Arts. Why would a professor give me room to tell my story and stay to listen? Why would a client urge me to embrace leadership? Why would a friend risk our friendship with his straight talking? Why, if not because they were prepared at that moment to put my interests before their own. Sometimes I wonder if all the Patterns and the Arts are not in fact always leading us to Grace.

Reflection

Take the time to think about your own story. The exercise 'Map Your Brilliance' in *Chapter 8: Brilliance* (see page 160) is a good place to start.

- Find some people who will listen to your story. Each time you tell it, ask what has changed and why.
- Where are you putting the emphasis?
- When you are ready, think about where you see the Patterns and the Arts in your story.

Q. # What do you hope we get from your story?

A. Two things. First, the encouragement to tell your own story. That starts with knowing it. I meet people in their 50s and 60s who when they do the exercise on brilliance at a retreat say it's the first time they ever told their story to anyone. They always say this with surprise at that fact and joy at having done so. Second, the encouragement to surround yourself with good people who will tell you the truth. Coaches and mentors can be really helpful for holding you to what you say you want to learn. And nothing matches dear friends. The key is opening yourself to be known and searching for what matters most.

To change a life is
to change a story.
Sometimes it is our
own life and our own
story that (must)
change the most.

CHAPTER 12

Leading One

We enter the other's story

Leading wisely through story

To lead wisely is to help others find their stories, their identity, their brilliance. In the last chapter I suggested it can be confronting to look at our own stories and to grapple with what we see there.

Walking alongside someone brings another dimension of this challenge. Reading and disclosing our own story requires considerable vulnerability: we have to be attentive and present to ourselves. Drawing out another's story requires us to be and to remain attentive and present to the other.

We can't do this well at arm's length. As we draw out a person's story to some degree we enter into it. If we hold back from a person while trying to draw out his story, our intervention will be contrived and distort the relationship.

It takes authenticity to open space for people to explore their brilliance. It takes presence and attentiveness to keep it open. Anyone who has ever tried to walk with someone this way knows how easily it exposes our own motives, assumptions, and expectations.

Sometimes we discover that we're the problem. I know I have. Some of my deepest learning about leading others and being the problem has come through my own family.

Here, with his blessing, is the story of such a journey with my son Luke.

The purposes of the heart are deep waters, but one who has insight draws them out.[1]
SOLOMON

MARK ON
MARK AND LUKE'S STORY

Most leaders face a time when they have no idea what to do. There is no way ahead except through the darkness. This is such a story.

Sue and I are blessed with rich friendship with our three adult children. Luke is our second child, and only son. He has been a bundle of energy since the Leap Year's Day he was born.

In early adolescence Luke began a slide into an all too common story for teenage boys. Life shrinks. School 'sucks'. Fear of being uncool drowns interest and initiative.

I can't count the times and ways I tried to connect with him. But nothing worked. We would argue and he would retreat to his room or take off on his bike. School became a disaster.

During this time I was often away on business. I began to dread the calls home after work. Chatting with the girls would be lovely and we would talk about what they had done that day. If Luke came to the phone it was difficult to get more than a grunt — have you ever noticed how teenage boys have an entire language system based on grunts?! Then Sue would tell me the latest unwelcome news from school.

Some days after these phone calls I would feel shrouded in a sense of helplessness and pretence. I was advising clients on how to bring deep changes for their people, while feeling powerless to help my own son. The sense of hypocrisy gnawed at me.

Outwardly I threw myself into action; inside I knotted up in fear. I grabbed for any strategy to put Luke back on course. The more I tried, the worse everything became. The more I tried to talk about my concerns, the more he withdrew. I kept telling myself I had to do something fast.

I turned to the obvious strategy. Where did everything seem to be at its worst? At school. If we could get school to work for him, I reasoned, then everything else would come right. But the more we focused on school, the more it frustrated Luke, and us.

One night Sue and I were talking, again, about Luke. Over and over the same old ground. I knew I had to reconnect with him but everything had failed. I had no more ideas. Slowly I began to sense there was only one thing left. I had to change, but again I had no idea how. All I knew was that somehow I had to walk toward my boy and into the terrifying darkness of not knowing what to do.

Sometimes Luke seemed like a stranger to me. I loved him of course but he seemed worlds away. His only interests were the things that got him into trouble, along with his friends, and tearing about on his bike. If only we knew what hope that bike held.

Have you ever found yourself saying what you always knew but didn't know that you knew? One night, talking about Luke, Sue and I discovered we had both noticed something though neither of us had thought any more about it.

I CAME TO A CROSSROAD. COULD I LET GO OF MY EXPECTATIONS? COULD I DEAL WITH MY FEARS? COULD I ENGAGE WITH LUKE IN HIS WORLD RATHER THAN MINE?

The one thing Luke cared about — his 'sweet spot' — was in our garage. It was his bike. As a young boy he had loved his bikes and that passion was still there. On his bike, something of the old energy came back. When the talk turned to bikes, he spoke rather than grunted. His world was a little bit bigger around his bike.

I'd love to say we saw all this and hatched a plan. But it didn't happen like that. Sue was talking with a colleague at work one day who also had a troubled son. It turned out that her boy raced mountain bikes (MTB). She asked if Luke would like to try. A few weeks later Luke entered his first cross-country MTB race.

At the starting line, Luke held back from the other boys. Desperately wanting to be cool, the truth was his bike and equipment was decidedly uncool and he had no idea about racing. But once the race began, he came alive. Determined. He led that race until a flat tyre sidelined him. You might imagine how sour he was. But to our surprise he came back. And he won the next race and many more. It was obvious he had ability. Soon he started to look beyond XC racing.

Have you ever seen downhill MTB racing? It is feral. You may have seen it on extreme sports shows or YouTube. Think ski resorts in summer. A track coming down the slope into the trees and boulders between the ski runs. Think crazy rocks, tree roots and mud on impossible slopes. Now imagine a bike on that track — at speed. That's downhill. And that, more than anything, was what Luke wanted to do.

What's a parent to do? Reason says this is madness. But he wanted it with a passion. The more I said no, the more he pushed back. Finally I relented. He could have one race. And he was to race sensibly with no injuries. I had no idea then how ridiculous that sounds now.

Well, he won that first downhill race — on a flat tyre! So much for one race only. And he came back and won again and again.

For the first time in a very long time, Luke wanted to excel at something. With the physique of a sprinter, he was never going to reach the peak of cross-country. But even on very inadequate bikes, he was good at downhill.

I came to a crossroad. Could I let go of my expectations? Could I deal with my fears?

MARK ON MARK AND LUKE'S STORY

Could I engage with Luke in his world rather than mine? Could I let go of trying to make school work? Did I really believe what I taught others about the whole of life being the context for learning?

Sue and I made some choices and I began to spend a lot more time with Luke travelling to races and helping him in between. Sue also travelled to many races especially when I couldn't be there. Sue and the girls were magnificent supports, encouraging me to spend the time with Luke and lifting my spirits when I grew despondent.

MOUNTAIN BIKING HAS BEEN GOOD FOR ME. I DON'T WANT TO BE LIKE THOSE OLDER GUYS WHO TELL ME TO GET LOST. I WANT TO GIVE SOMETHING BACK.

Downhill MTB racing is expensive. It's basically motocross technology with pedals. Luke was riding and quite often winning on bikes not much above the department store bikes handed out in thousands each Christmas. And he was breaking them every other race. His winning margins decreased as other kids moved up to better bikes.

Sooner or later Luke would have to get a real racing bike but I resisted just giving it to him. I believed he needed to commit to getting it as much as me. This was a tough time. We had grown a little closer and he liked me being part of his racing. But he resented me not buying everything for him.

Luke had attracted the attention of Paul, a former racer with business interests in MTB. One day after being with Paul, Luke said that Paul had called him an asshole. Rough diamond as he was, I couldn't imagine Paul just bad-mouthing Luke. And he hadn't.

Paul had been trying to fix Luke's bike — again — when he told Luke he would have to get a better bike. Luke's response was to bad-mouth me for not buying him one. Paul suggested sponsorship. Luke bad-mouthed sponsors as not being interested in kids like him. Then Paul hit the nail on the head:

'No-one', Paul said, 'wants to sponsor an asshole. If you want to get to the Worlds, and you have the potential, then you need sponsors. Your old man's not going to pay up and nor should he. You're going to have to show people you're worth their money. And that means not being a jerk'.

Knowing what Luke's behaviour could be like, Paul presented scenarios to him of how he could ruin his chances of being sponsored. Like blaming his own mistakes on his bike and equipment. Or bad-mouthing some other bike without realising the man who started talking to you is the guy who imports and sells them. That, Paul was saying, was the kind of 'asshole' no-one wants to sponsor.

That conversation was a godsend. For the first time, someone had made a link for Luke between his 'sweet spot', the bike, and the rest of his life and especially his behaviour. Luke was fast but not fast enough for people to just throw sponsorship at him. He had to prove himself. He didn't like it, but he began to see the point.

Paul's comment offered me a key to 'translation': a way to make links between Luke's riding and relationships, his racing and responsibility, and even his talent and personal character. School did not work for Luke. But now we had another avenue for his learning. In effect, the bike became his school.

As Luke progressed as a racer he moved on to state and national level competitions. And as the competition got higher so did the mountains. In Australia, a very flat land, that can mean driving six, ten, even twelve hours each way.

Some trips were great. Many were not. All this time I was thinking about translation. On the way to races I'd start a conversation around a great link I thought he'd relate to. More often than not I got it very wrong.

But sometimes I got it right. We'd connect, there'd be five minutes of real connection then, in mid-sentence, he'd turn up the stereo. (You may have no idea how loud a car stereo can play Megadeth or Nirvana. I do.) I'd want to keep the conversation going but the moment would be gone. There'd be no more talk that day or the next.

One day I was lamenting this lack of progress to my dear older friend Jim. Now Jim is a gentle man so I was stunned when he told me to shut up. My talking, Jim said, was probably driving Luke underground. I had to learn to shut up. Then Jim made me a strange promise:

'If you can get five minutes of real connection with Luke in a twelve hour

drive, and not stuff it up when you're at the race', Jim said, 'I guarantee you'll get ten minutes three days later on the way home. And don't expect five or ten continuous minutes'.

But if, in my worst fears, Luke was throwing away his future, what could be the value of five or ten minutes' connection? Yet Jim was right. I was making it worse. I did have to shut up. And we were both learning. I wish this came easily for me but it didn't.

One trip I decided to raise something I had noticed at races. High level races begin with a day or more of practice. One of the keys is to learn fast lines through the rough stuff. Less experienced riders like to watch or follow the better riders to see what they do. I knew this and I knew the culture that went with it.

'Hey Luke', I asked as we drove, 'what happens when you ask the older guys if you can follow them down practice runs?'
'Some guys are alright', he replied, 'but others tell me to get lost'.
'How does that make you feel?'
'Pretty angry!'
'Fair enough', I said. 'They're the good riders and you're just a kid'.

Luke looked at me as if to say, 'I can't believe you said that!' I could hear Jim: shut up. Time to let it go. Let Luke make the links.

Now there was this funny little kid who pestered Luke at races. He would hang around asking questions till Luke would tell him to get lost. So who should walk in while Luke was putting his bike together!

MARK ON MARK AND LUKE'S STORY

And as if on cue the pesky kid started pestering Luke with questions, and Luke told him to …!

That night I mentioned that I'd seen the kid hanging around him. We made light of it for a while and then I dared to make a link:

'Why do you think he hangs around?'
'Maybe he's just a jerk. I suppose he reckons I'm a hot rider and he wants to learn from me?'
'A bit like you and the older riders', I cautiously inferred.
'Aw, I s'pose'.

The next day Luke was about to ride off for a practice run when, you guessed it, the pesky kid rode up and asked to follow Luke down the hill. Luke was about to tell him to '#@$% off!' when our eyes caught. Luke shrugged, turned back to the kid, and let him ride with him. In fact, they did two runs together.

Luke won the race. As we drove home he was on a high and he didn't shut up for the first hour or so. I waited a while then decided to try the link. I mentioned how he had let the pesky kid follow him down the track. Then he told how he helped another kid fix a flat tyre. Luke obviously felt pretty good about this.

'Luke, why did you let that kid hang around and ride with you?', I said, trying to sound perplexed.
'He's a pain', Luke replied, 'but he just wants to learn. After a while I just took off with the other guys'.
'But you didn't tell him to get lost'.
'Nah'.

'Why not?'

Again, he gives me the look. And again I can hear Jim: 'Shut up, Mark! Say nothing more!' Miles later Luke lets out a sigh and says to me: 'Aw, this is that leadership #$%# you talk, isn't it?'

It was killing me, but I had to shut up just a little longer. I asked what he meant and began to talk about him and the older guys, and him and the pesky kid. He saw the connection. Then he floored me:

'Mountain biking has been good for me. I don't want to be like those older guys who tell me to get lost. I want to give something back'.

In that moment, his pride was complete. He had won a national, and he had helped someone generously. I was so excited and looked forward to a great conversation as we kept driving. But, no, that was all I got: that was the ten minutes Jim had promised.

Luke began to make his own connections. Watching a rider throw his bike down in disgust and bad-mouth it in front of a crowd would lead us to talking about why I hadn't bought everything for him. We'd discuss what it meant to value things and to enjoy the feeling of having worked to achieve something: like the mud bricks he made for our home that earned him the money for a new bike.

Reflecting on the way races were organised led us to talking about what it meant to think ahead and to put yourself in someone else's shoes. Mechanical problems were a classroom in themselves! Each setback was an opportunity to model how to deal with adversity. I showed him how to network to find help. And we usually did. He learned to stay calm and to persevere — in fact, way better than me.

Over time, we worked our way through a remarkable curriculum: leadership, appreciation, responsibility, character, facing the future, financial wisdom, generosity, friendship, to name but a few. Every topic translated through the bike.

Away from the bike we worked with him to help him make some changes. He decided he wanted to try a new school to have a fresh start. It didn't solve everything but it certainly helped. Near the end of his first year at the new school, Luke began a scary conversation with us. He wanted to leave school to train and find sponsors so he could race professionally. We figured he would ask us one day, but it was none the easier when it happened.

We talked it through. It was a huge step. He had huge potential, but he hadn't fully shown it yet. Not everyone makes it. And there's not a huge amount of money out there. But it wasn't about the money. It was what he loved.

It was hard for me not to revert to the past and to my fears. I didn't want him lying around in bed all day. He would need to get a proper training schedule, find some work, and maybe do a course or something. He said he was prepared to do all that. The truth was we wanted him to chase his heart's desire but we were scared of what could happen.

And we knew he had to work it out for himself. We asked him to seek the counsel of others he respected.

Luke sought out some of our older friends, his sponsors, and some guys racing on the world scene. They all endorsed his potential but recommended he stay at school. He listened to them and decided to stay. It was his decision and he felt he had chosen wisely. Luke calls it the year he discovered he had a brain. He still didn't like school but his attitude shifted. He learned. And he taught.

People often say we learn best when we teach others. One day Luke asked if we could take a young guy with us to a race. With a twinkle he added, 'He's kinda in the same place I used to be. I thought maybe we could talk with him a bit like you and I do'. He was mentoring his peers!

Coming to the end of the next National Series Luke was leading by a long way. Barring a complete disaster he looked certain to wrap up his first National Series Championship. And he was determined to finish the series on a high. He was going to turn heads on this, his sixteenth birthday.

But it wasn't to be. The rear axle slipped and he finished fourth. It was more than enough to clinch the championship but he was deeply disappointed about the race. He took it out on me as though it were my fault. After a sullen presentation, we packed up and left in silence. It felt as though the clock had been turned back two years. Deep down, I feared that nothing had really changed.

MARK ON MARK AND LUKE'S STORY

A little way out of town we came upon a police roadblock. There had been a very bad accident and we would have to take a long detour. It gave us enough time to get things off our chests. I let him know that I didn't appreciate the way he blamed me for what happened at the race. And he fired some heavy shots back at me. They hurt — because he was right.

Sometimes when you fight with someone you love you can get to a better place. Until this fight we had been enjoying an increasingly open level of conversation. Now I feared it was gone. But slowly our frigid silence melted. Still driving home, and without notice, Luke asked me, 'Dad, what's it been like for you these years we've been going to races together?'

I told him about the hotel rooms, phone calls, and tears; the anxiety, my love for him, the mess of school, and lots more. I talked about the times I felt I was losing him and had no idea how to help him. He told me what he saw and we talked freely about what the bike meant to both of us. Then he floored me again:

'Dad, I'm very proud of you. I love you for sticking with me through all that crap and never being violent like so many other kids' dads. I hope I can do the same with my own kids one day'.

Then his voice quavered. With tears framing his face in the oncoming headlights, he said, 'Dad, if I hadn't finished fourth today, we would never have had this conversation. This is worth more than any championship'.

Later that year, Luke volunteered to race up a category in the next series to give younger riders a chance at winning the junior series, and to push himself. From the very first race, he banished all doubts as to whether he could race competitively against the older riders. He secured selection in the Australian team for the first time and took the silver medal in the Oceania Junior Championships, a second behind his older team-mate who became Junior World Champion that year.

As the start of his final year at school approached he asked again about leaving school. We followed the same process and this time he decided to leave. He threw himself into training and securing sponsorship. It was a good call and we backed him.

The sponsorship hunt taught him more than he could have learned at school. In the end, he phoned, emailed, or faxed about one hundred and twenty organisations. A handful replied. Three asked to learn more about him. Two offered him small product sponsorships. One increased this to a small cash sponsorship.

You can imagine the ebb and flow of emotion in all this. And the learning. School could never have done this for him.

Everything seemed on track for the World Championships that year: the training, the bike, the mental preparation. One week before the team left, he fractured his wrist in a training ride. The team left without him. A week later the wrist was pinned and he flew out on his own.

Sitting out the warm-up races, he was able to get on a bike a few days before the race in Vail, Colorado. His wrist was very painful and weak. Two days later he qualified. But on the very next run he fell and freakishly broke only the radius in his lower left arm. No Worlds. A week after he returned, the arm was plated by the surgeon who had pinned his wrist. You can imagine the magnitude of the disappointment. I felt crushed for him. But he learned from it and he came home fired to train for the Worlds in Austria the following year.

Early that next year, Luke achieved his highest success to that point. Having previously won silver in the Oceania Championships, he went one better in New Caledonia to clinch the Oceania Junior Championships and in a time that also won him bronze in the Elite Men category.

In 2002 I joined Luke in Austria for the World Championships, his last race ever as a junior. On the first night together we sat on a hill overlooking the village and reminisced about our journey. It seemed only the other day he was thirteen, we were driving to club races, and he was dreaming of one day racing at the Worlds. The night before the race one of his bikes was stolen. More learning!

It's now almost ten years since I first wrote our story. Luke raced professionally based in the USA, France or Italy for seven seasons. He represented Australia in mountain-cross and downhill at every World Championship except one. He achieved some great results but never the level of success he most wanted. He had several more significant injuries. Most importantly, he continued to grow. And so did I.

Luke stopped racing professionally a few years ago but his learning continues at a whole new level. When he finished racing he made a few other big calls and found himself invited to an internship in a think tank. There a new world of possibilities opened for him. As I write, Luke is in his third year of university studies in philosophy and law. Best of all, he shares life now with his beautiful wife Jo and they are expecting their first child.

The bike was never the final word on Luke's ability to shine. It was a sweet spot through which he learned about himself, about life, and about how to bring himself wholeheartedly to every challenge and opportunity. He still does.

LUKE ON
MARK AND LUKE'S STORY

So what was the story like for Luke? Now a husband and soon to be a dad, how has the story shaped him?

Luke, in 2002 when we first wrote our story you added this final note:

I had a shocker at the Worlds in Vail. But I was sixteen and travelling the world, doing what I love best, seeing new places, experiencing whole new cultures — it doesn't get much better than this!

When I was in Vail I read Lance Armstrong's book, *It's Not About the Bike*. I kinda know what he means. In one sense it is about the bike. I love to ride. I don't ride because I have to or feel I ought to: I ride because I love it. I love to race. But the bike has given me much more than an interest or career. It's taught me about life and myself and the kind of life I want. It's been my school.

THE THINGS I LEARNED IN MY 'SCHOOLING' HAVE FUNDAMENTALLY SHAPED ME TO THIS DAY. IT IS A CONTINUAL REMINDER THAT REAL CHANGE CAN COME FROM UNLIKELY PLACES.

It's really important to me that I don't leave you with the wrong picture of how I see myself. I don't think I'm better than anyone. Or smarter. I told Dad last year that I want to start a foundation for kids one day. I still do, but I haven't thought about it a lot since. I'm not sure how to do it or even what will happen. But I do want to give back to the sport and the kids. That's why I like coaching and encouraging the younger riders.

I stuffed up big time and I learned heaps. I still stuff up and I still learn. It's not like I learn something once and that's it. Maybe I do with technical stuff like fixing my bike. But not the stuff in my head. I've learned to handle disappointments, but I still get disappointed. I've learned to read people better, but I'm still learning about what I do and don't say to people.

When it comes to staying focused or getting over crashes and fear, I don't learn this stuff once and for all. I still compare myself to others sometimes, rather than going it alone. I have to remember and focus again. Like I said, I'm still learning.

It's ten years since you wrote that and you were just starting your professional career as a cyclist. What were some of the highlights?
There are many highlights and they are all quite different. What particularly stands out is the sense that I did

something different and extraordinary with my passion. What was once a childhood thrill became a career that took me around the world. I got to see amazing places and meet amazing people. Some of the race highlights were winning Oceania and Australian Championships and representing Australia at five World Championships.

What have been the toughest challenges for you both in the early period and later racing professionally?

In my younger years racing felt like being dropped in one 'deep end' after the other. I remember feeling out of place at my first race with all the other fast kids with good bikes. I remember having that same feeling when I went to my first state and national races, then my first World Cups and World Championships. Everywhere I raced felt so much bigger than myself. The challenge was whether I would sink or swim. Sometimes the pressure and gravity of the situation got to me and felt too much; other times I would put all that to one side and do what I knew I could do.

In the later years of racing the challenge was to remain focused. There were more injuries, upsets, and even a sense of burn-out. At times I lost the desire to ride but I painfully kept training and racing. I had to keep reminding myself that the things affecting me were ephemeral and in no time I'd be having fun again.

I remember trying to do homework with you when you were fourteen. You've now finished your third year of philosophy and law, won

two first in class awards and an academic scholarship. It's been a huge change. What happened for you?

I wanted to do something interesting after racing. I found a passion for law and philosophy and applied everything I learned from years of racing to my studies.

Our journey lives on for me in lots of ways. How does it live on for you?

The relationship with you and the family has been the foundation for me to realise my potential. My biggest encouragement and supporters are the people closest to me. This has helped me to appreciate how others too can reach their potential with sufficient encouragement and support.

The things I learned in my 'schooling' have fundamentally shaped me to this day. It is a continual reminder that real change can come from unlikely places.

We need to make sense of our stories

Many people have heard our story and told us how it helped them. So, without turning the story into a formula, here are some themes you might find helpful in your own challenges of relating and leading.

Cherish the people you lead

Nothing creates strength and heart like love. The more we live and lead by grace, the more we give up control. Will you cherish the person enough to give up wrongful control?

Face the future

We need to name truly and strongly what is really happening. Our own expectations and preferences are not always a good guide to a better future. So what really matters most?

Face your own need to change

We cannot extend grace from fear or self-justification. At some level we cannot know what to do or even if we are up to the challenge. Can you walk into the darkness of not knowing?

Identify the 'school'

We need to name any 'sensible-dead-wrong-strategies' getting in the way, like my unhelpful emphasis on 'school'. What will it take to walk away from a strategy that isn't working?

Find the 'bike'

This was Luke's sweet spot. We need to value what others value no matter how insignificant it seems. The 'bike' may not be obvious. The only way to find it

is to know the person's story. Where do you see the light in their eyes?

Enter their world

We need to become part of their stories. It was difficult to stop rationalising my own preferences as what was best for Luke. I might have been right, but I made things worse. What's your greatest fear about entering the other's world?

Translate

Bridging two worlds is the art of making new meaning possible. We search for links and take tentative steps toward conversation. What rich life themes could your friend access through her or his own sweet spot?

Ask, don't tell

Second-hand learning is not learning. As a parent, or leader, it's hard to step down from feeling we know better (even if we do). What matters is what the other knows. How can you come alongside the other in her or his learning?

Share the journey

When we stand with others the relationship and challenge becomes our story too. We can't journey as intimately when it's not family or close friends. Yet nothing changes at arm's length. Are you open to *you* being the one who changes?

LOOK FOR THE PATTERNS AND THE ARTS

As you read Luke's and my story, and the reflections above, perhaps you recalled some of the patterns and arts we have discussed. Here are a few links I have made.

Wisdom — the challenge of reading the patterns of our own lives

I searched for answers when what I truly needed was wisdom. I failed to see the patterns of my own fear and behaviour. More than anything, I learned to be attentive to Luke and his world and to be present with him — even when all I got was five minutes down, and ten minutes back!

Leadership — the challenge to choose relationship over power

Leadership is only rarely about authority and position. It's about drawing alongside others on their behalf. Sue and our girls Miriam and Hannah, and a handful of friends, helped me see what I couldn't or wouldn't. Sometimes when things went wrong, Luke's calmness made him a better guide than me.

Naming — the call to challenge the realities we build with words

Time and again I had to confront not only the language that held Luke back, but also my own self-defeating language. I was naming him and myself falsely and weakly. I learned to rename what it meant to me to be his dad. Luke named the world as against him; he came to name it in terms of choices and responsibilities. None of this happens easily or quickly, or in a straight line. It's hard to reach a strong, true naming without weak and false detours.

Conversation — learning to shut up and listen

Despite my facilitation experience, there were arts of conversation I sorely lacked. I had to learn that five minutes could be enough. And if you really want to talk, try walking or making something together; not talking eyeball to eyeball.

Influence — shifting from self-protection to genuine commitment

I threw myself at influencing Luke and his world at school. I was clueless. The commitment I made was self-protective. No new meaning could come from there. It took a long time to truly believe in him. Only then did we start to find each other. Only then could I influence. It's fascinating now to watch how Luke influences others.

Character — learning to follow love into the void

I tried to run away from the void before me. I named the darkness as being about Luke and his future. But the deeper darkness was in my own heart. Perhaps I was a failure as a father and a man. Luke had his own darkness about where his life was heading, and the huge setbacks he faced as a racer. I smile at something he once said: 'Dad, I know all this (setbacks, crashes, disappointments, and so on) is character building, but frankly I'm a bit over it'.

Story — waiting for my story and his story to become our story

Something deep shifted for both of us the night Luke asked me what the journey had been like for me. The only way I could answer was to relive some of the moments by telling the stories. And as I said what I remembered, and he said what he remembered, we began to tell a story that was ours. That remains hugely special to us, as do my stories with my girls.

Brilliance — it rarely looks like what we expected or wanted

If to lead is to bless, then few things bless as deeply as being helped to see and name our brilliance. But what if you can't see the brilliance any more than they can? Then comes the long, hard work of paying attention not to our expectations but to the other's story. Even after we acknowledged Luke's sweet spot was his bike, it was hugely challenging to honour what he loved, to believe in him, and to let him fail and shine.

Promise — the impact of a few apt words

What does it mean to speak with promise? Think of Jim telling me to stop talking, and his encouragement that five minutes was enough. Think of Paul telling Luke he was an asshole! Think of Luke asking me about my story. One of my fondest memories in this whole story is not about Luke but my elder daughter Miriam. I worried a lot about spending more time with Luke than the girls. Mim said to me one day, 'Dad, we're worried about him too. You spend time with him. It'll be our turn later'. That is promise.

Grace — the cornerstone of leading wisely

Jim once told me that liking Luke wasn't the point; the point was to love him. Love doesn't depend on performance. Love comes from grace: a deep regard of the other person as my equal and worthy of honour and kindness. I had to go back to this again and again. I think the grace Luke showed me was remarkable.

Reflection

- Where have you created room for others to shine?
- Who would you love to help find her or his brilliance?
- Where do you need to change to better help others to change?
- What quiet acts of grace could open new space in the relationship?

Q. # What if I can't take time out like you did?

A. Being self-employed for most of that time allowed me to adjust my work to be with Luke. But your relationship is more important than your situation. When I share our story, I'm usually approached by people to talk about what's happening for them and their kids. I always say the same things: examine your own expectations, look for the bike, and come alongside your child. Sometimes I hear back from people. It seems no matter how hard it remains, they say something has shifted for the better. Like with me, the biggest shift is usually in them. And it happens whether they are self-employed or in a regular job.

No-one can plan, manage or deliver transformation. It is a by-product of relating and leading with wisdom. What we can do is care, be present, be attentive, and engage.

CHAPTER 13

Leading Many

We embody the story and sustain the conversation

People follow a leader before a vision

'Organisation' is such an inadequate word. You may have sensed my struggle with it throughout this book. Whatever term we use — organisation, team, community, group, 'those we lead' — we are talking about more than random individuals grouped together.

Purpose is the context of leadership: a group has a purpose and asks or expects someone to lead. Sometimes that purpose is clear. Sometimes it is blurry. The group may struggle to name it truly and strongly. Whether they know it or not, a group looks for a leader who will articulate a purpose that resonates with their own stories and that is worthy of giving their best.

No-one commits to a vision or mission statement. Sometimes these are very helpful. Too often they are not. Either way, people commit to a purpose they count as worthy held out by a leader they count as worthy.

People will commit to a noble purpose held out by a leader with integrity. Ultimately, leadership is about creating new realities through our words and our lives.

So leadership is deep. At their best, leaders create spaces where people learn to deepen their understanding of reality and participate in the unfolding of the world within them and around them.

My friend Tony Golsby-Smith says that 'ultimately leadership is about creating new realities'. I agree. Every leader must stand before her or his group — small or large, intimate or public — hold out a story with hope for their future, and bring to life the conversations where they can design for it.

Here, from another time and place, is the story of such a leader …

THE SURPRISING UNTOLD
STORY OF PAUL

Time to check our baggage. On my reading, Paul did not found a religion or moral system. He was the architect of profound change.

The shape of Western thought and society derives largely from the contradictions between, and synthesis of, its two founding traditions — the classical world of the Greeks and Romans, and the peculiar worldview that grew in Jewish soil.

As Westerners, or as those living in a world heavily influenced by Western ideas and traditions, we have inherited their richly contradictory notions and practices. In this creative tension we seek an understanding and practice of wise leadership for our own times.

This is the surprising story of Saul of Tarsus.[1]

From Saul to Paul

Saul was a Jewish man and a citizen of the Roman city of Tarsus, an important trading city in the vicinity of far south-eastern Turkey today. Palestine in the first century had been deeply Hellenised (influenced by Greek culture) for over a century and many Jewish people living throughout the Roman Empire held positions of high rank.[2]

Saul was likely trained in both Jewish and Roman law. His Roman citizenship was an honour passed through his family, perhaps from forebears who had merited high standing through their civic benefactions. Although immersed in Hellenism, Saul had not forgotten his Jewish roots. He was likely a member of a Jerusalem-based party some of whose members supported terrorism against the Roman forces occupying Palestine.

Saul's extremely rare dual education enabled him to operate in two very different worlds: as a fierce champion of Jewish nationalism, and an urbane Hellenised professional. After his experience on the Damascus Road, and now known by his assumed or perhaps second Roman name, Paul was to become the foremost advocate of a radical third option.

Many things Paul said have passed into our speech; like 'all things to all people' and 'speak the truth in love'. All Paul. Think how contemporary this advice sounds: Don't conform to the prevailing paradigms, but be transformed by a renewed mindset. This is the mindset of an innovator and an improviser.[3]

Paul is unprecedented in classical and Hellenistic literature and history as a radical advocate and leader of change. I think his contribution and 'methods' offer significant insights into the tensions we face today as leaders, and shed unusual light on what we call innovation and engagement.

From rationalism to story

We noted in *Chapter 1: Wisdom* how the earliest Greek philosophers were preoccupied with the problem of the One and the Many. We saw too how Plato's answer set the course for Western thought. Plato left us the legacy of thinking about life as though ordinary experience was separate from some other and purer reality. We call it dualism — a dual world. The world we apprehend through reason is perfect; the world we experience is imperfect.[4]

Plato's perfect reality in the Forms had to be unchanging, balanced, ordered, uniform, symmetrical, harmonious, rational, smooth, and serene. Unsurprisingly, these were also the virtues of a superior man. By contrast, everyday reality was imperfect, changing, chaotic, emotional, even evil. Again unsurprisingly, this is how the superior man regarded the rest.

Paul knew this intellectual and social legacy. Like other free-born boys, he learned his Greek by copying the texts of Homer and other literary greats. But Paul had also been schooled in his countrymen's traditions, the story-filled world of the Hebrew writings. Despite a long history of Judaism absorbing the intellectual and cultural patterns of Hellenism, the two mindsets were very different.

Paul was convinced that the success of his work hung on his hearers embracing a fundamentally new mindset, equally free from Greek dualism and rationalism and from Jewish nationalism. He knew they must sustain this mindset through a new kind of conversation that was grounded in a startling story. Here they found a basis for a new identity and purpose.

When Stoic and Epicurean philosophers in Athens heard Paul speaking in the marketplace, they presumed he was peddling some new philosophy, theology, or religion. And there was enough parallel to make the connection likely. He was clearly conversant with the main themes of Greco-Roman philosophy and quoted their own sources confidently. But the more he talked, the more the parallels dissipated.[5]

Paul began from an entirely different mindset. Gone was the old dualism between gods and men; Paul described a creation that was good. Gone were the abstract attributes of deity; Paul told a scandalous story in which God showed love (never a virtue for a Greek or Roman god or man) without respect for rank, gender, or ethnicity.

Steeped in the Jewish writings and tradition, Paul brought all questions back to a single, all-encompassing story and its recent surprising climax. Where Paul parted from Judaism, it was not to defer to the abstraction of the Greco-Roman tradition, nor to the universal claims on loyalty by the Roman Emperor. Paul grounded life in the story of a Jewish building worker from the back-country town of Nazareth.

Paul never developed any abstract conceptual system in the style of the

THE SURPRISING UNTOLD STORY OF PAUL

classical philosophers and theologians. Story was the shape of the new mindset. And a radical story gave birth to a radical mindset.

In effect, Paul told his fellow Jews that they had the right story — in the ancient covenant with Abraham — but had missed its recent dénouement.[6] While to the Romans, he in effect said they had the wrong story entirely — in the claims of *pax Romana* brought by Augustus.[7]

The great clash was not over ideas but over the implications of those ideas for society. To see this we must understand how Greco-Roman society worked.

From pyramid to community

Imagine a social network like a modern pyramid scheme. Think of a vast web of patron-client relationships carrying formal obligations and conventions. One worked to create obligations to oneself and called upon the conventions of enmity when slighted.

People in the top layers of the pyramid never worked a day in their lives. Work with one's hands was unseemly, including what we would call administration or management.

Those above took a share of what was achieved below. Strange as it may seem to us, money also flowed down as well as up the pyramid. So what did patrons stand to gain? Support. Prestige. Influence.

The harmony and well-being of the *polis* (the city or state) depended on public works, the availability of dole in times of famine, and on festivals and games. Relatively few of these works or events were financed by public monies. The money came from benefactors — the men at the top, and those keen to impress.

Friendship meant reciprocity. There were no free lunches in Athens or Rome. Layer upon layer of free-born men and not a few entrepreneurial freedmen, spent the bulk of their days in lobbying and intrigue, subterfuge and toadying. Litigation was rampant.

Ancient demarcations of rank defined social life. 'Free', 'freed' or 'slave' stamped a person for life. For example, a papyrus from Oxyrhyncus in Egypt provides the documentary evidence of sustaining rank for six generations on his father's side and eight on his mother's to show that a boy is eligible to enter a prestigious gymnasium.[8]

Household slaves gave themselves ranks with special prominence for the literate. You can see this in the occupational references on their tombstones and in the wills of unusually benevolent masters. As a freedman, you might rise to great prominence but there was always someone of inherited rank ready to rub your lowly origins in your face.

In the ancient worlds of Greece and Rome, leadership meant rank. Position, not role. Leadership was a right and responsibility attached to a man (overwhelmingly a man) by birth, marriage, or adoption. Leadership did not depend on competence, gift, intellect, or experience.

The purpose of leadership was to maintain the order of a highly stratified society. Good order depended on people staying in the places allotted to them by birth, by Fate, by the gods or by personal accomplishment.[9]

Status always complicated rank. One's rank was largely fixed by birth with some possibility of change through marriage or adoption. (We read of great men with sons many years their senior.) The marks of status are familiar to us: education, wealth, fame, achievements, friendships, personal appearance, memberships, lifestyle and, in Paul's day, oratory. A man might live many steps above or below his rank according to how well he fared in business and in securing the right friends.

Talent, piety, virtue, and citizenship could each offer a platform for new status. Divorce, marriage and adoption might offer a rare opportunity to lift one's rank. It was in everyone's interest to keep the system going. The costly business of benefactions brought status to those of means. Plutarch, a contemporary of Paul, wryly observed: 'Most people think that to be deprived of the chance to display their wealth is to be deprived of wealth itself'.[10]

Ever heard the line, 'Know thyself'? Whatever inner reflection it was meant to trigger, it first of all reinforced social convention. We know of over 250 such sayings. Four maxims are found far more frequently than any others. The original 3x5 motivational pack, the first fridge magnets, were:

Know yourself = know your place.

Nothing to excess = stick to what is expected.

Cost to every commitment = assess the risk to your honour.

Pick your time = seize the moment to improve your position.

Intellectuals, inscriptions, and pithy sayings only projected what everybody knew. This was the bottom line: know and maintain your rank. Compassion and humility will only hinder ambition. Keep compassion for those who deserve it. And don't exceed what's socially expected, or there'll be a price to pay. So stay in your place while you await your chance to move up.

From status to subversion
Enter Paul. What would an educated and urbane Greek man or woman make of a similarly educated and urbane Jewish man publicly declaiming or writing the following: 'there is neither Jew nor Greek, slave nor free, male nor female, for you are all one'? Or 'do nothing out of selfish ambition or vain conceit, but in humility consider others better than yourselves'? Or 'think not of yourself more highly than you ought but with sober judgement', 'associate with people of low position', and 'give greater honour to those without honour'?![11]

Here are perhaps the ultimate lines for (not) endearing oneself and one's message to a first-century patron: 'not many of you were wise, brothers. But God chose the foolish things of this world to shame the wise ... I did not come to you with superior wisdom or

THE SURPRISING UNTOLD STORY OF PAUL

eloquence … We messengers are the scum of the earth!'[12]

Today we prize adaptability. In Paul's world it was shameful. Grace, he said, drove him to adapt to those he sought to serve: 'I have become all things to all men'. To most, that meant he was unstable and inconstant.

Paul set himself on a collision course with Greco-Roman social expectation and convention. And for good reason. The social implications of his story were profound.

First, the story was anchored in a man who, in Paul's words, 'emptied himself, made himself nothing, and subjected himself to death',[13] even execution by the Romans. If Paul wanted to cast the central figure of his message as eminently embarrassing and dismissible, he couldn't have done a better job of it.

Second, Paul claimed that on the basis of this inexplicable act of self-sacrifice, grace was now available impartially to all. It was inconceivable to Greeks or Romans that a deity would subvert the social system. Yet this was Paul's claim and he insisted on modelling it in his own life.[14]

The way Paul worked
So did Paul set out to transform Greco-Roman society? I think we have to take an each-way bet on that one.

No, in that he was pragmatic about living in society. Patrons, he said, should not stop benefactions, but do so with generosity freed from the need for personal honour or reciprocity. Clients

should busy themselves with meaningful activity rather than endless lobbying for patrons (what else do you do all day if you don't have to work?).

But yes, in that he sponsored a quiet revolution from within. His groups formed communities around the simple convention of gathering for dinner. Inside this gathering, Paul expected the group to maintain a high standard of propriety, but to disregard social distinctions, even to honour the less honourable.

We should not intellectualise what Paul was advising. It involved inverting the normal conventions of honour. Paul expected his associates to break with the convention of allocating food and seating according to rank. He expected wives, children, even slaves, to be allowed, no, invited, to recline at meal with those of rank and to participate fully in the conversation.

This was entirely scandalous. He might as well have advised them to sit around in their underwear (not a few neighbours probably had their suspicions about that too, what with all this new talk about love)!

This realignment of social behaviour was critical. Paul was building something entirely new and had set himself an ambitious program of nurturing co-workers for the task. He had to neutralise the grip of every social convention that tied their hearts and minds to the old world. His strategy included undermining virtually every assured premise and outcome of the social system. But he did so by showing them what the new order looked like in his own relationships and lifestyle.

Paul was no less radical on leadership. He left no room for personal power or office. In a world where leadership was rank, and only rank, Paul was anti-leadership.

This is difficult for us to grasp. Paul exerted profound influence. He founded communities. He taught and modelled a reordering of social relations that would eventually reshape the social order. We are accustomed to calling all of this leadership.

Yet Paul avoided the vocabulary of leadership. Instead, he described himself with simple, demeaning metaphors like slave, servant, or gardener. He reframed friendship away from personal gain. In time, the new language (servant) would come to delineate rank (minister). But not for Paul.[15]

Paul showed no conscious dependence on any one school of thought. Rather, as an independent thinker, he simply built on whatever was to hand. As Edwin Judge has remarked, Paul was creatively 'exploiting the material rather than subjecting (him)self to it'.[16]

Paul's conversations were peppered with the phrases and thought of Hellenistic education and of popular philosophy and morality. Yet though he largely accepted the civil order of life in the cities, he promoted a distinctive set of social relations in his groups. He was in effect ambivalent or pragmatic about rank, but savage on status. No simple formula can account for how he worked this out.

Paul engaged with the world rather than retreating into an intellectual or religious ghetto. He was a thoroughly urban man. He readily employed his audiences' vocabulary, literary techniques, intellectual models, social conventions, and even clichés. He seems to have improvised from whatever was to hand in order to engage the needs and world views of his audiences. Today we take such adaptability for granted, but there was little precedent for Paul.

Paul was conscious of the conventions of friendship. Indeed, he deliberately exploited the theme, reframing it in the light of his story. When Paul described himself as a debtor to those with whom he had no prior relationship, he reversed the normal expectations of Greco-Roman friendship.

He recast the common honorific and moral term *philotimia* (love of honour, ambition) to advertise his choice, *not* to compete with others. He used the building as a metaphor for social relations in a remarkable innovation that enabled him to dismantle the traditional indicators and expectations of status.[17]

Nor was he interested in uniformity of behaviour in others. His own life embodied the dynamics that he sought to open up within his groups. His message was provocative, not prohibitive. It avoided the pettiness of philosophical and legal controversies. And in a remarkable move it did not embrace the classical virtues.[18]

Unlike the practices of later Christian leaders and groups, Paul did not prescribe any pattern for the gathering.

THE SURPRISING UNTOLD STORY OF PAUL

His advice left room for spontaneity and diversity.[19] His message offered no formula to settle in advance which way to respond to contemporary intellectual and social issues.

Paul used the common political metaphor of the body to drive home the reversal of status. The image was well-known and commonly used to reinforce the greater necessity and worth of the head over the lesser parts. Once again, Paul reframed convention. The greater part could not say to the least, 'I don't need you'. Nor vice versa. Each part, each member, had its role to play.[20] If you will pardon the pun, Paul turned the metaphor of the body on its head.

In one of the most remarkable innovations in the history of thought, Paul then added the metaphor of gifting to this inverted image of the body. Every person, Paul claimed, had talent and ability. Each should see this as a gift, a trust on behalf of others.

Together the metaphors of body and gifting as Paul envisaged them were to revolutionise the Western understanding of humanity and society.[21]

New understanding for new circumstances emerged within the communities through conversation. Indeed, the power of the story was realised in its ability to inform and reorient the changing circumstances of social life.

Paul, his colleagues and their communities were working out the meaning of their message as they went. Yet even as his thought matured,

Paul continued to show no interest in formulating final statements in the sense of the debates and creeds that subsequent generations would base on his writings. Paul remained focused on specific people and contexts. New contexts continued to stimulate fresh readings of the story.

What Paul offered was neither abstract nor idealised. He gave voice to a relationship. He was constantly reflecting and learning, yet he had no time for abstraction. He was gripped by the possibilities of the present moment, and of the next. He gives the impression of working out his thought on the run, with both remarkable clarity and surprisingly little formula.

The rhythm of Paul's choices — alternately conforming and innovating — was far from easy to pick up. This metaphor of rhythm is deliberate. Paul was more akin to a jazz musician improvising than to a lawyer, philosopher or theologian assembling a tight argument or system of thought.

I believe Paul creatively adapted his message and methods to match new challenges raised by new circumstances. His thinking and practice were contextual — shaped by and for each new context. Strong patterns and defining experiences linked all that he said and did. This coherence lay in his story and its central figure.

Living with Paul's legacies

Paul's life and work centred on the story of Jesus' resurrection. Whether or not we subscribe to that story as Paul did, we nonetheless live with his legacy.[22]

Paul's exposition of this extraordinary story, and his flimsy, messy, risky social experiment based upon that story, somehow changed the face of the Western world.

If it is hard for us to grasp Paul's significance, it is because we have read him for almost two thousand years through the lens of religion. But that is an anachronism.

Contemporary observers did not know how to characterise the groups known only as followers of 'The Way'. [23] Believing they were not religious, their contemporaries eventually named them christianoi.[24] The –ianoi is akin to our '–ism'. It signalled a political group, and the early groups did not want the tag.[25] Their groups used ekklesia, the common word for a meeting. If it had any connotation, it was political not religious. So since the groups had no marks of religion—no temple, sacrifices, idols, or priests (all of that came later)— some contemporary observers regarded them as atheists.[26]

Given all we have seen it is easy to imagine that Paul's story and groups would have been crushed by the weight of Roman power, Greek social convention, and Jewish nationalism. Certainly many who confessed 'Jesus Christ is Lord' were executed under imperial decree. But three hundred years later, one had to make that confession to be the emperor. This shift reshaped the political and cultural canvas.[27]

This success came at a huge cost. Paul's original vision was sustained, plagiarised, corrupted, and creatively adapted. There is no simple picture to what happened in the fusion of church and empire in the centuries that followed.

Every institution of social care and reform as we know them in the Western world—political systems, jurisprudence, public health, and education—indeed, even the very idea of social reform— depends to a very large degree on Paul's legacy.

Today most Westerners prefer some form of democracy for the ordering of society. That is the legacy of classical Athens. But most would add that democracy requires the idea of equality. Equality is the legacy of Paul; an idea, Alasdair MacIntyre rightly notes, about which Aristotle most certainly 'would have been horrified'.[28] As my old professor used to say, 'Western thought is the product of a contradiction—that's what makes it so fascinating'.

We need to make sense of our stories

No formula can capture the brilliance and subtlety of Paul's innovations and improvisations. But here are eight facets of what I think Paul was doing. For each I give first a précis of what I think it meant for Paul in his context, then a few thoughts on translating to our own contexts:

1. Shape and reshape the story

Paul's letters show him working out the story and translating it as he went along. The story stayed strong and retained its internal coherence in part because of his confidence in telling and retelling it in the marketplace of ideas and events. Every new context brought some measure of reframing.

Vision is a story. Tell it more than present it. Tell it often and differently. Tell it to enrich it. Tell it to know it.

2. Subvert unhelpful abstractions

Paul adopted contemporary language and conventions on many occasions. But he refused the story to be recast in terms of nationalism, religion, philosophy, theology, or morality. He undercut these dominant schemas even as he interacted boldly with their champions. He kept the story grounded in relationships and concrete contexts.

Push for the stories beneath the problems and opportunities. Story animates strategy. Use story to bring reality to planning and change initiatives.

3. Maintain the core conversations

Paul's groups gathered at dinner parties. They were conversations. At the heart of each group was a commitment to sustain the central conversation. They met to remind themselves of the central story and to think through its implications for their own lives. Paul's letters refreshed the conversation.

There is a central conversation to every enterprise. Name it. Honour it. Promote it. Place it at the heart of strategy, culture and practice.

4. Craft new meaning

No two of Paul's letters told the story the same way. Each retelling reflected the changing relational, social, intellectual, and political circumstances of his groups. Their conversations drew their own stories into the central story. There were massive implications to work through. Paul laboured to equip them to take up the conversations and to assure them of his confidence that they were gifted to do so.

Story must be given room to evolve and adapt. Make the conversations real. Leave room for people to chase the questions that matter most. Show people you are confident in their capacity to craft new meaning.

5. Embody the story

Paul knew that grace and freedom, equality, and gifting would stay mere subjects of discussion unless they were seen. For Paul, grace meant stepping down in the world. It meant embodying the paradoxical dynamics of weakness in strength, wisdom in foolishness. He would stay at the 'Hilton' on one occasion and sweat it out at the wrong end of town on another. He accepted rank pragmatically but detached his identity from marks of rank and status.

The old adage 'Walk the talk' is crucial, but doesn't say enough. It's not just about consistency and integrity. A leader's life needs to model the heart and wisdom of the story.

6. Subvert status with grace

He mixed freely with people of all backgrounds. He broke convention and taboo to honour those deemed dishonourable. He played down his education and intellectual capacity. He could also rise to the full height of his powers of argument and persuasion to oppose those who defrauded the poor. He didn't advise the wholesale emancipation of slaves since they had no legal identity or protection. Instead he modelled the master/slave relationship as brother/brother.

Every social system has conventions that foolishly and often unjustly discriminate. Find one that you can dismantle. Show yourself to be a fair leader who regards all with equal dignity and value. Make this a little hinge to turn a big door.

7. Aim at congruence not copied

Paul made no attempts to standardise the communities he founded (another irony of subsequent history). His letters show wide diversity in vocabulary, perspective and practice wrapped around the central non-negotiable story.

He expected they would translate with a high degree of local nuance.

Conformity kills community and brilliance. Diversity around a shared story fosters richness. No two groups will ever be identical. Give up trying to make them so. Organisations will never have one culture and don't need to. Foster a robust dynamic and dialogue that ensures diversity of expression around an honouring of the central story and identity.

8. Aim at maturity

Paul presumed and promoted maturity. This was no easy task as the groups struggled to come to grips with an alien story and worldview which cut across ideals and conventions. It required a new kind of rigour and growth grounded in speaking the truth in love.

Conformity, best practice, and ideals are not the marks of maturity. Aim instead for strength of character. Foster and model the commitment and ability to speak truthfully and respectfully. Promote the freedom to acknowledge and draw from one another's brilliance without embarrassment. This is a gutsy grace.

LOOK FOR THE PATTERNS AND THE ARTS

As you read Paul's story and the reflections above, perhaps you recalled some of the patterns and arts we have discussed. Here are a few links I have made.

Wisdom — reading the 'schemas' of the age

Some philosophers critiqued convention but Paul broke new ground. Drawing on equality and gifting, Paul judged rationalism, dualism, nationalism, and imperialism as diminishing human dignity and relationship. The need remains in our own context to inquire into the human impact of organisational faith in certainty, statistics, systems, structures, and processes.

Leadership — learning to lead from relationship, not position

Paul carried authority but reframed it in terms of a life in imitation of the story. He never used the language of leadership for himself. He used the shameful metaphors of gardener, builder, steward, and slave. He even reframed the positional metaphor of father as carer. Pragmatic on rank, harsh on status, his own practice was more egalitarian. Leaders who nurture innovation and engagement always flatten hierarchy by what they do.

Naming — the power of reframing language for new identity

Paul named his friends 'in Christ'. To our ears this sounds religious or moral. To Paul, the story gave a sense of identity that stood quietly against status and the power of Rome. An aristocrat and slave could stand side by side. The name was universal; but its meaning had to be embraced uniquely. This is powerfully relevant to modern contexts. People need to name themselves within a larger story and hear the value of their distinctive contribution.

Conversation — the challenge to nurture congruent conversations

Paul's groups met for dinner and conversation. His letters suggest their conversations ranged across marriage to work to politics and more. Paul *didn't* standardise these groups. He equipped them to translate what the story meant in their language, contexts, and relationships. He wanted congruence, not conformity. This is a huge challenge today: not to insist on identical conversations but to nurture diverse, congruent conversations that enrich the larger vision.

Influence — the impact of a life that models the story

Paul's group struggled between embracing his radical implications and clinging to the familiar. Every letter begins with warm greetings and thanksgivings. A big shift had to happen before a wealthy man would show slaves compassion. Paul staked his calls for reform on his story and on the integrity of his own life and relationships. He asked no-one to do more than he did. Nothing has changed. No amount of slides and emails can match an unhurried coffee.

Character — the courage to stand against demeaning conventions

The Corinthians (and others) insisted Paul play the leader under patronage: take the money, support politically, and parade his oratory to boost a patron's reputation. Paul refused and earned enmity. He was improvising a different model of social relations: equal, interdependent, and free from reciprocity. Leaders who choose to operate outside the privileges of position and the markers of certainty are likely to face incomprehension, gossip, and that bureaucratic favourite, stone-walling.

Story — the brilliance of improvising story-telling in each context

Paul had no standard way of telling the story. He creatively blended three sources: (1) Jewish texts; (2) Graeco-Roman themes; and (3) issues in the local context. He shaped this creative synthesis around a different dominant metaphor: law court, renewal, adoption, family, body, building, horticulture, slavery, education, clothing, warfare/peace, and more. At college we varied our telling of the vision through the lenses of heritage, culture, equality, excellence, change, groundedness, openness, and more.

Brilliance — naming our uniqueness as a gifting on behalf of others

Edwin Judge regards Paul's use of the body metaphor and idea of gifting as a major innovation in the history of ideas that triggered major changes in social expectations. In the first hundred years there's evidence of groups ignoring ethnicity, class, and gender. Convictions about the dignity and uniqueness of every person spawned initiatives in hospitality and education. The only change programs I've seen succeed have been built from employees' own craft (gifting) and community (body). Honour people and they change.

Promise — the fine line of speaking the truth with love

Paul opens every letter with affirmation, affection, and praise; he also critiques and rebukes. He expects change in relationships without a new moral code. He improvises between convention and radicalism. It's shockingly unstable. No group was more chaotic than at Corinth. Yet he urges them to resolve their disagreements by love. I've seen this in highly effective executives. They speak plainly and boldly out of mutual respect. Their people hear conviction, integrity, and hope.

Grace — the challenge of stepping down in the world

As we saw in *Chapter 10: Grace* the revolutionaries' cries of 'liberté, égalité, fraternité' presumed and distorted grace with violence and injustice. Grace was not a classical virtue. Aristotle said a low-born man was incapable of virtue. Every time Paul let go a privilege, he inverted rank and discredited status. I've seen values statements made contemptible by leaders who cling to position. And I've seen loved leaders who let go privilege to make vision and values credible.

Reflection

- Where does the story of Paul encourage and challenge you as you seek to lead with wisdom?

Q. # What is the tension we still live?

A. From the classical world, we continue to see
leadership in terms of rank, mental toughness,
a certain dispassionate decisiveness, an eye
for preserving the status quo, and a degree of
matter-of-factness about using position to further
one's status. From Paul, we place high value on
humility and compassion, censure the worst of
elitism, expect leaders to curb their own ambition
on behalf of the greater good, and desire some
degree of non-conformity and improvisation.
I don't think we can or need to choose between
these visions. Nor find a balance. I think the key
is to hold them in tension and, perhaps, to let the
latter reframe the former.

CONCLUSION

I began *Lead with Wisdom* by saying that leadership is a lot like laying bricks and that wisdom is the mortar. The mud. I began my working life as a labourer and spent a lot of that time mixing mud. When the bricklayers let me, I laid bricks. There's a funny thing about a finished brick wall: it gives completely the wrong idea about how to lay bricks. A finished wall is trowelled clean. The mortar is flush with the bricks or pointed with that nice inward groove. Either way, it's neat. But laying bricks isn't neat. You can't measure out mortar; you throw it on and clean up later. With some practice you can move fast and not waste much mud. All the same, you still have to use an excess of mortar every time so you can tamp the bricks down and along the course. That's what gives the bond strength. That's what makes the wall strong. A skilled application of excess. It's a lot like leading. The strength is in the insubstantial stuff. You get skilled at it but still have to put down more than is necessary. Attention. Presence. Naming. Conversations. Grounded questions. Relationships. Character. Story-telling. Brilliance. Words of promise. And grace. You can't measure any of it. It has to be excessive. Some people talk about the glamour of leadership. All I know is that it takes mud to lead with wisdom.

'IT TAKES MUD
TO LEAD WITH
WISDOM'.

ACKNOWLEDGEMENTS

And now the happiest though least read page for an author to write. I want to thank a few people who took a punt on me, worked with me, helped shape my thinking, walked with me for some large chunk of life, and helped bring this book to birth. Happily many people fit several categories.

Tony and Anne Golsby-Smith took a punt on me in their fledgling business that is now Second Road. It has been a marvellous friendship of hearts and ideas. Along the way there have been bosses and clients who became friends: Carl Luttig, the late Terry Ogg, Gary Seabury, Mark Benham, Karl Mociak, Jim Varghese, Terry Kearney, Peter McNee, Paul Henderson, and Graham Burt.

Terry Kearney and Jim Varghese warrant a further mention for encouraging me to think, all evidence to the contrary, that I might have something to say on leadership. In the same spirit, many joined in the ideas and various ventures along the way, including David Jones, Jim Ireland, Tom Morris, Ann Austin, Lindley Edwards, Geoff Strong, Martin Tan, Brad Turnbull, Tony Weir, and Bessi Graham.

My sojourn in Aotearoa, New Zealand, was rich in itself but made all the more so by the friendship of Sir Robert 'Bob' Harvey, Matua John Komene, and Esther Sila'ila'i. A warm thank you also to the staff, students, and friends of Laidlaw College and Compass. My heart remains in Aotearoa along with two of my children.

A special mention belongs to Emeritus Professor Edwin Judge, retired professor and pioneer of ancient history at Macquarie University. Edwin graciously took me on as a doctoral student on an informal basis even though, as he kept reminding me, I was not 'a proper historian'. Edwin's writings, then friendship, showed me the possibility of a different dialogue between classical thought and times, and our own.

Principals Toni McKinnon, Mark Diamond, and Natalie Brookton trusted me with their schools. It was at Toni's school that I had the privilege of working with Michelle Spagnollo, the 'teacher who paints with children'.

Pierre Gurdjian and Laurent Ledoux invited me to the other side of the world and into the stimulating company of their friends and colleagues, first in Belgium, then France and Switzerland. Brussels is now my third home.

How do I say thanks to friends who have carried me, kicked me in the pants, and sat through way too many episodes of me thinking out loud? To my dear friends, young and old, of the Hawkesbury, Blue Mountains, Auckland, and Christchurch, there's a little bit of you in these pages (only the good bits).

When I took up the role of CEO at Second Road, Tony and Anne generously encouraged me to push on with the book. There I had the extraordinarily good fortune to meet Alex Modie. Alex exemplifies true design, where content provokes design, and design provokes content. Some ideas would never have materialised if it were not for Alex's design instincts, and certainly none would be conveyed as clearly. From the overall concept of the book, to her delightfully whimsical images (many of my clunky originals), Alex has made evocative what might otherwise have been plain. At Wiley, Lucy Raymond took a punt on the idea, and Sarah Crisp, Alice Berry, and Kristen Hammond saw it through to completion.

And to my family. Mum, you and Dad kept me alive and gave me dreams. JB, thanks for believing in me. You too Charis. George and Merle, thanks for taking a punt on me 34 years ago with Sue. Mim, Luke, and Han, you taught me far more than you will ever realise and now I thrill to watch you lead. Jo and Leon, thank you for joining our family and loving my kids. And finally, always, Sue. The bloody book is done! You proofed, edited, kept track of things, stimulated — and contributed — countless ideas on the many walks of our Balmoral extravagance. Simply: none of this would be, without you.

All the above should take some blame for this book. If not for the actual content, then certainly for encouraging me one way or other to persist with the ideas. May 'mud' be yours in abundance.

And finally, a Japanese proverb states, 'If a man has no tea in him, he is incapable of understanding truth and beauty'. The marvellous staff and atmosphere of the Bathers Pavilion and Burnt Orange cafés at Balmoral and Mosman kept me happily philosophical while writing this book.

ENDNOTES

Chapter 1: Wisdom

[1] Hugh Mackay, *Turning Point: Australians Choosing Their Future.* Sydney: Macmillan, 1999, page 106.
[2] Proverbs 4:7.
[3] Tao de Ching 33.
[4] Quoted in Fung Yu-Lan, *The Spirit of Chinese Philosophy.* London: Kegan Paul, 1947, page 20.
[5] Attributed to Democritus in Stobaeus, Anthology, III vii 74 (B216).
[6] Antigone 710.
[7] Euthydemus 282.
[8] Politics 1323.
[9] Bhagavad-Gita IV: 38.
[10] Miles Gloriosus, Act III.
[11] De Finibus, book I, 1:3.
[12] Satires XIII. 20.
[13] Meditations V: 9.
[14] The Art of Worldly Wisdom, #20, page 12.
[15] *The Rock,* Chorus 1.
[16] Proverbs 26:4 5.
[17] Works and Days II: 383–392.
[18] 'The Instruction for King Meri-ka-re', in J B Pritchard, ed., *Ancient Near Eastern Texts.* Princeton: Princeton University Press, 1969, page 417. An Egyptian text dating as early as 2300 BC. Most texts in Pritchard were written on stone and the surviving sources are often fragmented and broken. The renditions cited here presume the educated guesswork of the translators.
[19] Native American Ute Prayer. (n.d). From www.coyoteprime-runningcauseicantfly.blogspot.com.au. Accessed March 11, 2012 from http://coyoteprime-runningcauseicantfly.blogspot.com.au/2011/05/native-american-ute-prayer-earth-teach.html.
[20] 'The Instructions of Shuruppak', in Pritchard, *Ancient,* page 595. An Akkadian fragment possibly dating as far back as 2500 BC. Mesopotamia includes the area of modern Iraq.
[21] Analects, book xiv, 31.
[22] 'The Words of Ahiqar', in Pritchard, *Ancient,* page 429. A collection of Aramaic proverbs and precepts from around the sixth century BC.
[23] 'The Instruction of Amen-em-opet', in ibid., page 423. Egyptian wisdom text from period tenth to sixth century BC.
[24] 'The Words of Ahiqar', in ibid., page 429.
[25] Proverbs 12:18–19.
[26] Attributed to Democritus in Stobaeus, Anthology, II xv 33 (B53a). Possibly as early as c. 700 BC.
[27] Ibid., II xv 40 (B177).
[28] Analects, book xv, 8.
[29] Paraphrased from the sources cited in notes 2–28.
[30] Attributed to Empedocles in Simplicius, Physics, B17.1 2.
[31] Republic, 507B.
[32] Frederick Winslow Taylor, *Shop Management.* New York, Harper and Brothers, 1912, page 98.
[33] Edwin Judge, 'St. Paul as a Radical Critic of Society', *Interchange* 16 (1975), page 191.
[34] David Tracy, *Plurality and Ambiguity.* San Francisco: Harper & Row, 1987, page 9.
[35] See my talk from TEDxPlainpalais, Geneva, February 2013: http://www.youtube.com/watch?v=tElSLatc57I titled 'Grounded questions. Rich stories. Deep change'.
[36] Mencius, book VII, A.
[37] Commonly attributed to Paulo Coelho. Source unknown.
[38] Proverbs 2:2.
[39] Proverbs 5:1.
[40] Commonly attributed to Buddha. Source unknown.
[41] Meditations IV:10.
[42] Henry David Thoreau, *Walden.* 1854, page 16.
[43] Richard Rorty, *Contingency, Irony, Solidarity.* Cambridge: Cambridge University Press, 1989, page 52.
[44] Usely attributed to José Ortega y

Gasset. Source unknown.

[45] Thoreau, *Walden*, page 19.

[46] Analects, book xiii, 6.

[47] Discourses, book II:5.

[48] Discourses, book III:2.

[49] From the entry for April 21 in Leo Tolstoy, *A Calendar of Wisdom: Daily Thoughts to Nourish the Soul*, 1908.

Chapter 2: Leadership

[1] See David Crystal, ed. *As They Say In Zanzibar: Proverbial Wisdom From Around the World*. London: HarperCollins, 2006, page 196.

[2] Ibid.

[3] Ronald Heifetz, Alexander Grashow, and Martin Linsky, *The Practice of Adaptive Leadership: Tools and tactics for changing your organization and the world*. Cambridge: Harvard Business Press, 2009, page 24.

[4] Analects, book xiii, 6.

[5] Ronald Heifetz, *Leadership Without Easy Answers*. Cambridge: Belknap, 1994, page 193.

[6] Sue Ebury, *Weary: The Life of Sir Edward Dunlop*. Melbourne: Penguin, 1995, page 547.

[7] Philippa Tyndale, *Don't Look Back: The David Bussau Story: How an Abandoned Child Became a Champion of the Poor*. Sydney: Allen & Unwin, 2004, page 286.

[8] I learned the Reader to Author heuristic from Tony Golsby-Smith. See his ground-breaking research in 'Pursuing the Art of Strategic Conversations: An investigation of the role of the liberal arts of rhetoric and poetry in the business world', PhD thesis, University of Western Sydney, Sydney, 2001, page 126. See also his articles: 'Fourth Order Design: A Practical Perspective', *Design Issues*, 12:1 (1996), pages 5–25; and 'The Second Road of Thought: How design offers strategy a new toolkit', *Journal of Business Strategy*, 28:7 (2007), pages 22–29. On the Reader-

Author heuristic, see also John Shotter, *Conversational Realities: Constructing Life through Language*. London: Sage, 1993, pages 148–159. Shotter writes: 'a good manager should also be … a practical ethical author, conversational author, able to argue persuasively for a landscape of next possible actions' (page 157).

[9] Politics, book 3, chapter 9 (1280b).

[10] Ibid.

[11] See Tom Morris, *If Aristotle Ran General Motors: The New Soul of Business*. New York: Owl Books, 1997.

[12] Thomas Mann, *Essays on Three Decades*. New York: A A Knopf, 1947.

Chapter 3: Naming

[1] David and I have studied and worked together over many years. In fact, it is hard for me to tell now what ideas about naming are mine and what are David's. For his reflections on philosophy, design, and business, see his website: www.justknowledge.com.au.

[2] See http://conversationdesignbydj. wordpress.com/2013/07/15/respecting-the-habitats-of-conversational-cogntion-naming-is-different-to-labelling/.

[3] This section is based on H Rubin, 'The Power of Words', Interview with Fernando Flores, *Fast Company*, January 1999. All quotes are from that article.

[4] David Tracy, *Plurality and Ambiguity*. San Francisco: Harper & Row, 1987, page 25.

[5] Hans-Georg Gadamer, *Philosophical Hermeneutics*. Berkeley: University of California Press, 1976, page 65.

[6] 'The self-awareness of the individual is only a flickering in the closed circuits of historical life. That is why the prejudices of the individual, far more than his judgements, constitute the historical reality of his being'. Hans-Georg Gadamer, *Truth and Method*. New York: Continuum, 1975, page 276.

[7] Ludwig Wittgenstein, *The Blue Book*. Oxford: Basil Blackwell, 1958, page 26.

[8] Ludwig Wittgenstein, *Philosophical Investigations*. New York: Macmillan, 1958, I.7.

[9] Thomas Kuhn, *The Structure of Scientific Revolutions*. Chicago: University of Chicago Press, 1962, page 5.

[10] Paulo Freire, *Pedagogy of the Oppressed*. New York: Continuum, 2005, pages 89–90.

[11] Ibid.

[12] David Jones. See http://conversationdesignbydj.wordpress.com/2013/07/15/respecting-the-habitats-of-conversational-cogntion-naming-is-different-to-labelling/.

[13] Vickers, G, 'The Poverty of Problem Solving', *Journal of Applied Systems Analysis,* 8 (1981), pages 15-21.

[14] Arthur Koestler, *Roots of Coincidence*. New York, Random House, 1972, page 43. Koestler was offering a paraphrase of Part II Act V from *Faust* by Johann Wolfgang von Goethe.

[15] John 1:13–15.

[16] Wittgenstein, *Investigations,* page 6.

[17] Ursula LeGuin, *The Earthsea Trilogy.* London: Penguin, 1979, page 19.

[18] Ibid., page 23.

[19] Ibid., page 25.

[20] Ibid., page 48.

[21] Ibid., page 50.

[22] Ibid., page 152.

[23] Ludwig Wittgenstein, *Culture and Value*. Oxford, Blackwell, 1980, 39e.

[24] Ibid., 56e.

[25] Ibid., 76e.

[26] Freire, *Pedagogy,* page 88.

[27] These thoughts first took written form in an unpublished paper I wrote with David Jones, 'Naming', August 1994. David and I have collaborated on the idea of Naming over many years.

Chapter 4: Conversation

[1] The theme of conversation has long been of interest philosophically and professionally. I have been privileged to pursue these questions in dialogue with friends and colleagues including David Jones, Tony Golsby-Smith, Tony Weir, Jim Ireland, and Anne Deane. Tony developed one aspect of this work in his thesis, 'Pursuing the Art of Strategic Conversations: An investigation of the role of the liberal arts of rhetoric and poetry in the business world', PhD thesis, University of Western Sydney, 2001.

[2] Thomas Lewis, Fari Amini, and Richard Lannon, *A General Theory of Love*. New York: Vintage Books, 2001.

[3] The heuristic of Two Roads based on Aristotle was first developed by Tony Golsby-Smith, 'Strategic Conversations', pages 178–209. This section is based on a blog piece I wrote while CEO of Tony's firm Second Road. See www.secondroad.com.au.

[4] Posterior Analytics, 71b.

[5] See the wonderful account of a mechanic's work as ways of knowing in Matthew Crawford, *Shop Class as Soulcraft: An Inquiry into the Value of Work*. New York: Penguin, 2009.

[6] Hans-Georg Gadamer, *Truth and Method*. New York: Continuum, 1975, page 345.

[7] David Tracy, *Plurality and Ambiguity*. San Francisco: Harper & Row, 1987, page 18.

[8] My comments on how conversation functions follow in part the work of Terry Winograd and Fernando Flores, *Understanding Computers and Cognition: A New Foundation for Design*. Norwood: Abtex, 1986. Like them, I am influenced here by the work of Gadamer in particular.

[9] See the works by Plato known as the Phaedrus, Theatetus, Protagoras and Meno. Plato's dialogues are our primary source for Socrates. It is an open question as where we are reading Socrates, who never wrote, or Plato.

[10] See http://www.youtube.com/watch?v=tEISLatc57I.

[11] The saying possibly derives from

philanthropist W Clement Stone (1902–2002). See also, Lao Tse: 'Difficult things in the world must needs have their beginnings in the easy; big things in the world must needs have their beginnings in the small'. Tao Te Ching, book 2, lxiii (149a).

[12] Or: 'The fox knows many things, the hedgehog just one, but a decisive one'. From Archilochus, fragment 201 in M L West, ed., *Iambi et Eligi Graeci*. Vol I. Oxford: Oxford University Press, 1971. The fragment probably stems from the pseudo-Homeric Margites. Cited in Isaiah Berlin, *The Hedgehog and the Fox*. Chicago: Elephant Paperbacks, 1978.

[13] Jim Collins, *Good to Great: Why Some Companies Make the Leap ... And Others Don't*. New York: Harper Business, 2001, pages 90–117.

[14] The AcdB® model is a proprietary tool of the strategy and design firm Second Road mentioned earlier in this chapter. Again it builds on the integration of rhetorical theory with design and strategy pioneered by Tony Golsby-Smith, 'Strategic Conversations', and his extensive experience facilitating strategic conversations at the most senior levels of corporations and governments.

[15] Tracy, *Plurality*, page 13.

Chapter 5: Influence

[1] John Maxwell, *The 21 Irrefutable Laws of Leadership*. Nashville: Nelson, 1998, pages 11–20.

[2] The discussion here follows the 1993 movie *Gettysburg* written and directed by Ronald Maxwell. The movie is in turn based on Michael Shaara, *Killer Angels*. New York: Ballantine Books, 1974.

[3] See for example John Pullen, *Joshua Chamberlain: A Hero's Life and Legacy*. Mechanicsburg: Stackpole, 1999.

[4] On Western rhetorical tradition, see Thomas M Conley, *Rhetoric in the European Tradition*. Chicago: University of Chicago Press, 1990. On ancient Near Eastern and Egyptian rhetorical traditions, see Carol S Lipson and Roberta A Binkley, eds. *Rhetoric Before and Beyond the Greeks*. Albany: State University of New York Press, 2004. On ancient Chinese rhetorical traditions, see Xing Lu, *Rhetoric in Ancient China, Fifth to Third Century B C E: A Comparison with Classical Greek Rhetoric*. Columbia: University of South Carolina Press, 1998. On Maori whaikorero or oratory, see Poia Rewi, *Whaikorero: The World of Maori Oratory*. Auckland: University of Auckland Press, 2010. For a broad study of non-Western rhetorical traditions, see George A Kennedy, *Comparative Rhetoric: An Historical and Cross-Cultural Introduction*. Oxford: Oxford University Press, 1998.

[5] See Gorgias, Helen, 8. Gorgias was a renowned intellectual and orator in Athens in fifth century BC, a contemporary of Socrates, and the subject of Plato's dialogue Gorgias.

[6] Others, like Isocrates, criticised the sophists but shared their pragmatism: '(we cannot) attain exact knowledge ... (but) those are wise who are able by opinion to hit upon what is for the most part the best course of action'. Isocrates, Antidosis, 271.

[7] 'When the rhetorician is more persuasive than the physician (i.e. philosopher), the ignorant is more persuasive with the ignorant than he who has knowledge'. Plato, Gorgias, 459.

[8] Gorgias, 465a.

[9] Rhetoric, 1.2.1.

[10] From the Greek verb *heurisko* meaning to find or discover.

[11] Aristotle offered three key heuristics for rhetoric. First, logos, pathos, and ethos: the public life of words is shaped by reason, emotion, and character. Second, deliberative, forensic, epideictic: speech can open us to the future, ground us in the past, or open the significance of the present. Third,

invention, arrangement, style, memory, delivery: the arts of rhetoric.

[12] Cicero, De Inventione, De Oratore, Brutus, De Optimo Genere Oratorum, and De Partitionibus Oratoriae. Quintillian, The Institutio Oratoria.

[13] Dio Chrysostom, Oration, 32.7–12.

[14] The saying possibly derives from philanthropist W Clement Stone (1902–2002). See also, Lao Tse: 'Difficult things in the world must needs have their beginnings in the easy; big things in the world must needs have their beginnings in the small'. Tao Te Ching, book 2, lxiii (149a).

[15] This saying may derive from Jesus' parable of the talents in Matthew 25:14–30. 'You have been faithful with a few things; I will put you in charge of many things'. It also bears significant similarity to two ancient sayings: 'Practise yourself, for heaven's sake, in little things; and thence proceed to greater'. Epictetus, Discourses, 18. 'Big things must needs have their beginning in the small'. Lao Tzu, Tao Te Ching, book 2, lxiii (149a).

[16] This section is based on the article by David Dorsey, 'Positive Deviant: An Interview with Jerry Sternin', Fast Company 41 (Dec 2000), pages 284–292. See also Dennis Sparks, 'From hunger aid to school reform: Positive deviance approach seeks solutions that already exist', National Staff Development Council 25:1 (Winter 2004), pages 46–51. A Day, 'The Answer Is on the Ground', Stanford Social Innovation Review 7:4 (2009), pages 63–64. T Brown and J Wyatt, 'Design Thinking for Social Innovation', Stanford Social Innovation Review 8:2 (2010), pages 30–35. M Sternin. J Sternin, and R Pascale, 'Bring the Outliers Inside', OdeWire, September 2010. M Sternin and S Sternin, 'Best Behaviours', RSA Journal (Summer 2011), pages 39–41, available at: http://www.thersa.org/large-text/fellowship/journal/archive/

summer-2011/features/best-behaviours. Accessed June 28, 2013.

[17] Marian Zeitlin, Hossein Ghassemi, and Mohamed Mansour, Positive Deviance in Child Nutrition: With emphasis on Psychosocial and Behavioural Aspects and Implications for Development. Tokyo: United Nations University, 1990.

[18] Adapted from Dorsey, 'Positive Deviant'.

[19] There is no record of this quote anywhere in the 98 volumes of The Collected Works of M K Gandhi. New Delhi: The Publications Division. See http://www.gandhitopia.org/forum/topics/a-gandhi-quote. Accessed June 29, 2013.

[20] Mahatma Gandhi. From an article in the Indian Opinion 9/8/1913. Reprinted in ibid., volume 13, chapter 153, page 241.

[21] From Jerry Sternin's theory of amplifying positive deviance. See Dorsey, Deviant, pages 284–292.

Chapter 6: Character

[1] Tom Morris, If Aristotle Ran General Motors: The New Soul of Business. New York: Owl Books, 1997, page 133. Note the sentiment commonly attributed to Heraclitus (c.535–475 BC): 'A man's character is his fate'. Heraclitus, fragment 119.

[2] Proverbs 11:3.

[3] Moral Letters, Letter 52: On choosing our teachers, line 12.

[4] From the Doctrine of the Mean, 29:3, attributed to Zisi, grandson of Confucius. On the mean, see Confucius, Analects, 4:26.

[5] Psalm 139:14.

[6] 'All human beings are born free and equal in dignity and rights. They are endowed with reason and conscience and should act towards one another in a spirit of brotherhood'. Opening statement of the Universal Declaration of Human Rights.

[7] Genesis 1:26–28. Image of God is an integrating thread in Jewish and Christian scriptures. See Psalm 8 and Hebrews 2:6–8.

[8] See the hymn of Philippians 2:6–11 where Jesus is portrayed as a humble and humiliated Lord. The language was an affront to the Caesars. See Richard Horsley, ed., *Paul and Empire: Religion and Power in Roman Imperial Society*. Harrisburg: Trinity Press, 1997.

[9] 'There is neither Jew nor Gentile, neither slave nor free, nor is there male and female, for you are all one in Christ Jesus' (Galatians 3:28). On the intellectual revolution presented by the writings of Paul, see my, '"To know as we are known": Locating an ancient alternative to virtue', in Mike Thompson and David Bevan eds, *Wisdom and Organizational Complexity*. London: Pallgrave-Macmillan, 2013, pages 83–105.

[10] See Colin Gunton, *The One, the Three and the Many: God, Creation and the Culture of Modernity. The 1992 Bampton Lectures*. Cambridge: Cambridge University Press, 1993, page 118.

[11] Not everyone is convinced that rights need the idea of dignity. When Steven Pinker asks and affirms, 'Is dignity 'stupid?'', he confuses what I am calling deep and surface dignity — and the history. He begins with deep dignity: 'We should not ignore a phenomenon that causes one person to respect the rights and interests of another'. He then lapses into surface dignity: 'Dignity is skin-deep: it's the sizzle, not the steak … We may be impressed by signs of dignity without underlying merit, as in the tin-pot dictator'. It is ironic that he then (rightly) urges us not to 'fail to recognize merit in a person who has been stripped of the signs of dignity, such as a pauper or refugee'. The word he needs, and assumes, is not 'merit' but 'dignity'. Surely we affirm not the merit of someone so disadvantaged but their intrinsic dignity no matter how bereft of 'the signs of dignity'. See Steven Pinker, 'The Stupidity of Dignity: Conservative bioethics' latest, most dangerous ploy', *The New Republic* (May 28, 2008).

[12] Morris, *If Aristotle*, page 215.

[13] Michel de Montaigne, *The Complete Essays*, book 3, chapter 13.

[14] Psalm 8:5–8. The Psalm recalls Genesis 1:26–28 and the idea of man and woman as equally 'image of God'.

[15] Ralph Waldo Emerson, *Essays and English Traits*. The Harvard Classics. 1909–14, Essay V Compensation, page 39.

[16] See Joseph Badaracco, *Leading Quietly: An Unorthodox Guide to Doing the Right Thing*. Boston: Harvard Business School Press, 2002. See in particular pages 169–179.

[17] Susman famously traced the shift from a 'Culture of Character' to a 'Culture of Personality' by collating the changing emphases from the self-help manuals of the nineteenth century ('citizenship, duty, reputation, morals, and integrity') to the early twentieth century ('magnetic, attractive, glowing, dominant, and energetic'). See his, 'Personality and the Making of Twentieth-Century Culture', in *Culture as History: The Transformation of American Society in the Twentieth Century*. New York: Pantheon Books, 1984, pages 271–285.

[18] Tom Peters, 'The Brand called You', *Fast Company*, August/September 1997, pages 83–94.

[19] Glenn Llopis, 'Personal Branding is a Leadership Requirement, not a Self-Promotion Campaign', *Leadership* 4/08/2013. Available at: http://www.forbes.com/sites/glennllopis/2013/04/08/personal-branding-is-a-leadership-requirement-not-a-self-promotion-campaign/.

[20] Anthony Giddens, *Modernity and*

Self-Identity: Self and Society in the Late Modern Age. Cambridge: Cambridge University Press, 1991, page 201.

[21] From Diogenes Laërtius, Lives of Eminent Philosophers, 2:60. Diogenes attributes this saying to 'Apollodorus in his work on the Philosophic Sects'. Solon (638–559 BC) was responsible for a series of far-reaching economic, social, and political reforms in Athens. Though largely unsuccessful at the time, his reforms may have contributed to aspects of later Athenian democracy.

[22] I am fortunate to know Theary as a friend. In addition to our conversations and correspondence, I have drawn from her autobiography Theary Seng, Daughter of the Killing Fields: Asrei's Story. London: Fusion Press, 2005. See the websites: http://www.thearyseng.com/biography and http://www.asianfortunenews.com/article_0213.php?article_id=36. See also her speech at TEDx Phnom Penh: http://www.youtube.com/watch?v=Qn1_KKl1irg.

[23] Seng, Daughter, page 244.

[24] Ibid., page 259.

[25] Romans 5:3–4.

[26] Seng, Daughter, page 262.

[27] Ibid., page 241.

[28] Ibid., page 259.

[29] For first-hand accounts of the epic rescue, see Ernest Shackleton, South: The Story of Shackleton's 1914–17 Expedition. London: Century, 1919, and Frank Worsley, Endurance: An Epic of Polar Adventure. London: Philip Allen, 1931. For a discussion of Shackleton as a leader, see Margot Morrell and Stephanie Capparell, Shackleton's Way: Leadership Lessons from the Great Antarctic Explorer. New York: Viking, 2001.

[30] Genesis 2:25.

[31] Most scholars read Genesis 1–3 as arising from two traditions reflected in 1:1–2:4a and 2:4b–3:23. On the themes shared with other ancient Near Eastern literature and legend, see O Keel, The Symbolism of the Biblical World: Ancient Near Eastern Iconography and the Book of Psalms. Winona Lake: Eisenbrauns, 1996. Also Nick Wyatt, Space and Time in the Religious Life of the Near East. Sheffield: Sheffield University Press, 2001.

[32] The Tree of Life features in many ancient traditions.

[33] Genesis 2:9.

[34] The Tree of the Knowledge of Good and Evil appears nowhere else in Jewish or Christian scriptures. The Tree of Life occurs as a symbol of wisdom (Proverbs 3:18, 11:30, 13:12, 15:4), and in association with restoration (Ezekiel 47:1–11; Revelation 22:1–5).

[35] See Viktor Frankl, Man's Search for Meaning. New York: Pocket, 1984.

[36] For the conference papers see Mike Thompson and David Bevan eds. Wisdom and Organizational Complexity. London: Pallgrave-Macmillan, 2013. See also: Barry Schwartz and Kenneth Sharpe, Practical Wisdom: The Right Way to Do the Right Thing. New York: Riverhead, 2010. Stephen Hall, Wisdom: From Philosophy to Neuroscience. New York, A A Knopf, 2010. Prasad Kaipa and Navi Radjou, From Smart to Wise: Acting and Leading with Wisdom. San Francisco: Jossey-Bass, 2013.

[37] Satires, II line 83.

[38] I say 'rarely' in hope. I actually have not come across the themes of foolishness or brokenness in modern secular treatments of wisdom. Some seem at pains to remove the concepts altogether.

[39] Seng, Daughter, page 262.

[40] Peter Senge, The Fifth Discipline. Sydney: Random House, 1992, pages 13–14.

[41] Helen Keller from 'The Heaviest Burden of the Blind', a speech given in New York on January 15, 1907 and reproduced in Outlook for the Blind 1 (1907), pages 10–12.

[42] Helen Keller, Optimism: An Essay. New York: Crowell, 1903, page 56.

Available from http://archive.org/details/optimismessay00kelliala. Accessed July 18, 2013.

[43] From an interview with Helen Keller by Barbara Bindley titled 'Why I Became an IWW' New York Tribune, January 16, 1916. From http://www.marxists.org/reference/archive/keller-helen/works/1910s/16_01_16.htm. Accessed July 21, 2013. IWW refers to the International Workers of the World, which Keller had joined in 1912. In 1920 she helped found the American Civil Liberties Union (ACLU) and was a member of the Socialist Party of America.

[44] Helen Keller from a letter to pacifist Senator Robert La Follette, 1924 supporting his presidential candidacy. From http://www.yesmagazine.org/people-power/the-radical-dissent-of-helen-keller. Accessed July 21, 2013.

[45] All quotes in this column from Ronald Heifetz, *Leadership Without Easy Answers*. Cambridge: Belknap, 1994, page 180.

[46] Robert Herrick, To the Virgins to Make Much of Time, from Alfred Pollard, ed. *Works of Robert Herrick*. Volume I. London: Lawrence & Bullen, 1891, page 102.

[47] William Barrett, *Irrational Man: A Study in Existential Philosophy*. London: Mercury, page 201.

[48] Ibid., pages 201, 202.

[49] Moralia, Vol. I, The Education of Children 4.3.

Chapter 7: Story

[1] Anthony Giddens, *Modernity and Self-Identity: Self and Society in the Late Modern Age*. Cambridge: Cambridge University Press, 1991, page 54.

[2] With thanks to Sam Bloore.

[3] Stephen Denning, *The Secret Language of Leadership*. San Francisco: Jossey-Bass, 2007, page 44.

[4] Hannah Arendt, 'Isak Dinesen: 1885–1963' in *Men in Dark Times*. New York: Harcourt Brace & Company, 1983, page 147.

[5] Alasdair MacIntyre, *After Virtue: A Study in Moral Theory*. Notre Dame: University of Notre Dame Press, 2007, page 182.

[6] Modern organisational writing employing wisdom literature and themes draws on Aristotle and Confucius as its two major ancient sources. Access to Aristotle is almost always via the work of MacIntyre, *Virtue*. For recent examples see the essays in Mike Thompson and David Bevan, eds. *Wisdom and Organizational Complexity*. London: Pallgrave-Macmillan, 2013.

[7] For a fuller discussion of faith, hope, and love as epistemic rather than moral or spiritual, see my article, '"To know as we are known": Locating an ancient alternative to virtue', in ibid., pages 83–105.

[8] This point has been made forcibly in recent times by several philosophers who share no personal affiliation to Paul or his message. See for example A Badiou, *Saint Paul: The Foundation of Universalism*. Stanford: Stanford University Press, 2003.

[9] Edwin Judge, 'St. Paul as a Radical Critic of Society', *Interchange*, 16 (1975), page 191.

[10] 1 Corinthians 8:11. See also 1:18–31, 4:10–13, 2 Cor 10:1–6.

[11] For a full discussion illustrated from the primary sources, see my book *Reframing Paul: Conversations in Grace and Community*. Chicago: Intervarsity Press, 2001, pages 58–67.

[12] See the very different accounts in Anthony Gottlieb, *The Dream of Reason: A History of Philosophy from the Greeks to the Renaissance*. London: Allen Lane, 2000, and Marjorie Grene, *The Knower and the Known*. Los Angeles: University of California Press, 1974.

[13] Sermon 126.

[14] N Wirzba and B Benson (Eds) *Transforming Philosophy and Religion:*

Love's Wisdom. Bloomington: Indiana University Press, 2008, page 4.

[15] Eva Illouz, 'Love and Its Discontents: Irony, Reason, Romance', *The Hedgehog Review*, 12:1 (2010), page 19.

[16] Badiou, *Universalism*, pages 90–91.

[17] Universally attributed to Danish author Karen Blixen (1885–1962) who wrote *Out of Africa* and *Babette's Feast* under the pseudonym Isak Dinesen. No source is ever cited for the quote.

[18] Daniel Pink, *A Whole New Mind: Why Right Brainers will Rule the World*. New York: Riverhead, 2005, page 117. The phrase does seem to be more widely attributable. Among scholarly accounts see Anthony Rudd, *Self, Value, and Narrative: A Kierkegaardian Approach*. Oxford University Press, 2012. Dan McAdams' work has been particularly influential. Among others, see his, 'The Psychology of Life Stories', *Review of General Psychology* 5 (2001), pages 100–122. The general point that we need stories to know ourselves seems supported for the most part by both anthropology and neuroscience. Thus the anthropologist Owen Flanagan suggests that 'people of all cultures cast their own identity in some sort of narrative form'. *Consciousness Reconsidered*. Boston: MIT Press, 1992, page 198. Also neuroscientist Antonio Damasio argues that 'consciousness begins when brains acquire the power … of telling a story'. *The Feeling of What Happens: Body and Emotion in the Making of Consciousness*. New York: Harcourt, 1999, page 10. There are some dissenters to this view. Galen Strawson, 'We live beyond any tale that we happen to enact', *Harvard Review of Philosophy* 18 (2012), pages 73–90. For a general review and critique of narrative theories of knowing, see Paisley Livingston, 'Narrativity and Knowledge', *Journal of Aesthetics and Art Criticism*, 67:1 (2009), pages 25–36.

[19] Daniel Dennett, 'The Self as a Center of Narrative Gravity', in F Kessel, P Cole and D Johnson, eds, *Self and Consciousness: Multiple Perspectives*. Hillsdale: Erlbaum, 1992. The analogy is useful though I see no need to embrace the scepticism he associates with the image.

[20] Rudd, *Kierkegaardian*, page 179.

[21] MacIntyre, *Virtue*, page 216.

[22] Edwin Judge, 'Ancient Beginnings of the Modern World', *Ancient History: Resources for Teachers* 23:3 (1993), pages 125–126.

[23] Ibid., page 135.

[24] Ibid., page 135.

[25] Ibid., page 125.

[26] Ibid., page 126.

[27] Ibid., page 134.

[28] Ibid., page 135.

[29] French filmmaker Jean-Luc Godard, possibly from an interview; source otherwise unknown.

[30] Alistair Mant, *Intelligent Leadership*. Sydney: Allen & Unwin, 1997, pages 102–103.

[31] From H Rubin, 'The Power of Words', interview with Fernando Flores, *Fast Company*, January 1999.

[32] See Denning, *Secret*, pages 65–68.

[33] Tony Golsby-Smith first drew my attention to Lincoln's speech and the relation to Aristotle's *topoi*. This is a significant influence in his model of strategic conversation. See Tony Golsby-Smith, 'Pursuing the Art of Strategic Conversations: An investigation of the role of the liberal arts of rhetoric and poetry in the business world', PhD thesis, University of Western Sydney, Sydney, 2001, pages 107–120, 173–209.

[34] From secondroad.com.au. Accessed August 2, 2013.

[35] Ibid.

[36] Again, the AcdB® model is a proprietary tool of the strategy and design firm Second Road based on Tony Golsby-Smith, 'Strategic Conversations'.

[37] See http://www.ted.com/talks/barry_schwartz_on_the_paradox_of_choice.html.

[38] C S Lewis, *The Horse and His Boy*, Book 5 in *The Chronicles of Narnia*, London: Macmillan, 1954, page 32.

Chapter 8: Brilliance

[1] Joseph Epstein, 'Celebrity Culture', *The Hedgehog Review* 7:1 (2005), page 9.

[2] They include: Terrific Mentors International at http://www.terrificmentors.com/tag/wisdom-quotient-wq/. Sageadviser at http://www.sageadvisor.org/book/wisdom-iq-test. First Christian Church of Lake Butler, Florida, USA at http://www.firstchristianfamily.org/_blog/Manna_in_the_Morning/post/What_is_your_Wisdom_Quotient/. And the University Belt church in Manila, Philippines at http://www.victoryubelt.org/wisdom-quotient.html.

[3] Salespeople can get RQ (Relational Quotient) from http://www.stevesaccone.com/blog/improving-your-rq. Or the folks with a trademark on RQ over at http://www.relationalcapitalgroup.com/apps/. Or those behind the RQ test at http://www.3smartcubes.com/pages/tests/relationship-quotient-test/relationship-quotient-test_instructions.asp.

[4] Howard Gardner, *Frames of Mind*. New York: Basic Books, 1983.

[5] Daniel Goleman, *Emotional Intelligence*. New York: Bantam Books, 1995. Before Goleman was P Salovey and J Mayer, 'Emotional Intelligence', *Imagination, Cognition, and Personality*, 9 (1990), pages 185–211. A crucial earlier work was W Payne, A study of emotion: developing emotional intelligence; self integration; relating to fear, pain and desire', PhD thesis, Union Graduate School, 1983.

[6] See the discussion by Stephen Murdoch, *IQ: How Psychology Hijacked Intelligence*. London: Duckworth Overlock, 2009.

[7] See the sage review by Jim Holt, 'A Word About the Wise', *New York Times* (March 11, 2010). See http://www.nytimes.com/2010/03/14/books/review/Holt-t.html?pagewanted=all. Accessed August 9, 2013. Holt refers to Stephen S Hall, *Wisdom: From Philosophy to Neuroscience*. New York: A A Knopf, 2010. See also Stephen S Hall, 'The New Middle Ages: The Older-and-Wiser Hypothesis', *New York Times*, May 6, 2007, and 'Can Science Tell Us Who Grows Wiser?' *New York Times Magazine*, May 6, 2007.

[8] Lauralee Alben, 'At the Heart of Interaction Design', *Design Management Journal* (Summer 1997), pages 9–27. The article is available at: http://www.albendesign.com/downloads/heart_of_interaction.pdf.

[9] This text and that which follows are taken from http://www.templegrandin.com/. See also Temple Grandin, *Thinking in Pictures: And Other Reports from My Life with Autism*. New York, Vintage, 1995.

[10] Temple Grandin, *Emergence: Labeled Autistic*. New York: Warner Books, 1986.

[11] Perceptions of autism are changing. See the many self-published videos and other productions by autistic people. For example, http://www.youtube.com/watch?v=POIJG3qmV9Q. In particular, see the remarkable production at http://www.youtube.com/watch?v=JnyIM1hl2jc. Do not stop watching — text and voice over will start at 3:14. There is a profound challenge here to the idea that only 'high-functioning' autistics like Temple Grandin are epistemologically aware and reflective.

[12] You can view a portion of a documentary on his life at: http://www.youtube.com/watch?v=ZWtZA-ZmOAM. You can also view extracts from a movie made of Lesley: http://www.youtube.com/watch?v=9C21FZAN6Rg. Other portions are also available on YouTube.

[13] See for example, Thomas Lewis, Fari Amini, and Richard Lannon, *A General Theory of Love*. New York: Vintage Books, 2001.

[14] Albert Szent-Gyrgyi (1893–1986) was a Hungarian physiologist who won the Nobel Prize in Physiology or Medicine in 1937. He is credited with discovering vitamin C and the components and reactions of the citric acid cycle. He was also active in the Hungarian Resistance during World War II and entered Hungarian politics after the war. I have been unable to verify the source of the quote.

[15] City of God, In Praise of Creation, #24.

[16] Hymn to Apollo, 189–193. Translation is by Robin Lane Fox, *The Classical World: An Epic History from Homer to Hadrian*. London: Basic, 2006, page 48.

[17] See I Corinthians 12:12–26, and Romans 12:5. In a couple of instances the image is used conventionally — as head over the body — but controversially and seditiously by replacing Caesar with Christ. See Ephesians 5:23 and Colossians 1:18.

[18] Gianozzo Manetti, On the Dignity and Excellence of Man in Four Books, completed 1452 or 1453.

[19] Peter Miller, 'The Renaissance Republic of Letters and the Genesis of Enlightenment' in *Europäische Bildungsströme. Die Viadrina ima Kontext der europäischen Gelehrtenrepublik der frühen Neuzeit (1506-1811)*. ed. Reinhard Blänkner. Berlin: Schöneiche, 2008, pages 45–46.

[20] This quotation and those that follow are from Robert Pirsig, *Zen and the Art of Motorcycle Maintenance*. New York: William Morrow and Company, 1974, pages 32–34, as cited in Matthew Crawford, *Shop Class as Soulcraft: An Inquiry into the Value of Work*. New York: Penguin, 2009, pages 95–99.

[21] Crawford, *Shop Class*, page 5.

[22] Pirsig, *Zen*, pages 32–34.

[23] Crawford, *Shop Class*, pages 98–99.

Chapter 9: Promise

[1] Both promise and hope can of course have lesser, even opposite, meanings to how I'm using them here. Promises can be mere words without substance, such as in this German proverb: 'Promise is a bridge of words, unsafe to walk across'. Hope can have the sense of wishing that leaves us disappointed, such as in this English proverb: 'Hope is a good breakfast but a bad supper'. See David Crystal, ed. *As They Say In Zanzibar: Proverbial Wisdom From Around the World*. London: HarperCollins, 2006, pages 170, 447. I think the older, positive use of both words is worth preserving.

[2] Max de Pree, *Leadership is an Art*. Lansing: Michigan State University, 1987, page 11.

[3] Crystal, *Zanzibar*, page 432.

[4] Ibid., page 558.

[5] Ibid., page 434.

[6] See H Rubin, 'Interview with Fernando Flores', *Fast Company*, January 1999.

[7] Ibid.

[8] David Tracy, *Plurality and Ambiguity*. San Francisco: Harper & Row, 1987, page 9.

[9] Rubin, 'Flores'.

[10] Ibid. In the interview Flores associates hope with wishing and, to that degree, rejects the term. We agree on the larger picture but I'm holding hope for hope!

[11] Again, see Tony Golsby-Smith, 'Pursuing the Art of Strategic Conversations: An investigation of the role of the liberal arts of rhetoric and poetry in the business world', PhD thesis, University of Western Sydney, Sydney, 2001, page 126.

[12] Crystal, *Zanzibar*, page 156.

[13] Proverbs 27:17.

[14] Again, the AcdB® model is a proprietary tool of the strategy and

design firm Second Road. See www.secondroad.com.au.

[15] Al-Anbiya` 21:37. Translation by Amatul Rahman Omar. See also Surah al-Ma'arij, 70:19–20.

[16] John Ralston Saul, *On Equilibrium*. London: Penguin, 2001, page 148.

[17] Ibid., page 7.

[18] See further on Second Road's methodologies, Tony Golsby-Smith 'The second road of thought: how design offers strategy a new toolkit', *Journal of Business Strategy*, 28:4 (2007), pages 22–29. See also: http://blogs.hbr.org/cs/2011/02/hold_conversations_not_meeting.html, and the three-part article beginning at: http://www.leadingwithlift.com/blog/2010/12/20/strategic-innovation-part-i/.

[19] John Bury, *The Idea of Progress: An Inquiry into its Origin and Growth*. London: Macmillan, 1920. Bury is often cited as arguing the ancients had no idea of progress. In fact Bury argued that the ancient idea of progress lacked the sense of history and society that animates our idea of progress.

[20] 'All things from eternity are of like forms, and come round in a circle'. Marcus Aurelius, *Meditations*, Book 2.14. It is too simplistic however to read every writer who thought in terms of 'recurrence' as ruling out progress. See Gary Trompf, *The Idea of Historical Recurrence in Western Thought: From Antiquity to the Reformation*. Berkeley: University of California, 1979.

[21] For example: 'Not from the start did the gods reveal all things to mortals, but in time, by inquiring, they make better discoveries'. Xenophanes, Fragment B18 in Stobaeus, Anthology I viii 2. 'For one thing after other did men see grow clear by intellect, till with their arts they've now achieved the supreme pinnacle'. Lucretius, De Rerum Natura V.1448. A century later, Seneca (54 BC–39 AD) anticipated a day when 'our posterity will marvel at our ignorance of causes

so clear to them'. Seneca, *Naturales Quaestiones*, vii. 25, 31.

[22] Romans 12:2. This may be the first positive use of *metamorphoo* in classical literature. Alain Badiou calls Paul 'an antiphilosophical theoretician of universality'. See Alain Badiou, *Saint Paul: The Foundation of Universalism*. Stanford: Stanford University Press, 2003, page 108. I'd add 'and transformation'. Jacob Taubes goes so far as to call Paul's message a 'declaration of war against Rome'. Jacob Taubes, *The Political Theology of Paul*. Stanford University Press, 2004, page 13. On the political background to Paul's writings, see Richard Horsley, ed. *Paul and Empire: Religion and Power in Roman Imperial Society*. Harrisburg: Trinity Press, 1997.

[23] City of God, book X, chapter 14.

[24] This discussion is based on the transcripts of five speeches given in South Africa June 4–9, 1966 by Senator Robert F Kennedy. The texts are available at the website for the documentary made about the visit titled RFK in the Land of Apartheid: http://www.rfksafilm.org/html/visit.php. I have also drawn on other primary sources and background information from that site. See also Senator Robert F Kennedy, 'Suppose God is Black', *Look Magazine*, 23 August 1966. See http://www.rfksafilm.org/html/media/magazines/look.php.

[25] For example: 'It is hard to see what useful purpose Senator Kennedy is achieving in South Africa ... The suspicion must be that Mr Kennedy simply wants to advance his presidential prospects by creating a stir'. 'Two Wrongs', *The Express*, June 1966.

[26] An article in the UK newspaper *The Guardian* noted: '(O)ccasionally in politics it is given to a man to say the right thing, at the right time and in the right place, and so strike a chord that is both sympathetic and lasting' (as

quoted in *Newsweek,* June 20, 1966).
[27] From his Day of Affirmation speech to the student union at the University of Cape Town, June 6, 1966.
[28] Robert F Kennedy speech at the University of the Witwatersrand, Johannesburg, June 8, 1966.
[29] Vaclav Havel, 'The Politics of Hope', in *Disturbing the Peace: A Conversation with Karel Hvizdala.* New York: Vintage Books, 1990, page 113. Havel wrote the essay while in prison as a political dissident.

Chapter 10: Grace

[1] See http://www.rembrandtpainting. net/rembrandt's_prodigal_son.html. Accessed at September 16, 2013.
[2] See for example, Edwin Judge, *Rank and Status in the World of the Caesars and St. Paul: The Broadhead Memorial Lecture 1981.* Christchurch: University of Canterbury Press, 1982.
[3] Ramsey MacMullen notes the profound influence of status and ambition over Roman society: '*Philotimia* ... No word, understood to its depths, goes further to explain the Graeco-Roman achievement'. Ramsey MacMullen, *Roman Social Relations: 50 BC to 284 AC.* New Haven: Yale University, 1974, page 215.
[4] There is a powerful picture of this in the history of ancient Corinth. The city's history stretches back to 6500 BC. But in 146 BC the Romans destroyed it and removed all its people. Then in 44 BC Julius Caesar re-established Corinth with an imported, mixed population with few social demarcations beyond free, freed, and slave. Three generations later a contemporary critic could write to his pompous friends, 'Consider that ... not many of you were influential; not many were of noble birth'. Ouch! See I Corinthians 1:26.
[5] From the poem 'All That is Gold Does Not Glitter' from JRR Tolkien, *The Lord of the Rings.* The poem

appears several times in the trilogy. It first appears in Gandalf's letter to Frodo in Chapter 10, Strider, of volume one, *The Fellowship of the Ring.* New York: Ballantine, 1965, page 231.
[6] Directed by Kay Pollak. See http:// www.imdb.com/title/tt0382330/ for credits. All quotes are from the dialogue.
[7] Warning: This is a spoiler. The final scene can be viewed at http://www. youtube.com/watch?v=m6mi5jTsLBc.
[8] Matthew 6:9–13.
[9] From the entry for April 21 in Leo Tolstoy, *A Calendar of Wisdom: Daily Thoughts to Nourish the Soul,* 1908.
[10] 'Where is the wisdom we have lost in knowledge? Where is the knowledge we have lost in information?' From TS Eliot's play, *The Rock.* London: Faber & Faber, 1934.
[11] I Corinthians 13:5.
[12] For an introduction to Pearson's perspectives, see http://www. youtube.com/watch?v=QLpll1- gnxk&feature=youtu.be. Start listening at 2:50. Accessed September 16, 2013. See also his *Up from the Mission: Selected Writings.* Melbourne: Black, 2009. His views are not shared by all Indigenous Australian leaders.
[13] Heather Warren, 'Authority and Grace: A Response to Robert Bellah', *The Hedgehog Review,* 4:1 (2002), page 34.
[14] From the album *All That You Can't Leave Behind,* Island, 2000. It is somewhat ironic that copyright prevents me from quoting a handful of beautiful words on grace from a song called Grace!
[15] See for example the famous works of Michael Polanyi and Thomas Kuhn. Michael Polanyi, *Personal Knowledge: Towards a Post-Critical Philosophy.* Chicago: University of Chicago Press, 1958. Thomas Kuhn, *The Structure of Scientific Revolutions.* Chicago: Chicago University Press, 1970.

[16] See for example the discussion in Richard Creel, *Thinking Philosophically: An Introduction to Critical Reflection and Rational Dialogue*. Oxford: Blackwell, 2001, pages 91–111. Creel also offers overviews of materialism and rationalism.

[17] Humberto Maturana Rowesin and Gerda Verden-Zöller, *The Origin of Humanness in the Biology of Love*. Exeter: Imprint Academic, 2008, pages 39–40.

[18] Rob Riemen, *Nobility of Spirit: A Forgotten Ideal*. London: Yale University Press, 2008, page 101.

Chapter 11: Leader's Journey

[1] A saying commonly attributed to Johann Wolfgang von Goethe. It bears some similarity to Wagner's words on childhood to Faust in Part II of *Faust*. Otherwise I have not been able to locate an original source.

Chapter 12: Leading One

[1] Proverbs 20:5

Chapter 13: Leading Many

[1] The ideas of Saul/Paul of Tarsus, called the apostle, have been obscured by anachronistic 'Christian' readings of his letters — a fault sometimes as ubiquitous in critical readings as in conservative readings. Whenever Christianity has been complicit in patriarchy, intolerance, neuroses, and political agendas, the apostle is usually singled out as the source. Those claims may be substantial, but blaming Paul is to read him back to front, a point acknowledged by the French neo-Marxist philosopher Alain Badiou, *Saint Paul: The Foundation of Universalism*. Stanford: Stanford University Press, 2003, page 4. See also Giorgio Agamben, *The Time that Remains: A Commentary on the Letter to Romans*. Stanford: Stanford University Press, 2005. What subsequent theologians and churchman have done with Paul's legacy is another story.

[2] See most recently, Mark Strom, '"To know as we are known": Locating an ancient alternative to virtue', in Mike Thompson and David Bevan eds. *Wisdom and Organizational Complexity*. London: Pallgrave-Macmillan, 2013, pages 83–105. This portrait of Paul is based on my doctoral research, published in modified form as *Reframing Paul: Conversations in Grace and Community*. Chicago: Intervarsity, 2001. It is a pleasure to acknowledge my indebtedness to my supervisor Edwin Judge. See the representative articles of Judge's near six decades of scholarly leadership in James Harrison, ed., *E A Judge: The First Christians in the Roman World: Augustan and New Testament Essays*. Tübingen: Mohr Siebeck, 2008, and David Scholer, ed., *Social Distinctives of the Christians in the First Century*. Peabody: Hendrickson, 2008.

[3] I Corinthians 9:22, Ephesians 4:15, Romans 12:2.

[4] For example: 'We must in my opinion begin by distinguishing between that which always is and never becomes from that which is always becoming but never is. The one is apprehensible by intelligence with the aid of reasoning, being eternally the same, the other is the object of opinion and irrational sensation, coming to be and ceasing to be, but never fully real'. Plato, Timaeus, 27D–28A.

[5] See the still pertinent conclusions of the late Colin Hemer, *The Book of Acts in the Setting of Hellenistic History*. Wissenschaftliche Untersuchungen zum Neuen Testament 49, Tübingen: Mohr, 1989, and 'The Speeches of Acts: II. The Areopagus Address', *Tyndale Bulletin* 40 (1989) pages 239–259.

[6] On Paul and Judaism see N T Wright, *Paul: Fresh Perspectives*. London: SPCK, 2005, and John Dominic Crossan and Jonathan Reed, *In Search of Paul: How*

Jesus' Apostle Opposed Rome's Empire with God's Kingdom. London: SPCK, 2005.

[7] On the political implications of *pax Romana* and Paul's unavoidable collision with it, see Richard Horsley, ed., *Paul and Empire: Religion and Power in Roman Imperial Society.* Harrisburg: Trinity Press, 1997, and *Paul and Politics: Ekklesia, Israel, Imperium, Interpretation.* Harrisburg: Trinity Press, 2000.

[8] The *epikrisis* is dated 4 August 272 and lists the family and its rank back to 4/5 AD. See Stephen, 'The Preservation of Status and its Testing', in S Llewelyn, ed., *New Documents Illustrating Early Christianity.* Vol 6. Sydney: Macquarie University, 1992, pages 132–140.

[9] See Aristotle, Politics for a classic articulation of superiority on the Greek side. On the Roman side, see Seneca, Essays. See also Tom Hillard, 'Augustus and the Evolution of Roman Concepts of Leadership', in J Beness ed., *Studies in Honour of Margaret Parker: Part II,* pp. 107–152. Sydney: Macquarie Ancient History Association, 2008.

[10] Plutarch, Life of Cato the Elder, 18.4, in the Parallel Lives.

[11] Galatians 3:28, Philippians 2:3, Romans 12:3, 16, 1 Corinthians 12:23. See my 'Humility', In C Baker, ed., *The Seven Heavenly Virtues of Leadership.* Brisbane: McGraw-Hill, 2003, pages 3–15, and more recently John Dickson, *Humilitas: A Lost Key to Life, Love, and Leadership.* Grand Rapids: Zondervan, 2011, pages 83–96.

[12] 1 Corinthians 12:23, 1:26 27, 2:1, 4:13.

[13] Philippians 2:6–8. Reading Paul's letters as moral or religious homilies we will miss the highly political references. See Horsley, *Imperial.* The profession 'Jesus is Lord' was an affront to 'Caesar is Lord'. In a hymn (Colossians 1:15–20) Paul's description of Christ appropriates imperial titles. Taubes goes so far as to call Paul's message a 'declaration of war against Rome'. Jacob Taubes, *The Political Theology of Paul.* Stanford: Stanford University Press, 2004, page 13.

[14] 'Paul was attracted to *charis* as a leitmotiv for divine beneficence because the Augustan 'age of grace' had ensured that nobody would be able to compete against the munificence of the Caesars'. James Harrison, *Paul's Language of Grace in its Graeco-Roman Context.* Wissenschaftliche Untersuchungen zum Neuen Testament 2. Reihe 172 Series, Tübingen: Mohr Siebeck, 2003, page 351.

[15] For the evidence, see Winter, Sophists, Andrew Clarke, *Secular and Christian Leadership in Corinth: A Socio-Historical and Exegetical Study of 1 Corinthians 1–6.* Leiden: E J Brill, 1993, and Hillard, *Augustus.*

[16] Edwin Judge, 'St. Paul and Socrates', *Interchange* 14 (1973), page 110.

[17] 'Roman *principes* sought fame, and to get to the top. Self-advertisement and the proclamation of achievement were essential tools in the armoury', Hillard, *Augustus,* page 107. This is the background to the scandal of Paul's unseemly boasting in 2 Corinthians 10–12: not that he boasted, for that was expected of a great man. See Chris Forbes, 'Comparison, self-praise and irony: Paul's boasting and conventions in Hellenistic rhetoric', *New Testament Studies,* 32 (1986), pages 1–30.

[18] This is an admittedly difficult point to grasp on the back of two millennia of associating faith and virtue. From Homer through Aristotle to writers contemporary with Paul, the classical virtues of wisdom, justice, temperance, and courage were understood to be exemplified in the self-contained man (e.g., Dio Chrysostom, Oration 49.8–11; Seneca, 'On the firmness of the wise man', 6:3–8). The classical ideal remained *ataraxia,* detachment (e.g.,

Plutarch, Moralia, 83E, 86A, 83BC). In Phil 2:3 Paul turned *tapeinos* (humbled, abased), a term only used negatively in classical literature into the virtue of *tapeinophrosune* (humility, modesty). For the evidence from non-literary sources, see the discussion of three first-century eulogies in Greg Horsley, ed. *New Documents Illustrating Early Christianity*. Sydney: Macquarie University Press, Vol 2 (1982) pages 33–36, 40–43 and Vol 4 (1987) pages 10–17. What is lacking in Paul is the crucial nexus of virtue and social privilege. In classical and Hellenistic society, wisdom was that which upheld social stratification, justice that which gave a man the reward/punishment due to him (i.e. according to his rank), self-control was the mark of a superior man, and courage was exemplified in a man who upheld his own honour. See the extensive citation and discussion of Graeco-Roman moral texts in Abraham Malherbe, *Moral Exhortation: A Greco-Roman Sourcebook*. Library of Early Christianity 4. Philadelphia: Westminster, 1986.

[19] I have argued elsewhere that Paul does not fit the patterns of a theologian, philosopher, moralist, or religious figure. His thinking may be likened to a jazz musician improvising on a theme more than a classical musician following a score. Strom, *Reframing*, pages 182–197.

[20] See the descriptions of early gatherings in Romans 12 and 1 Corinthians 12–14.

[21] See the classic study by Charles Cochrane, *Christianity and Classical Culture: A Study of Thought and Action from Augustus to Augustine*. Indianapolis: Amagi, 2003.

[22] Neo-Marxist and atheist philosopher Alain Badiou argues that Paul's proclamation of the resurrected Christ is the turning point of Western thought. See 'The Antidialectic of Resurrection' in Badiou, *Universalism*, pages 66–74.

[23] Acts 9:2, 19:9, 24:14.

[24] Acts 11:26, 26:28.

[25] See Edwin Judge, 'St Paul and Classical Society', *Jahrbuch für Antiquity und Christentum*, 15 (1972), pages 19–36.

[26] See the evidence in Robert Wilken, *The Christians as the Romans Saw Them*. London: Yale University Press, 1984.

[27] Julian the Apostate is the only exception after Constantine (272–337). In his Letter to Arsacius (c.362), Julian pins the Galileans' (i.e. Christians') subversion of the order of *Romanitas* on their novel conventions of open dialogue, literacy, and hospitality. His advice: plagiarise! Though his own agenda died with him soon after, he needn't have bothered: the emerging synthesis of Paul's radical message with classical thought was already well underway. In time it would sustain that which it had subverted, *Romanitas*, under the twin (and often opposed) guises of the Church of Rome and the Holy Roman Empire. See Cochrane, *Augustus*.

[28] Alasdair MacIntyre, *After Virtue: A Study in Moral Theory*. Notre Dame: University of Notre Dame Press, 2007, page 184.

Dr Mark Strom

KEYNOTES. RETREATS. CONSULTING.

Thousands of leaders have heard Mark's keynote addresses or participated in his leadership seminars in Australia, New Zealand, Asia, Europe, and North America.

His retreats, based on the material in *Lead with Wisdom*, are unique learning experiences acclaimed by leaders in many sectors.

Mark has consulted to commercial corporations, government bodies, not-for-profits, and individual leaders. His expertise lies at the intersection of strategy and leadership, the reframing of innovation and engagement initiatives, and the creation of leadership programs for senior leaders.

Mark can be reached at:
mark@markstrom.co
www.markstrom.co

Linkedin: DrMarkStrom
Facebook: DrMarkStrom
Twitter: StromDrMark

CPSIA information can be obtained
at www.ICGtesting.com
Printed in the USA
BVHW040523180122
626118BV00014B/244